The Innovative Bureaucracy

Bureaucracy has been largely criticized throughout much organization theory and management literature, having been seen as inefficient and incapable of being able to respond to external changes. Contrariwise, Alexander Styhre argues that an empirical study of bureaucracy underlines the merits of a functional organization, the presence of specialist and expertise groups and hierarchical structures.

Styhre examines the literature of bureaucracy and the new forms of post-bureaucratic organization and shows that the discourse on bureaucracy includes a number of competing and complementing themes. His two empirical studies, of the Volvo Car Corporation and AstraZeneca, offer affirmative views of bureaucracy and a final chapter, drawing on the bio-philosophy of Henri Bergson, presents a vitalist model of bureaucracy, capable of both apprehending its functional organization and its continuous and ongoing modifications and changes to adapt to external conditions.

This book will be of great use to advanced students of organization and management theory, seeking alternative views and perspectives on bureaucracy and its relative merits. It will also be of considerable interest to managerial strategists and decision-makers world wide.

Alexander Styhre is Professor at the Department of Technology Management, Chalmers University of Technology, Gothenburg, Sweden.

RIOT!

Routledge studies in innovation, organization and technology

The Innovative Bureaucracy

Bureaucracy in an age of fluidity

Alexander Styhre

LONDON AND NEW YORK

First published 2007
by Routledge
2 Park Square, Milton Park, Abingdon, Oxon OX14 4RN

Simultaneously published in the USA and Canada
by Routledge
270 Madison Ave, New York, NY 10016

Routledge is an imprint of the Taylor & Francis Group, an informa business

© 2007 Alexander Styhre

Typeset in Times by Wearset Ltd, Boldon, Tyne and Wear
Printed and bound in Great Britain by TJI Digital, Padstow, Cornwall

British Library Cataloguing in Publication Data
A catalogue record for this book is available from the British Library

Library of Congress Cataloging in Publication Data
A catalog record for this book has been requested

ISBN10: 0-415-39597-6 (hbk)
ISBN10: 0-203-96433-0 (ebk)

ISBN13: 978-0-415-39597-7 (hbk)
ISBN13: 978-0-203-96433-0 (ebk)

For Simon and Max

The strongest is never strong enough to be always the master, unless he transforms strength into right, and obedience into duty.

Jean-Jacques Rousseau, *The Social Contract*: 184

All that we ask of the men is to do the work that is set before them.

Henry Ford, cited in Thompson 1969: 29

Contents

Illustrations

Figures

Tables

Preface

It probably matters that I was born, raised and have spent most of my life in a modern Western social-democratic country praising egalitarian values, and, most importantly, spending a considerable amount of resources on the public sector – but I have never been fully able to understand all the ready-made complaints and critiques about bureaucracy in popular culture and the social theory and organization theory literature that I have engaged with over the last ten years. For me, bureaucracy is not part of the problem but part of the solution to a range of social concerns and objectives. Without doubt, my own personal experiences from reasonably well-functioning bureaucratic organizations catering a range of services in Swedish municipalities and the state administration are not fully compatible with other's experiences of bureaucracy. I have, over the years, heard numerous complaints, anecdotes and more or less amusing stories from my friends and colleagues about encounters with Belgian immigration officers, Italian university administrators, the Chinese railways, the Philippinian police corps and a variety of other representatives of bureaucratic organizations that have been deemed by my interlocutors to function less smoothly and transparently than one may hope for. Furthermore, newspapers continuously report about the presence of corruption, bribery, nepotism and oligarchies in most parts of the world. Such news is discouraging for anyone having faith in public administration, so I am fully aware that I may have been lucky to be able to testify to my belief in bureaucracy.

However, this book is the outcome of my own inability to really understand the problem with bureaucracy *as such*; isn't bureaucracy just one type of organizational arrangement whose content rather than form determines its outcome and effects? What struck me is that it is, in fact, the very form as such that seems to enrage both the proverbial "wo/man on the street" and the more theoretically inclined social scientist. Contemporary everyday speech is infested with a rich variety of derogatory remarks on bureaucracy and stories of how it fails to function or fails to provide meaningful work assignments abound. This veritable mythology of the shortcomings of bureaucracy is shared between folk psychology, popular culture and scholarly works. Moreover, what is confusing for us – perhaps not too many, one may ask? – having positive experiences of bureaucracy is that most dismissive remarks on the subject appear to be based on what is often referred to as "anecdotal evidence" by positivists; that is, idiosyncratic and contextualized experiences, or even by mere hearsay and common-sense thinking. Like in all mythologies, the deeply imbued belief that bureaucracy is a suspicious thing is a self-perpetuating axiom that one cannot easily falsify without deconstructing underlying and rarely articulated assumptions. Bureauphobia – the systematic disbelief in bureaucracy – is here fixed in the form that Pierre Bourdieu calls *doxa*. In order to defamiliarize what one already knows, empirical studies may hopefully play a role. This book is therefore an attempt at critically examining the literature on bureaucracy and the various organizational arrangements that have been jointly referred to as "post-bureaucratic organization". In addition, the book presents two studies of large Swedish companies employing a bureaucratic form to organize their activities. Finally, a more affirmative image of bureaucracy than the conventional mechanistic metaphors is sketched in the final chapter.

The aim of the book is thus to make bureaucracy a domain of empirical research anew, rather than serving as a "straw man" or a signifier denoting an antiquated organization form always already dismissed as being out of step with contemporary times. The other aim is to speak of bureaucracy in terms of change, movement and adaptation rather than stability, closure and even petrification. Therefore, notions such as vitalism, organism and becoming, derived from a bio-philosophical discourse, are brought into discussion in the sixth and final chapter. As we learn from, for instance, Alfred North Whitehead and Gilles Deleuze, in order to defamiliarize *what is*, one needs to conceive of images of *what may be*; thinking emerges through concepts and therefore new images, vocabularies and metaphors may help us to think along new routes. Rather than reproducing trite mechanistic images of bureaucracy, an organic image of an organization form maintaining its form, yet responding to external changes and influences may be enacted. For me, no matter how naive such a view may be regarded, that is how bureaucracy works: through ceaseless differentiation and integration, through oscillating between openness and closure.

Acknowledgements

I am indebted to Sten Setterberg, Volvo Car Corporation, Mats Sundgren, AstraZeneca, Mölndal, Jan Wickenberg, AstraZeneca, Mölndal and especially Sofia Börjesson, Chalmers University of Technology, for all of their support and help during the research project on which this book is based. I am also grateful for the time spent on the research project by the busy co-workers and managers at Volvo Car Corporation and AstraZeneca. I would also like to thank the participants at the first OLKC Conference at the University of Warwick, UK, in March 2006, in commenting on my paper and helping me to reformulate some of my ideas.

The study was funded by a grant from The Bank of Sweden's Tercentenary Fund.

1 The supplementarity of bureaucracy in management thinking

Introduction

In a paper published in 1970, Warren Bennis speaks about the "end of bureaucracy": "Every age develops an organization form appropriate to its genius, and ... the prevailing for today – the pyramidal, centralized, functionally specialized, impersonal mechanism known as bureaucracy – [is] out of joint with contemporary realities" (Bennis, 1970: 166). Bennis continues and predicts a future where new organization forms are developed and widely used:

> Organizations of the future ... will have some unique characteristics. They will be adaptive, rapidly changing *temporary systems*, organized around problems-to-be-solved by groups of relative strangers with diverse professional skills. The groups will be arranged on organic rather than mechanical models: they will evolve in response to problems rather than to programmed expectations. People will be evaluated, not in a rigid vertical hierarchy according to rank and status, but flexibly, according to competence. Organization charts will consists of project groups rather than stratified functional groups, as now is the case. Adaptive, problem-solving, temporary systems of diverse specialists, linked together by coordinating executives in an organic flux – this is the original form that will gradually replace bureaucracy.
>
> (Bennis, 1970: 166)

Bennis is here sketching a future society less dependent on the bureaucratic organization model. Instead, a variety of more fluid and flexible organization forms, capable of responding to new challenges and new human demands and expectations, are advocated. Bennis's text is representative of a utopian stream of thinking in the management literature, a genre of writing that thinks of forms of organization as a vehicle for the democratic society and other virtues praised in the Western world. In many cases, such utopian thinking has joined hands with a tradition of critical views of bureaucracy. Here, bureaucracy, portrayed as an embodiment of deranged instrumental rationalities and the mistaken expectations on the positive effects of economies of scale, is one of the abiding concerns for management writers. For instance, in 1966, Warren Bennis portrayed bureaucracy in the following terms:

> If does not take a great critical imagination to detect the flaw and problems of the bureaucratic model. We have all experienced them: bosses without technical competence and underlings with it; arbitrary and zany rules; an underworld (or informal) organization which subverts or even replaces the formal apparatus; confusion and conflict among roles; and cruel treatment of subordinates, based not upon rational or legal grounds, but upon inhumane grounds.
>
> (Bennis, 1966: 5)

Bureaucracy is, for its detractors, one of the predicaments of modern life and must be examined as what is, at best, a functional solution to administrative problems and, at worst, an immediate and living threat to the open society. In management writing, bureaucracy critiques are a staple food, a trite gesture and what is very much grist for the mill for a variety of management writers subscribing to various theoretical and methodological orientations. "Bureaucracy is a term so loaded with negative meaning for most people that it is mainly used as a negative rhetorical resource and it is difficult to make an explicit ideological case for bureaucracy" (Thompson and Alvesson, 2005: 105). Bureaucracy has many detractors and few friends. Such anti-bureaucratic sentiments are by no means a recent cultural phenomenon. Honoré de Balzac, the great French novelist, published no less than ninety-five interconnected novels and short stories under the label *La Comédie Humaine*, capturing the French society of his time, the period 1830–1850. One of the novels is entitled *Bureaucracy* (*Les Employés*, 1837, also translated as *The Bureaucrats*) and accounts for the intrigues and political games in a French *bureau* when a new director is about to be appointed. Balzac portray the French bureaucracy in the following terms:

> No one comes or stays in the government offices but idlers, incapables, or fools. Thus the mediocrity of French administration has slowly come about. Bureaucracy, made up entirely of petty minds, stands as an obstacle of prosperity of the nation; delays for seven years, by its machinery, the project of a canal which would have stimulated the production of a province; is afraid of everything, prolongs procrastination, and perpetuates the abuses which in turn perpetuate and consolidate itself. Bureaucracy holds all things and the administration itself in leading strings; it stifles men of talent who are bold enough to be independent of it or to enlighten it on its own follies.
>
> (Balzac, 2000: 10–11)

Here, bureaucracy is portrayed in comical terms and as being subject to political struggles. For instance, one of the *dramatis personae* frankly says: "Of course bureaucracy has its defects. I myself think it slow and insolent; it hampers ministerial action, stifles projects, and arrests progress. But, after all, French administration is amazingly useful" (Balzac, 2000: 137). Perhaps Balzac is here the spokesman of a common view of bureaucracy in mid-nineteenth-century French society.

The purpose of this book is to critically review the literature on bureaucracy and to present a two-year study of how two major multinational firms are organizing their innovative capacities to support a more affirmative view of bureaucracy. In the contemporary management literature, in the media and in popular culture, the bureaucratic organization form is generally portrayed as an inefficient, outmoded and poorly functioning form of organization unable to provide meaningful job opportunities for its members. This overtly negative view of bureaucracy is by no means a recent idea but, rather, has been one of the consistent themes in both the organization theory literature and in other disciplines in the social sciences. "Nearly everyone," Starbuck (2003a: 162) writes, "who has written about bureaucracies has complained about it; almost the only authors who found value in bureaucracy were German economists and sociologists writing between 1870 and 1915."

In many cases, bureaucracy has been invoked to serve the role as what Derrida (1976) calls a *supplement*, what is additional to, complementing, or external to something but nevertheless fails to achieve the same status as the primary and most accomplished form. The terms "supplement" and "supplementarity" are here adopted from Jacques Derrida's seminal account on the role of writing in Western thinking as being a mere supplement to speech. For Derrida, the Western canon rests on what he, drawing on Heidegger, calls "logocentrism". Logocentrism is the "metaphysics of presence", an ontological and epistemological position favouring presence in every single instant, that things are not in the making but contain their innate essences exclusively enclosed within themselves. For Derrida, logocentric thinking is observable in the literature on writing in Western thinking, especially in Plato but also in less central figures in the philosophy of metaphysics such as Jean-Jacques Rousseau. Rousseau declares: "Languages are made to be spoken, writing serves only as a supplement to speech" (quoted in Derrida, 1976: 303). Writing is a corrupted form of speech, a form of speech fixed by certain symbols and always less closely associated with the human mind. For Plato, the written text can never substitute for the full presence of oral speech. Socrates, Plato's beloved master – "he who does not write", for Nietzsche – resisted writing for this reason. Rousseau, then, is following closely in this tradition. Writing as supplement; writing as mere image or representation of primary speech; "[W]riting, the letter, the sensible inscription, has always been considered by the Western tradition as the body and matter external to the spirit, to breath, to speech, and to the logos" (Derrida, 1976: 35). Derrida argues that Rousseau's disregard of writing is derived from this binary mode of thinking, the Platonist separation into dualities, opposing terms structuring being into a series of antagonist relations:

> [R]ousseau could not think this writing, that takes place before and within speech. To the extent that he belonged to the metaphysics of presence, he

dreamed of the simple exteriority of death to life, evil to good, representation to presence, signifier to signified, representer to represented, mask to
face, writing to speech. But all such oppositions are irreducibly rooted in
that metaphysics.

(Derrida, 1976: 315)

What we may learn from Derrida is that all thinking is located within a certain
tradition of thinking. The treatment of writing as something that is only sec-
ondary, additional, supplementary, and in many respects inferior to speech, is
one indication of the effects of the logocentric thinking proceeding along binary
categories. Writing is, then, Derrida argues, never supposed to be strictly
complementary to speech or the equal to speech but is, instead, what is merely
supplementary, always less credible and useful. As Gherardi (1995) points out,
Platonist thinking is problematic because such binary opposites are never supposed to be of equal importance: the supplementary concept is always less
valued, of less importance or directly condemned. Reality–appearance,
good–bad, original–copy, speech–writing, man–woman, is a series of Platonist
and opposing concepts. It is always the former that is privileged and given a
central importance. As feminist thinkers point out, women are defined in terms
of negativity, in terms of the absence of masculine qualities and features – de
Beauvoir's (1993) *le deuxième sexe* – and so is the case for all such binary opposites. For instance, Oseen (1997) writes, speaking of leadership:

> Maleness and masculinity are the templates for leadership. Within the con-
> fines of technological rationality, leadership has been constructed on the basis
> of male experience, but this experience has been universalized, and women
> have been labeled as deficient leaders. By definition, they lack what they can
> never attain. Men are the norm, women the deviant, the different, the lesser.
>
> (Oseen, 1997: 175)

Derrida sketches a programme of deconstruction examining instituted binary
opposites such as speech–writing in the following terms:

> Deconstruction first sets out to identify the conceptual construction of a
> given theoretical field, whether it is religion, metaphysics, or ethical and
> political theory, which usually makes use of one or more irreducible pairs.
> Second, it highlights the hierarchical ordering of the pairs. Third, it inverts
> or subverts their ordering by showing that the terms placed at the bottom –
> material, particular, temporal, and female, in this example – could with jus-
> tification be moved to the top – in place of the spiritual, universal, eternal,
> and male. While the inversion reveals that the hierarchical arrangements
> reflect certain strategic and ideological choices rather than a description of
> features intrinsic to the pairs, the fourth and final move is to produce a third
> term for each oppositional pair, which complicates the original load-bearing
> structure beyond recognition. If the first two moves take on the description

of a given conceptual construction, the final two are aimed at deforming it, reforming it, and eventually transforming it.

(Derrida, cited in Borradori, 2003: 138)

Bureaucracy – our object of study here – in many cases plays the role of the yardstick against which new organization forms are compared and evaluated. Therefore, a more detailed analysis of bureaucracy is demanded. This casting of bureaucracy as what is, at best, slightly inefficient and, at worst, a wholly perverted organization form, has numerous consequences. First, the image of bureaucracy is unnecessarily negative in terms of efficiency, performance, customer satisfaction and work-life experiences among co-workers. Almost daily, one is exposed to derogatory remarks concerning bureaucracy, pointing at a series of supposedly significant shortcomings of this organization form.

Second, the view of bureaucracy as some kind of primordial organization form, an instituted benchmark for what has supposedly proven to function poorly, has enabled a situation where numerous writers are allowing themselves to pass negative judgement on bureaucracy without bothering to provide empirical evidence or systematic research to support such arguments. As Jones *et al.* (2005: 148) say, "it is all very well to be 'against bureaucracy', as any politician knows." Therefore, the tradition of bureaucracy bashing has been going on for years with little systematic self-reflection regarding the underlying conditions in industry and administration.

Third, since the notion of bureaucracy is closely associated with social formations favouring large public sectors and other forms of administration not exposed to market forces and the pressure of competition, some authors tend to invoke bureaucracy when criticizing "predatory capitalism" and the emergence of an ideology of an enterprising self, emphasizing individualism, careerism and meritocracy. In this debate, bureaucracy is playing the role of a safe haven providing predictable careers, reasonably meaningful job opportunities and other increasingly valued and praised qualities and work-life opportunities (e.g. Sennett, 1998; Bauman, 2000). When it is portrayed in such rosy and nostalgic terms, the detractors of bureaucracy seem to be even more convinced that bureaucracy itself is what, of necessity, fails to adapt to the demands of today's business world in a globalized society. Taken together, bureaucracy becomes cast as what is either failing to institute mechanisms enabling continuous improvement and adaptation to external changes, or as what is representing supposedly past virtues and social formations. Therefore, bureaucracy is portrayed as a *supplement*, as what is always already different and less accomplished than other forms of organization. This supplementarity of bureaucracy is put into question in this book.

Rather than subscribing to the binary machine of bureaucracy/post-bureaucracy, the dichotomous thinking assuming a series of dualities in opposition to one another, this book will explore how bureaucracy can operate efficiently in an age favouring fluidity and change rather than past virtues of stability and predictability. Du Gay (2005: 3) argues:

[B]ureaucracy is not – as many critics assume – a simple singularity. Rather, whatever singularity it is deemed to possess is multiple or mono-lithic. . . . To be more specific, bureaucracy has turned out to be less a hard and fast trans-historical model, but rather what we might describe as a many-sided, evolving, diversified organizational device.

Newton (2005: 191) argues in a similar vein:

[F]ew "pure" bureaucracies have ever existed in public services: most organizations combine features of bureaucracy and professionalism, of bureaucracy and managerialism, and even bureaucracy and entrepreneur-ship. Bureaucracy, then, can be viewed as a set of principles and practices that may be articulated with others in particular organizational settings. These articulations can be loose or tight, and lead to more or less discomfort for those living with the tensions they produce.

In other words, bureaucracy is here not primarily regarded a fixed, immutable structure but is instead treated as the outcome from a rule-governed process of organizing complex undertakings. Therefore, the demands for more flexible forms of working and instant adaptation to market changes being addressed in a massive amount of research monographs and business paper articles are not, of necessity, in opposition to a bureaucratic form of organizing. Moving beyond the most ready-made and widely circulated narratives of the bureaucracy critique may provide alternative perspectives on bureaucracy.

In the remainder of this chapter, some of the main themes of the book will be addressed. First, the notion of fluidity and change, so central to our age, is dis-cussed as a principal characteristic of the contemporary society that needs to be theorized and taken into account when examining the role and functioning of bureaucracy. Second, the concept of bureaucracy is introduced. Third, the concept of innovation is discussed and the innovation management literature is reviewed.

The age of fluidity

Contemporary civilization differs in one particularly distinctive feature from those who preceded it: *Speed*. The change has come about within one gener-ation.

(Marc Bloch, cited in Virilio, 2004: 5)

Zygmunt Bauman argues that the modern project favoured immutable material embodiments:

Engineered, modern space was to be tough, solid, permanent and non-negotiable. Concrete and steel were to be its flesh, the web of railway tracks and highways its blood vessels. Writers of modern utopias did not distinguish between the social and the architectural order, social and territorial units and divisions; for them – as for their contemporaries in charge or social order – the key to an orderly society was to be found in the organization of space. Social totality was to be a hierarchy of ever larger and more inclusive localities with the supra-local authority of the state perched on the top and surveilling the whole while itself protected from day-to-day invigilation.

(2005: 62)

This view of modernity emphasizes the "solid" manifestations of human achievements; roads and railways are fixed and visible infrastructures. However, in our own time, a new invisible space or "dimension" (Virilio, 1991), that of cyberspace, is laid out over the solid and material networks. As opposed to the "modernity of solids", Bauman (2000: 23) speaks of a "society of fluid modernity" characterized by fluidity and change. Bauman conceives of what is fluid in the following terms in a passage worthy of being cited *in extensio*:

Liquids, unlike solids, cannot easily hold their shape. Fluids, so to speak, neither fix spaces nor bind time. While solids have clear spatial dimensions but neutralize the impact, and thus downgrade the significance, of time (effectively resist its flow or render it irrelevant), fluids do not keep to any shape for long and are constantly ready (and prone) to change it; and so for them it is the flow of time that counts, more than the space they happen to occupy: that space, after all, they fill but "for a moment". In a sense, solids cancel time, for liquids, on the contrary, one may ignore time altogether; in describing fluids, to leave time out of account would be a grievous mistake. Descriptions of fluids are all snapshots, and they need a data at the bottom of the picture.

Fluids travel easily. They "flow", "spill", "run out", "splash", "pour over", "leak", "flood", "spray", "drip", "seep", "ooze", unlike solids, they are not easily stopped – they pass around some obstacles, dissolve some others and bore or soak their way through others still. . . . The extraordinary mobility of fluids is what associated them with the idea of "lightness". There are liquids which, cubic inch for cubic inch are heavier than many solids, but we are inclined nonetheless to visualize them all as lighter, less "weighty" than everything solid. We associate "lightness" or "weightlessness" with mobility and inconstancy: we know from practice that the lighter we travel the easier and faster we move.

(Bauman, 2000: 2)

For Bauman (2000), the image of liquids and fluids is capable of capturing the continuously changing relations and institutions in contemporary society; it is an image that underlines *temporality* – it captures the transient nature of a fleeing event, the "snapshots". Schatzki (2002) speaks of the "decline of functionalism" in the 1970s as an important driver towards a recognition of fluid and transient social arrangements; "Today," Schatzki (2002: 16) says, "theorists are much more likely to emphasize the flux and becoming that pervade such formations." Contemporary social theory is affirmative of what Schatzki calls "transitory fixations": "Relations, positions, and meanings, like the arrangements of which they are aspects, are labile phenomena, only transitory fixations of which can be assured" (Schatzki, 2002: 24).

The flow and the movements and exchanges of information and know-how characterize modern society in "non-visible" and computer-mediated systems. But such flows have always been part of human society (de Landa, 1997); even the most "primitive" societies display modes of exchange and the passing around of tokens and artefacts, be they money, seashells or, as in the primitive proto-capitalist society lacking agreements on proper means of exchange, say, packets of cigarettes. Nevertheless, in our own society the dependency and reliance on forms of flow and exchanges are perhaps more accentuated than in previous social formations. Yet, as Law points out, talking about sociology, the dominant theoretical mindset privileges stability over fluidity: "[S]ociologists, like many others, tend to prefer to deal in nouns rather than verbs. They slip into assuming that social structure is an object, like the scaffolding round a building, that will stay in place once it has been erected" (Law, 1994: 14). Contrary to this view, Law suggests an analysis of networks of action bringing together social and material resources (see also Czarniawska, 1997): "[W]hat we call the social is *materially heterogeneous*: talk, bodies, texts, machines, architectures, all of these and many more are implicated in and perform the 'social'" (Law, 1994: 2). "[T]he social," Law (1994: 139) concludes, "is never purely social."

While the post-Second World War period, up to the early 1970s, was a remarkably stable period in terms of economic growth (Piore and Sabel, 1984), the period thereafter has been characterized by technological changes orchestrating the movement towards what have been labelled a "post-industrial society" (Dahrendorf, 1959; Touraine, 1971; Bell, 1973), an information society (May, 2002), a knowledge society (Burton-Jones, 1999; Mouritsen and Flagstad, 2005), or even a virtual society (Woolgar, 2002). Such new social arrangements are generally thought of as being increasingly influenced by diverse modes of thinking and pluralism. Urry (2000) suggests that classic sociology is impotent when examining these new fluid social arrangements and calls for new theoretical developments that can capture institutions in a society characterized by continuous change (see also Appadurai, 1996). Urry (2003) suggests that complexity theory represents one such theoretical development that can enable an understanding of the contemporary society. De Landa speaks of the abandoning of "conservative systems": "[A] century-old devotion to 'conservative systems' (physical systems that, for all practical purposes, are isolated from their surroundings) is giving was to the realization that most systems in nature are subject to flows of matter and energy that continuously move through them" (De Landa, 1992: 129). Nowotny shares this affirmative view of complexity as perhaps informing social theory:

The climax of high modernity with its unshakeable belief in planning (in society) and predictability (in science) is long past. Gone too is the belief in simple cause–effect relationships often embodying implicit assumptions about their underlying linearity; in their place is an acknowledgement that many – perhaps most – relationship are non-linear and subject to ever changing patterns of unpredictability.

(Nowotny, 2005: 16)

Tsoukas (2005: 5) speaks of such "changing patterns of unpredictability" as an "open-world ontology":

An open-world ontology assumes that the world is always in a process of becoming, of turning into something different. Flow, flux and change are the fundamental processes of the world. The future is open, unknowable in principle, and it always holds the possibility of surprise.

Beck (2000: 19) discusses interchangeably the terms "the second modernity" and "reflexive modernity" when addressing contemporary times wherein the old regime is overturned: "The term 'reflexive modernity' . . . refers to the transition away from the first modernity locked within the national state, and towards a second, open, risk-filled modernity characterized by general insecurity." Lash (2003), following Beck (2000), speaks of the second modernity as a period characterized by a high-speed society wherein the possibility for reflection is lost:

In the second modernity we haven't sufficient reflective distance on our-selves to construct linear and narrative biographies. . . . We may wish to be reflective but we have neither the time nor the space to reflect. We are instead *combinards*. We put together networks, construct alliances, make deals.

(Lash, 2003: 51)

The lack of time for reflection is also an issue emphasized by French social thinker Paul Virilio. In a series of books and interviews, Virilio has discussed the influence of increased speed in contemporary society. Virilio says: "We no longer have time for reflection. The power of speed is *that*. . . . Democracy is no longer in the hands of man, it's in the hands of computerized instruments, answering machines, etc." (Virilio and Lotringer, 1997: 61). This lack of time for reflection has significant effects for politics:

Today, we have no longer time to reflect, the things that we see have already happened. . . . Is a real-time democracy possible? An authoritarian politics, yes. But what defines democracy is the sharing of power. When there is not time to share, what will be shared? Emotions.

(Virilio, 2002: 43)

In addition to the influence of speed, Virilio examines the influence of new technology and speaks of the "three technological revolutions": the *transportation revolution* orchestrated by the development of the railways systems, the *transmission revolution* wherein media such as radio and information technologies evolve, and a forthcoming *transplantory revolution* wherein the human body is increasingly "colonized" by technology: Virilio writes: "In the future, just as the geographic world was colonized by means of transportation or communication, we will have the possibility of a colonization of the human body by technology. ... We are on the verge of the biomachine" (Virilio, cited in Der Derian, 1998: 20). For Virilio, our bodies are no longer "the ultimate matter" (Virilio, 2000: 11) but new opportunities emerge when nanotechnology is being developed and refined (see also Haraway, 1997; Jones, 2004; Milburn, 2004; Thomas and Ancuña-Narvaez, 2006).[1] In the future, the line of demarcation between human body and machine will no longer be uncomplicated or uncontested but will become permeable and fluid. Virilio explains what he means by the "transplantation revolution":

> By this term I mean that technology is becoming something physically assimilable, it is a kind of nourishment for the human race, through dynamic inserts, implants and so on. Here, I am not talking about implants such as silicon breasts, but dynamic implants like additional memory storage. What we see is that science and technology aim for miniaturization in order to invade the human body. This is already true of [the] cardiac stimulator, a device I am especially interested in, since much of my work is about rhythm and speed, and the cardiac stimulator is what *gives* the rhythm to the life of the human patient. ... Technology no longer spreads over the body of the territory, as with the railways, motorways, bridges and large factories, but now enters the innards of the human body.
>
> (Virilio, cited in Armitage, 1999: 49)

Turning from the human body to the macro-level of social organization, Urry (2005) wants to revitalize the analysis of globalization through drawing on a complexity theory framework affirmative of an epistemology of fluids. Urry (2005: 246) is talking about "global fluids" as an analytical category. Here "global fluids" travel "along various routeways or scapes" and "break free from linear clock-time". Using a similar vocabulary, Thrift (2005) speaks of a new form of capitalism that he calls "soft capitalism", increasingly capable of adapting to changes in the environment and employing the new technologies and subscribing to new managerial regimes of governance and control. He writes:

> I regard capitalism as a set of networks which, though they may link in many ways, form not a total system but rather a project that is permanently "under construction". Capitalism firms may be able to mobilize power and enroll allies but they are as uncertain about the future as we all are because the future unfolds as a virtuality – it is continually creating temporary

actualizations out of new questions – not a known quantity, or at least a distinct possibility. So capitalist firms may sit on the bridge of this world, able at their best to steer it in certain directions, but they still cannot know what is around the corner, whether it be an emerging energy crisis, a financial downturn, a set of protests that threaten a brand's image, or something more mundane like a cashflow crisis. This essentially performative notion of capitalism, conceiving of it as a continually renewed set of responses to new drivers, means that I see capitalism, to repeat, as a constantly mutating entity, made up of a field or networks which are only ever partly in its control. No matter how many assets are engaged, it must constantly face the pressure of unexpected events.

(Thrift, 2005: 3–4)

Such a fluid image of capitalism is also advocated by Hardt and Negri (2000) who conceive of capitalism as a distributed, de-centred, dynamic and flexible system that they name "Empire". Such a capitalist system is essentially "governing without government" and is therefore without the full control of any agent. Speaking in less-critical terms, Castells (1996) examines what he calls the "network society", a society distributed across a number of technical, cultural and social systems. These new forms of organizational arrangements, derived from an alternative epistemology recognizing the fluid and heterogeneous nature of the contemporary social reality, will be discussed in greater detail in terms of what is put forth as being inherently in opposition to the bureaucratic organization form. The main argument is that the virtues of transparency and predictability embodied and manifested in the bureaucratic organization form have lost a significant degree of their social and cultural capital in what Thrift (2005: 6) calls "the cultural circuit of capitalism", that is, an integrated cultural system including a variety of institutions and actors serving as carriers of business knowledge such as the business schools, management consultants and management gurus (see, for example, Clark and Salaman, 1996; Huczynski, 1996; Grint, 1997; Case, 1999; Collins, 2000; Jackson, 2001; Pfeffer and Fong, 2002). What were important and axiomatic virtues and praised qualities in the 1950s and 1960s are no longer of necessity favoured. On the contrary, the contemporary emphasis on qualities such as speed, diversity, pluralism, movement, individualism and so forth have wielded destructive effects on the social legitimacy of the bureaucratic organization form. In other words, as time has passed, stability and absence of change are no longer perceived as desirable conditions and, consequently, the idea of a bureaucratic organization becomes an obsolete construct, a reminiscence of a past period of time and an antiquated mode of thinking.

The concept of bureaucracy

In the literature on bureaucracy, reviewed and accounted for in Chapter 2, several *images* of bureaucracy (see Morgan, 1986) are presented. Albrow (1970: 14) writes:

The student coming to the field can be excused bewilderment. Sometimes bureaucracy seems to mean administrative efficiency, at other times the opposite. It may appear as simple as a synonym for civil service, or it may be as complex as an idea summing up the specific features of modern organizational structure. It may refer to a body of officials, or to the routines of office administration.

Still, few authors put into question Max Weber's foundational principles, the "ten commandments" of bureaucracy presented in his magnum opus, *Economy and Society*, but numerous writers associate bureaucracy with public administration. In this book, the concept of bureaucracy denotes a set of abstract organizational principles that are manifested in a variety of ways in organizations and companies. Such abstract principles include functional organization, hierarchical structure, the emphasis on and adherence to rules, the demands for specific skills and professional identities and careers, and the vertical chain of command so dear to Henri Fayol (1949). Fayol spoke of a "general theory of administration" while he was clearly making references to his work as a manager in industrial companies. For Fayol, administrative principles were by no means only of relevance for the public sector or for strictly administrative matters such as bookkeeping and so forth. Therefore, in this book, the view of bureaucracy is not strictly Weberian; Fayol is also regarded as a foundational writer in terms of referring to industrial firms exposed to full-scale competition as relying on "general administrative principles". As a consequence, in this present book, firms in the industries experiencing the fiercest of competition, such as the automotive industry and the pharmaceutical industry, are organized in accordance with bureaucratic principles and rules. If one strictly adheres to an ideology of *bureauphobia*, this may appear as an absurd statement: companies and firms operating in highly competitive industries can by no means remain viable when being organized as bureaucracies because they would of necessity fail to respond to the dynamics of such industries.

In opposition to such a view, here, bureaucracy is not what is by definition default and misconceived but is rather a set of administrative principles guiding a rich variety of organizations and firms in their pursuit of, in the vocabulary of strategic management theorists, sustainable competitive advantage. If one bothers to take a closer and more careful look into companies organized in accordance with bureaucratic principles, one may find a variety of processes, mechanisms, forms of working, communities, expert groups and other organizational resources safeguarding dynamic responses to external environments, yet adhering to certain bureaucratic principles and guidelines. In other words, bureaucracies are by no means strictly mechanical systems as conceived of in the anti-bureaucracy literature but, rather, are better conceived of in zoomorphic terms, as organisms structured in accordance with certain mechanical principles, yet capable of responding to and dealing with external changes. Biological organisms are structured in accordance with a number of principles suggesting order, rules and what may be called "routines" – for instance, the metabolism is structured around recurrent temporal events – but does not fail to maintain a close attention to the external world. Following Henri Bergson's (1998) view of biological life as that which is always in a state of becoming, in a continuous movement towards new constellations and forms of life, the metaphor of a biological organism is a more adequate image of a bureaucracy than, say, a mechanical apparatus. Even though a mechanical apparatus obeys the same Newtonian principles of entropy and enthalpy as a biological organism, it does not have the same intrinsic possibilities for responding to external changes in the course of time. The mechanical system is once and for all determined to operate along certain schemata while the biological organism is always already capable of developing along new lines. For the critics of bureaucracy, this organization form works like clockwork; you can have specific uses of such systems but you must not forget the limited functionality of the system and its fixed grids of operation. For us, conceiving of bureaucracy as what is intrinsically dynamic and capable of changing, along with a great many other things, the mechanical model is mistaken because is it inadequate and incapable of accounting for the changes bureaucracies can be proven to have orchestrated. These preferences for certain images may be one of the decisive differences between the critics and the defenders of bureaucracy.

In summary, for us, conceiving of bureaucracy not as what is already defined as a poorly functioning organization but instead as a set of organizational principles, Weber's classic introduction of the bureaucracy model needs to be supported by writers such as Henri Fayol, thinking of "general administration" as what is relevant not only for public administration but also for companies and corporations. Bureaucratic principles are then present to various degrees in most firms and organizations; in some cases, certain rules and principles are overturned and criticized, in other cases they are playing a central role. A great deal of variety in organizational practice is observable in the field.

The concept of innovation

Perspectives on innovation

Research on innovation, new product development and the management of R&D in organizations is a substantial domain of research in organization theory and management studies (for an overview, see Wolfe, 1994; Slappendel, 1996; Dougherty, 1999). In a seminal text by Peter Drucker (1955: 32), the management of innovation is introduced as one of the central tasks of the manager, and since the publication of Burns and Stalker's (1961) classic study, innovation has been a part of the management studies agenda. However, the *locus classicus* of the notion of innovation is Joseph Schumpeter's *The Theory of Economic Development* (1934). In a publication from 1939, Schumpeter speaks of innovation in the following terms:

> We simply define innovation as the setting up of a new production function. This covers the case of a new commodity, a well as those of a new form of

organization such as a merger, of the opening of new markets, and so on . . . innovation combines factors in a new way . . . it consists in carrying out New Combinations.

(Schumpeter, 1939: 87–88)

Later on, Schumpeter distinguishes between the *enterprise* and the *entrepreneur*: "For actions which consists in carrying out innovation we reserve the term Enterprise; the individuals who carry them out we call Entrepreneurs" (Schumpeter, 1939: 100). The two fields of research on innovation and entrepreneurship are therefore both indebted to Schumpeter's foundational work.

Today, there is a massive research literature on innovation in organizations; a rich plethora of theoretical perspectives in this body of literature is ranges from a narrow micro-level of individuals to the analysis of industrial clusters and regions. Wolfe (1994) identifies three distinct research questions and traditions within the innovation literature (see Table 1.1).

The first research question has engaged a number of researchers in exploring how innovations have been diffused in markets and industries. The second research question has produced a number of studies regarding the determinants of innovation, and the third research question deals with the actual innovation process. For Wolfe (1994), these three perspectives are complementary because innovation is too complex a practice or event to be captured by one single, unified model or perspective. He therefore suggests a pluralist view of innovation. Similarly, Slappendel (1996) talks in her review of the innovation literature about three complementary perspectives on innovation: (1) the *individual perspective*, emphasizing the individual actors that are the principal agents in innovative work; (2) the *structural perspective*, "assuming that innovation is determined by organizational characteristics" (Slappendel, 1996: 113); and (3)

Table 1.1 Schools of innovation research (adopted from Wolfe, 1994: 407)

Research question	*Research approach*	*Research focus*
1 What are the patterns of diffusion of an innovation through a population of potential adopter organizations?	Diffusion of innovation (DI) research	Addresses the *diffusion of an innovation* over time and/or space
2 What determines organizational innovativeness?	Organizational innovativeness (OR) research	Addresses the *determinants of innovativeness* of organizations
3 What are the processes organizations go through in implementing innovations?	Process theory (PT) research	Addresses the *process of innovation* within organizations

the *interactive perspective*, studying innovation as the outcome of a joint collaboration between groups of individuals, organizations and relevant resources. The three perspectives are summarized in Table 1.2 below.

For Slappendel (1996: 122), the three perspectives have evolved over time and, consequently, it is the interaction perspective that is the most recent contribution to the analysis of innovation. Both Wolfe's (1994) and Slappendel's (1996) reviews of the literature suggest that innovation is a substantial field of research that cannot be boiled down into one single unified model or theory. Thus one needs to approach the literature by discussing its heterogeneity.

In the innovation literature, some contributions have bearings on adjacent theoretical fields such as knowledge management (e.g. Von Hippel, 1998; Subramaniam and Venkatraman, 2001), human resource management (Bunce and West, 1996), or, more generally, philosophy (O'Shea, 2002). Among the various

Table 1.2 The main feature of the three perspectives (adopted from Slappendel, 1996: 109)

	Individualist	*Structuralist*	*Interactive process*
Basic assumption	Individuals cause innovation	Innovation determined by structural characteristics	Innovation produced by the interaction of structural influences and the actions of individuals
Conceptualization of an innovation	Static and objectively defined objects or practices	Static and objectively defined objects or practices	Innovations are subject to reinventions and reconfigurations. Innovations are perceived.
Conceptualization of the innovative process	Simple linear, with focus on the adoption stage	Simple linear, with focus on the adoption stage	Complex process
Core concepts	Champions Leader Entrepreneurs	Environment Size Complexity Differentiation Formalization Centralization Strategic type	Shocks Proliferation Innovative capability Context
Research methodology	Cross-sectional survey	Cross-sectional survey	Case studies Case histories
Main authors	Rogers March and Simon	Zaltman *et al.*	Van de Ven *et al.*

perspectives pursued, researchers have studied the impact of local cultures on innovation (Jassawalla and Sashittal, 2002), the ability to share knowledge within new product-development teams (Leonard-Barton, 1995) as well as between business units and firms (Powell *et al.*, 1996; Nobel and Birkinshaw, 1998; Hage and Hollingsworth, 2000; Jones, 2000; Spencer, 2003), the capacity to implement and use new technology (Tushman and Nelson, 1990; Hargadon and Sutton, 1997; Dodgson, 2000; Cardinal, 2001), the role of managerial control (Feldman, 1989), organization size (Romano, 1990; Damanpour, 1992), slack (Nohria and Gulati, 1996) and the influence of managers' cognition, identities and conceptualization of innovation (Scott and Bruce, 1994; Greve and Taylor, 2000; Harrison and Laberge, 2002; Salaman and Storey, 2002; Greve, 2003). Other contributors suggest that innovation is an outcome of a superior ability to combine existing resources (Galunic and Rodan, 1998; Hargadon, 1998), the establishment of a culture that supports experimenting and innovative thinking (Kamoche and Pina e Cunha, 2001; Thomke, 2001), to integrate human, social and organizational capital (Subramaniam and Youndt, 2005), or the capacity to manage expert knowledge (Blackler *et al.*, 1999). Some researchers have claimed that innovation is, of necessity, at least partially chaotic (Cheng and Van de Ven, 1996) or challenging to predominant beliefs and institutions (Dougherty and Heller, 1994) and, therefore, large organizations are poorly equipped for managing innovation work (Dougherty and Hardy, 1996). Others have stressed that innovation is co-dependent with the institutional milieu in which the firm is located (Whitley, 2000; Hargadon and Douglas, 2001). Furthermore, Argyres and Silverman (2004) show that organization structures determine innovation. In firms with a central R&D function, innovations were more general and of the "basic research type", while in firms with divisionalized R&D functions, innovation work was more focused on applications:

> We find that firms with centralized R&D organization structure (i.e., corporate-level R&D labs only) and centralized R&D budget authority (i.e., funds coming from corporate headquarters) generate innovations that are significantly different along several dimensions from those generated by firms with decentralized R&D organizations.
>
> (Argyres and Silverman, 2004: 930)

For the sake of simplicity and clarity, in this book the definition of innovation formulated by Andrew Van de Ven (1986: 591) will be adhered to. Here innovation is conceived of as "[t]he development and implementation of new ideas by people who over time engage in transactions with others in an institutional context". This is a broad and general definition, but it captures the long-term commitment to a specific practice and assignment. In addition, Van de Ven (1986: 591) speaks of innovation as a *combination of ideas*: "An innovation is a new *idea*, which may be a recombination of old ideas, a scheme that challenges the present order, a formula, or a unique approach which is perceived as new by the individuals involved." Van de Ven points at the managerial consequences of innovation work: "From a managerial viewpoint, to understand the process of innovation is to understand the factors that facilitate and inhibit the development of innovations. These factors include ideas, people, transactions, and context over time" (Van de Ven, 1986: 591). Needless to say, Van de Ven's definition is accompanied by a number of definitions and perspectives on innovation. Damanpour (1992: 376) defines innovation rather loosely as "[t]he adoption of an idea or behaviour, whether a system, policy, program, device, process, product or service, that is new to the adopting organization". Dougherty and Hardy (1996: 1121) talk about "sustained product innovation": "We define sustained product innovation as the generation of multiple new products, as strategically necessary over time, with a reasonable rate of commercial success." This definition is of interest because it indicates that commercial effects are an integral component of innovation. Harrison and Laberge (2002: 498) emphasize the distinction between technological and social innovations: "Studies of innovation generally distinguish between technological resources and social innovation. Technological innovation is often the result of a deliberate creation or invention while social innovation most often consists in the codification of a specific type of interaction." Hellström (2004) criticizes what he calls "naively functionalist process frameworks of innovation" for portraying innovation work as a linear process aimed at producing some artefact as its principal outcome. Instead, Hellström suggest that innovation is to be conceived of as a form of "social action":

> The key lesson from this analysis should be that, whereas in common usage innovation may exist *qua* artefactual representation, in the context of social action the actual thing could never be understood as having "a life of its own". Rather, reification should be conceived of as a parallel movement of continuous physical representation that acts eventually to reinforce the inno-vating actor in a Parsonian norm structure, as well as creatively set the foundations for practical consciousness.
>
> (Hellström, 2004: 644)

Innovations, then, are not solely a matter of producing artefacts but, prior to that, the ability to integrate a number of relevant actors and make them engage in social activities is of central importance for any innovation process. In perhaps the largest integrated innovation research programme, The Minnesota Innova-tion Research Program, directed by the University of Minnesota in the 1980s (Ven de Ven, Angle and Poole, 2000), the *process* of innovation was strongly emphasized. Van de Ven and Poole distinguish between *innovation* and *process of innovation*:

> A theory of innovation is fundamentally a theory of change in a social system. While *innovation* is defined as the introduction of a new idea, the *process of innovation* refers to the temporal sequence of events that occur as

people interact with others to develop and implement their innovation ideas within an institutional context. *Events* are instances when changes occur in the innovation ideas, peoples, transactions, contexts, or outcomes while an innovation develops over time. *Change* is an empirical observation of differences in time on one and more dimensions of an entity.

(Van de Ven and Poole, 2000: 32)

It is therefore important to integrate the broader organizational and institutional context into account when studying innovation work. In the same volume, Schroeder *et al.* (2000) are critical of the functionalist orientation of much innovation research:

[T]he innovation process has traditionally been viewed as a sequence of separable functional stages (such as design, production, and marketing) sequentially ordered in time and linked with transition routines to make adjustments between stages. These simple unitary stage-wise progression models are increasingly being discredited because of their lack of empirical validity or correctness.

(2000: 113)

They continue: "The tendencies to reduce complex innovation processes to simply unitary stages and their lack of empirical substantiation suggest that many of the process models in the literature are suspect or simply inadequate" (Schroeder *et al.*, 2000: 113). Hung (2004) is formulating a similar critique of the innovation literature and suggests that most models of innovation are either voluntaristic or deterministic in their design. As opposed to these two positions, Hung (2004) advocated a path-dependency model called a *technology path* mediating the actor–structure problem inherent to all innovation activities. Hung writes:

The power to innovate ... derives not so much from individual actors, but from their identification with, and appropriation of, the structural context. These distinctive notions in characterizing the structure are particularly identified: "regime" as a knowledge base; "paradigm" which embodies a model and a pattern of enquiry; and "tradition", which is cognitively based. The spread of regime, paradigm or tradition comes partly through the emergence of dominant designs and partly through the prevalence of technological guideposts.

(Hung, 2004: 1481–1482)

However, the success of a particular innovation is not solely a matter of activities and the deployment of resources internal to the firm (see, for example, Powell *et al.*, 1996: 118). Innovations need to be favourably received by external stakeholders such as investors and customers in order to become viable. Therefore, Hargadon and Douglas speak of the "cultural determinants" of innovation: "One cultural determinant of an innovation's value is how well the public, as both individuals and organizations comprehends what the new idea is and how to respond to it" (2001: 476). Other researchers reject the dominant image of the innovation process as a voluntaristic, purposeful and consciously managed process and conceive of innovation work as a distributed, haphazard and non-linear event. For instance, the sociological view of innovation advocated by Akrich *et al.* (2002a: 191) stresses the heterogeneity of innovation:

> An innovation in the making reveals a multiplicity of heterogeneous and often confused decisions made by a large number of different and often conflicting groups, decisions which one is unable to decide a priori as to whether they will be crucial or not.

The innovation process is not simply located in certain departments of individual firms; ideas may evolve from all kinds of settings. In addition, the innovator needs to be able to mobilize a variety of stakeholders to make an innovation become a final product launched in the market. They exemplify with the perhaps most emblematic figure of innovation, Thomas Alva Edison:

> Edison is everything but a handyman of genius. He is an organizer, an entrepreneur, a strategist, a researcher, a public relations man and if there is any genius, it is in this ability to pass from one role to the another and to play each of them with equal delight, that it must be situated.
>
> (Akrich *et al.*, 2002b: 215; see also Hargadon and Douglas, 2001)

Akrich *et al.* (2002a) thus speak of the importance of mobilizing interested and influential individuals or groups of individuals that support the new innovation (see also Bijker, 1995; Latour, 1996; Harrison and Laberge, 2002):

> Since the outcome of a project depends on the alliances which it allows for and the interests which it mobilises, no criteria, no algorithm, can ensure success a priori. Rather than speak of the rationality of decisions, we need to speak of the aggregation of interests which decisions are capable or incapable of producing. Innovation is the art of interesting an increasing number of allies who will make you stronger and stronger.
>
> (Akrich *et al.*, 2002a: 205)

Innovation, then, is not solely a matter of effectively integrating intellectual and technical skills, competencies and experiences but, equally, a matter of making the specific innovation become a desirable object of investment, something that heterogeneous groups can collectively collaborate around. In everyday life in innovating organizations, there is rarely too *little* innovation; on the contrary, managers and project leaders have to make decisions all the time regarding which innovations to prioritize. Knorr Cetina (1981: 60) writes: "Generally speaking, the interest of an 'innovative idea' is not that it is new, but that it is *old* – in the sense that it draws on available knowledge as a source for producing knowledge."

Innovations, then, are rarely, if ever, as the romantic image suggests, bolts from out of the blue but, rather, are ideas that are forged together with other ideas, material resources, laboratory practices and so forth, into assemblages that may qualify as innovations under favourable conditions.[2] The "aggregation of interests" is one of the central functions herein because it provides the social embedding that innovation demands to become viable (Latour, 1995).

In addition to the notion of innovation, the notion of "new product development" will be employed in this book (see, for example, Lindkvist *et al.*, 1998). Sheremata's definition (2000: 392) points at the major traits of new product development: "New product development includes all activities needed to conceive, design, produce, and deliver a product to market. It is a specific type of innovation, defined here as the commercialization of invention, where invention is an act of insight." To distinguish the two terms, one may say that innovation is made up of the activities prior to commercialization, while new product development is the commodification of an innovation.

In summary, innovation work contains intellectual, technical and social components and has cognitive as well as emotional consequences. Innovation, then, is never strictly a matter for engineers and scientists, but engages a broader set of functions within, as well as outside, the organization. Since innovation today, at least in the automotive and pharmaceutical industries, is largely a matter of communicating and collaborating across functions, departments, expertise groups and company boundaries, innovation processes are never solely located in one place but are always the outcome of a "dynamic synchronization" (Adler, 1999) between various organizations. Such dynamic synchronization increasingly demands large-scale operations and the integration of a number of functions. Therefore, the bureaucratic organization form is a fruitful domain for innovation work.

Innovation in large organizations

In their study of fifteen large firms, Dougherty and Hardy (1996: 1121) found poor capacities for sustained product innovation: "We found that most of these firms were not organized to facilitate innovation: occasionally innovation did occur, but it occurred in spite of the system, not because of it." In a similar negative account of the innovative capacities of large firms, Sharma writes:

> Many observers of innovation note that the bureaucracies that govern large firms suppress both the creativity necessary to generate radically new ideas and the initiative necessary to build them into businesses. The elaborate administrative systems and the accompanying risk-averse attitude burden entrepreneurial initiatives with seemingly mindless procedures that dampen flexibility and responsiveness. The mechanisms that facilitate predictability and order in existing operations smother the entrepreneurial flair necessary to deal with the unpredictable and disorderly innovation process.
>
> (1999: 146–147)

In general, large bureaucratic firms are regarded as poor performers in terms of innovation work. In Blau and McKinley's (1979) study of innovation – operationalized as the number of awards received by the firm – in 152 architecture firms, it was found that differentiation of tasks were negatively correlated with innovativeness.

> At least in architectural firms, a high degree of differentiation does not have the beneficial consequences for innovation that it has in other types of organizations. This implies that excessive subdivision of tasks and responsibilities reduce the flexibility and openness that are required for highly creative work. Moreover, social integration may be impaired by excessive differentiation. ... In short, organizations that create original products may require integration through personal contact; in these organizations, structural differentiation, by adversely affecting integration, is detrimental to innovation and creativity.
>
> (Blau and McKinley, 1979: 212)

Moreover, Blau and McKinley report that a close match between the organization and its environment did not guarantee any significant improvement terms of the number of innovations. They write:

> Our data show that there is little relationship between the complexity of the environment and that of the organization regardless of how innovative the firm and that a better match between environmental and organizational complexity is not more likely in successful firms.
>
> (Blau and McKinley, 1979: 214)

In general, Blau and McKinley conclude that firms that standardize their activities and work procedures are less likely to establish an innovative milieu:

> Firms with routine production emphasizes satisfying a relatively uniform market demand, and principals, in an effort to maximize profit and reduce risks, may seek to standardize further, for example by promulgating criteria for a widely accepted style. ... But award-winning firms stress maximizing efficiency and profit less than they do turning out unique, aesthetically or technically notable projects. These firms rarely standardize design concepts from project to project, and attempt to continually evolve new and creative solutions to particular problems. In this 'uniform' situation, it is necessary to look beyond an individual building project to find a stable set of values in which a permanent means–ends hierarchy and a continuously organized structure can be anchored.
>
> (Blau and McKinley, 1979: 216–217)

In a similar vein, Hlavacek and Thompson (1973: 371) predicted that large organizations would develop new "non-bureaucratic forms of organization" to promote innovative work procedures. Speaking in terms of the bureaucratic organization form, Dougherty and Hardy (1996), Blau and McKinley (1979) and Hlavacek and Thompson (1973) suggest that large, functionally organized firms are less capable of innovating and have poorer skills in organizing innovative work. As opposed to this view, Damanpour (1992: 389) found "[a] positive and statistically significant relationship between size and innovation". In other words, large firms demonstrate a more significant capacity to innovate than small and medium-sized firms. Damanpour suggests that this may be related to the actual size of innovative departments within large firms:

> A survey of 4,000 innovations and innovative firms in the U.K. over four decades has shown that the average size of innovative firms is increasing, but the average size of divisions within those firms is decreasing (Pavitt *et al.*, 1989). Therefore, it appears that large innovative organizations are creating the required flexibility and autonomy needed for innovation by founding smaller (more specialized) divisions, while maintaining the advantages associated with large size.
>
> (Damanpour, 1992: 395)

This proposition is also supported by the research of Nohria and Gulati (1996) who suggest that there is an inverted-U relationship between slack and innovation; organization with little or no slack and organizations with excessive resources are poorer performers in terms of innovation than firms that have a reasonable amount of slack (see also Feldman, 1989, on control *versus* autonomy in innovation work). Since the organization's size probably influences the amount of slack, it may be that large firms effectively organize smaller units better equipped for successfully managing innovative work.

In addition to the parameter of size, the literature suggests that innovation is also strongly affected by mergers and acquisitions in the firm in focus. In the empirical material discussed in Chapters 4 and 5 in this book, the two firms studied had recently experienced a merger (in the case of AstraZeneca) and an acquisition (in the case of the Volvo Car Corporation). Consequently, it is important to take into account the effects of such major organization changes. Hitt *et al.* (1996) found in their analysis of Compustat company statistics that firms which underwent a merger or an acquisition displayed a lower degree of innovation:

> These results strongly suggest that firms actively buying or selling businesses, or both, are likely to produce less internal innovation and rely more heavily on external innovation for a variety of reasons, including the structure and implementation of the internal control system derived from their strategic actions.
>
> (Hitt *et al.*, 1996: 1110)

They continue:

Our results suggest that an active acquisition strategy has direct, negative effects on the internal development of firm innovation. This effect is likely due to the transaction costs involved and to acquisition-related activities that absorb managers' time and energy. Because of these transaction costs, managers have little time left to manage other important projects, and target firm managers in particular become strongly risk averse. Thus, managers of acquiring and target firms may postpone major decisions regarding long-term investments such as R&D and thereby reduce the innovative capabilities of their firms.

(Hitt *et al.*, 1996: 1110)

It is therefore not only the bureaucratic organization form as such that influences the capacity to innovate. Major organization changes such as mergers and acquisitions have a decisive influence on the innovative capacities of the firm. It is thus important to recognize the consequences of the recent organization changes in the two firms investigated as well as the established bureaucratic procedures and routines.

Studying bureaucracy

In the 1950s and 1960s, a number of bureaucracy studies were published. Talcott Parsons translated Weber into English and introduced him to the Anglo-American community of sociologists in the 1940s. In the 1950s and 1960s, Parsons held a chair in sociology at Harvard University and his colleague, Robert Merton, published some foundational texts on bureaucracy portraying it as possibly "dysfunctional" because of the emphasis on stability and rule-governed behaviour. Merton's students, Alvin Gouldner (1954) and Peter Blau (1963), published influential studies of bureaucracy to verify Merton's arguments. Somewhat surprisingly, neither Gouldner nor Blau were as negative towards bureaucracy as other contributors, but thought of bureaucracy as being capable of responding to social changes and establishing new procedures to deal with such changes. In the 1960s and 1970s a number of studies regarding bureaucratization (e.g. Maniha, 1975) were published, whereas, in the 1980s, bureaucracy studies were a less fashionable domain of investigation. Other research questions, such as the influence of company culture and a number of "management fads" (Total Quality Management, lean production, just-in-time logistics) largely displaced bureaucracy studies. In the 1990s, a variety of organization forms derived from the use of new information and communication technologies were investigated and bureaucracy gradually slipped down to its status of a supplementary organization form, a form of organization anyone could criticize and take a stance towards without taking any substantial risks. Everybody *knew* bureaucracy was bad and ineffective; virtually nobody cared to articulate a defence for bureaucracy. In the new millennium, bureaucracy studies are not exactly in vogue, but there is an emerging debate on the long-term consequences of a work-life characterized by flatter organization structures, little formal hierarchy and few lines of demarcation. However, as there is an increasing formulation of new organization forms, there is a need for studying how bureaucracies actually work. For instance, talking about "post-bureaucratic organizations" implies that one knows what a bureaucratic organization is and how it operates and under what conditions it is effective. The construction of a proper theory of a "post-bureaucratic organization" cannot be built on hearsay, folktales and beliefs imbued with common-sense thinking. Hence the need for research on bureaucratic organizations – or, rather: organizations structured on the basis of bureaucratic principles.

Outline of the book

The purpose of this book is threefold:

1   First, the literature on bureaucracy and the various forms of "post-bureau-cratic organization" is critically reviewed.
2   Second, two empirical studies of how innovation work is organized in large, bureaucratic organizations are reported.
3   Third, bureaucracy is reconceptualized and theorized in terms of sharing certain features with biological organisms, capable of undergoing ceaseless change yet maintaining their form and their identity qua organism. This image of bureaucracy is presented as a critique of the predominant machine metaphor still to date subscribed to in the bureaucracy literature and is an attempt at bridging biophilosphical thinking and process philosophy and bureaucracy literature.

This book is structured as follows: in Chapter 2, the literature on bureaucracy is examined and discussed in terms of constituting a discursive formation on bureaucracy.[3] The discourse on bureaucracy, then, is what is establishing bureaucracy as a certain form of organization and inscribes various capabilities and potentialities but also deficiencies and shortcomings into such a structure. For instance, the persistent theme of the "bureaucratic personality" is a subject-ivity derived from enunciations embedded in discursive beliefs.

In Chapter 3, the literature on the post-bureaucratic organization is reviewed. In this chapter, the post-bureaucratic organization is based on what is here called an "epistemology of fluids" that favours fluids, fluxes, movements and processes of becoming as the ultimate matter of being rather than stable entities and fixed, immutable bodies as in the Newtonian canon. The epistemology of fluids is a multifaceted and multiplanar discourse and comprises and integrates a series of adjacent traditions of thinking. As a consequence, the literature on the post-bureaucratic organization includes a number of different themes and trajectories and is by no means a unified and coherent movement beyond the conventional organization form. Just as the literature on bureaucracy is characterized by het-erogeneity, the post-bureaucratic organization literature is similarly lacking a unified and integrated theme but is instead a patchwork of different perspectives and ideas.

In Chapters 4 and 5, the empirical studies of two major multinational firms, Volvo Car Corporation in the automotive industry, and AstraZeneca in the pharmaceutical industry, are presented. These two companies are structured in accordance with bureaucratic principles such as the emphasis on standardized procedures, functional organization, hierarchical chains of command, life-long specialization as a qualifying marker of the experts employed in the organization, and so forth. However, these two firms have demonstrated a persistently and continual innovative capacity in terms of new patents and new product innovation in Volvo Cars in the automotive industry and in terms of the amount of newly registered and blockbuster drugs in AstraZeneca in the pharmaceutical industry. Volvo and AstraZeneca, then, are good examples of how bureaucratic principles are fruitfully adhered to in innovative and creative work. It is important to notice that the purpose of the two empirical chapters is not to evaluate whether large firms can be innovative or not, but to examine under what conditions co-workers operate in large, multinational companies.

In the sixth and final chapter, theoretical and practical implications from the two studies are critically evaluated and accounted for. In this final chapter, the functionalist and instrumental procedures enacted within the ideal-type bureaucracy model formulated by Max Weber are regarded as providing a firm grounding and an adequate degree of transparency for an innovative and creative organization. In addition, the organization needs to be able to nourish an entrepreneurial mindset and an experimental sense of joie de vivre among central communities and actors, providing good opportunities for exploiting the innovative and creative potential of the organization, but under determinate and reasonably transparent conditions. Adhering to the image of the organization as functioning as a biological organism, drawing on the bio-philosophy of Henri Bergson, as that which is both functionally structured yet capable of orchestrating continual changes and modifications in order to remain viable, the innovative and creative bureaucracy is not some kind of oxymoron but is, on the contrary, a hybrid combining stability and functional organization with mechanisms and processes that manage to adapt to external conditions. In terms of theoretical contributions, the book is aimed at (1) making bureaucracy what is not always already cast and condemned as incapable of innovating and being creative, (2) revitalizing the tradition of empirical studies of bureaucracy, and (3) offering alternative images of bureaucracy derived from the fields of biology and biophilosophy.

Summary and conclusion

Bureaucracy is, and will remain, one of the most important organizational forms in modern society. The establishment of systematic management practices, a managerial class qua social strata, and a variety of institutions such as business schools, polytechnic universities, engineering associations, business and engineering magazines and newspapers, is a multifaceted and complex social movement that is always already theoretically overdetermined; that is, it can be examined from a variety of perspectives and angles. Even though the rational- ization movement orchestrated by the emergent engineering profession from the end of the nineteenth century was by no means a linear event, it gradually gained acceptance equally among workingmen, managers and capitalists. The rationalization of industry is a romantic narrative (Sköldberg, 2002) filled with heroes and villains, great battles and defeats, accomplishments and failures. In contrast, the history of bureaucracy is less grand and more of a tragic story, pointing at the shortcomings and failures of the bureaucracy to fulfil all of its objectives and goals. For some reason, bureaucracy has always played a sec- ondary and little-appreciated role. Even though it is perhaps the single most important organizational model in the modern society, bureaucracy is more or less treated as a failure or as being merely capable of satisficing rather low expectations. Therefore, there is a need for more systematic studies of bureau- cracy, that is, the bureaucratic organization form rather than administrative activities as such, in order to address this deeply ingrained belief.

2 The concept of bureaucracy

Introduction

In this chapter, the concept is bureaucracy is examined. Rather than conceiving of the concept of bureaucracy as a single and unified construct, isolated from external influences, bureaucracy will be examined within a *field of intertextuality*, that is, within a field where various texts and other resources are continually interconnected and folded into one another. "Bureaucracy", then, is by no means a singularity, a word with one single proper lexical definition, but is instead a multiplicity or a manifold, capable of embodying a variety of meanings (Du Gay, 2005). This post-structuralist approach to the analysis of the concept of bureaucracy is by no means attempting at relativizing the idea of bureaucracy, to make it become something different than what it generally denotes in everyday language, but is rather an analytical strategy for envisaging how the different texts on bureaucracy are co-dependent and co-evolutionary, mutually supporting one another or presenting fruitful antagonist views of the concept. In the following, bureaucracy will be examined from a historical perspective, then how it is discussed in Max Weber's foundational texts, and thereafter the research on bureaucracy in organization theory, sociology and political science will be accounted for. Bureaucracy will thus be explored from a number of perspectives and angles. The purpose is to show how the writing on bureaucracy more or less follows a certain narrative, that of bureaucracy as representative of the failure to develop organization forms that are capable of responding to external influences and providing meaningful work assignments for the organization members. This narrative is persistent in the literature on bureaucracy and needs to be examined as what Claude Lévi-Strauss calls a "mytheme", a recurrent mythological figure appearing in a specific culture.

Modernity, management, bureaucracy: organizing the modern society

While bureaucracy is very much what is inextricably bound up with the emergence of the modern state apparatus, examples of pre-modern bureaucratic organization exists. In order to understand the emergence of bureaucracy and its image in the public mind, one needs to examine the emergence of management thinking as being entangled with the Western canon of thinking. In this section, the roots and the various branches of managerial thinking are examined. In so doing, we start from the dawn of Western thinking and the derogatory view of economic activity in Greek philosophy.

Premodern and religious roots of management

The notion of management is of recent origin and inextricably bound up with modernity and its various institutions and new forms of social arrangement (Shenhav, 1995, 1999). When we in the following speak of modernity, we adhere to Anthony Giddens's definition:

> At the simplest, modernity is a shorthand term for modern society or indus-trial society. Portrayed in more detail, it is associated with (1) a certain set of attitudes towards the world, the idea of the world as open to trans-formation by human intervention; (2) a complex of economic institutions, especially industrial production and a market economy; (3) a certain range of political institutions, including the nation-state and mass democracy. Largely as a result if these characteristics, modernity is vastly more dynamic than say previous type of social order.
>
> (Giddens and Pierson, 1998: 94)

In more specific terms, Giddens and Pierson argue that "the emergence of modernity is first of all the creation of a modern economic order, that is, a capi-talistic economic order" (1998: 96).

However, prior to any management discipline or discourse on management, there have been economic and mercantile activities that have been structured, controlled and organized on the basis of systematic and partially formalized knowledge and more or less explicit ideologies. The first evidence of math-ematical thinking in Babylonia and in Assyria testified to agricultural calcula-tions. In Greek thinking, later on, Aristotle distinguished between "the art of household management" (*oekonomia*) and "the art of moneymaking" (*Chrema-tistike*) (Swedberg, 1998: 30). Household management was the practical under-taking, of the transformation of nature into utilities such as goods, food items and some specific services, while moneymaking was aimed at earning money out of money-lending and other financial operations and ventures. Aristotle associates the latter form of economic activity with a less moral form of life not worthy of the philosopher. In his *Politics*, Aristotle (1998a) tells the story of how Thales of Miletus bought all the olive presses on his own and the neigh-bouring island, just to rent them back to the olive-farmers at the time of harvest. Thales's venture was aimed at showing how easy it is to make money for the philosopher if he only wanted to, but that the philosopher should dedicate his valuable time to more intellectual demanding matters such as geometry, politics or rhetoric. The derogatory view of *Chrematistike* among the Greeks would persist long into the medieval times. The French medieval historian, Jacques Le Goff (1980), shows how the Church struggled to resolve the theological problems associated with money-lending. On the one hand, the growing economies of the late medieval times demanded an effective financial market that could deal with risk allocation; on the other hand, lending money was "to lend time", and since time belonged to God, money-lending was located within a theologically complex domain. The pragmatic solution was that the Jewish community – who did not obey the Christian credo anyway – was given the permission to handle the money transactions.

In general, in the emergence of the modern society and its institutions and organization forms, the Jews and their religious beliefs played a substantial role: "The Jews ... often chose trade as their occupation for religious reasons; it was much easier to follow the rituals of Judaism if one was a trader than an agriculturalist" (Swedberg, 1998: 15). The Jewish community thus championed the growth of non-agricultural activities beneficial for the economy. In addition, Swedberg (1998: 19– 20) argues, the Jews were preceding the ascetic Protestantism that Max Weber saw as the primary motor for modern capitalism in terms of rejecting mystic components of religion and turning religious practice into profane activities and everyday life striving for better living conditions:

> The most important contribution of Judaism was ... not that the Jews had opposed the economic doctrine of the Catholic Church and thereby set free modern capitalism. ... It was that Judaism had turned religion in a nonmagical [Judaism was hostile to magic] and to some extent also nontraditional direction.

In this view, the modern organization and managerial practices have their roots in theological discourses. The most prominent spokesman for such as view is Weber (1992) and his emphasis on Protestantism as the dominant mode of thought preceding capitalist ideologies. For Protestants, religious following did not only imply an adherence to certain rules and practices, but also implied a long-term commitment to hard work and value accumulation in the praise of God. Weber's thesis, however, is far from uncontested and has been subject to substantial critical reflections. For instance, as several historians have pointed out, Catholic city-states such as Venice and Genua in medieval Italy were the first capitalistic trade centres of Europe, and Muslim trade centres in the Middle East and on the shores of Africa flourished prior to any Protestant capitalism (Braudel, 1992). Other scholars have even argued that Weber has reversed the causality, that Protestantism was an effect of capitalism rather than its impetus (Wren, 1972: 28). Nevertheless, Weber's basic idea, that certain ideologies and beliefs have long-term and largely latent functions and unanticipated effects, is still often referred to as a major contribution to the history of capitalism. Guillén (1994: 235) points at more recent associations between religion and management, for instance in the case of the UK where a number of large corporations in a variety of businesses, including banking (Lloyds, Barclays), accounting

(PriceWaterhouse & Co.) and confectionery (Cadbury, Rowntree), were controlled by Quaker families.

The premodern forms of managerial control were therefore heavily dependent on what Barley and Kunda (1992) refer to as "normative control"; religious beliefs and practices determined which economic and financial ventures were legitimate or not. The modern forms of management thinking, strongly associated with *rational forms of control,* were primarily developed in domains such as accounting and book-keeping. One such rational method was the Venetian Luca Paciolo's double-entry book-keeping advocated in his *Summa de arithmetica, geometrica, proportioni, et proportionalita* published in 1494 (Wren, 1972: 21). The development of management thinking and practice prior to the industrial revolution and its radical transformation of European societies were unsystematic and largely embedded in the search for solutions to practical concerns. During the formative years of industrial capitalism – here opposed to the mercantile capitalism of the premodern period – the issue of management became of central importance in the process of modernization.

The demand for systematic management knowledge

The effects of division of labour had been known since the dawn of humanity, and the Scottish moral philosopher Adam Smith gave it a proper theoretical account in his *Wealth of Nations* (1776), a liberal economics book that spoke in favour of free trade and the importance of exploiting what David Ricardo later would call comparative advantages of different regions and nations. Although Smith pointed at the immediate and, in many cases, baffling effects of division of labour, he was also aware of the devastating effects that a far-reaching division of labour might imply for the working men. Many other writers would return to this perennial issue. One of the most influential was Charles Babbage, who was one of the first – Andrew Ure's *The Philosophy of Manufacturers* (first published in 1835) is another classic text – to apply the idea of division of labour directly to companies. According to Babbage, there are five forms of gains from the division of labour:

1   shorter time for learning a skill.
2   less waste in materials.
3   lower transaction costs.
4   no need for the change of tools.
5   skills acquired by repetition.

(Babbage, 1833: 170–172)

Babbage also points out that the mechanisms of division of labour are also applicable within "mental labour": "The division of labour can be applied with equal success to mental as to mechanical operations, and that it ensures in both the same economy of time" (Babbage, 1833: 191). In other words, specialization was one of the keys to a more effective and productive industry and administration of the state affairs. In terms of specialization and division of labour, two major trends can be discerned. On the one hand, the bureaucratic organization form evolved, based on a series of principles and rules. On the other hand, the management function was made a systematic field of inquiry and was *eo ipso* professionalized. Before the development of bureaucracy will be examined, the engineering-driven development of systematic management procedures will be examined in greater details.

However, before engaging with the "official history" of management thinking, one may address the managerial innovations developed in the agrarian economy in the European colonies and in the American South in the eighteenth and nineteenth centuries. In a seminal paper (2003), Bill Cooke discusses the relatively marginalized topics of the influence of slavery in management thinking and practice. Cooke points to the size of the plantations as a decisive factor and a driving force behind the development of systematic managerial practice:

> Throughout the eighteenth century, the great plantations of the sugar colonies . . . were the largest private enterprises of the age, and their owners were among the richest of men. The same can be said of the cotton plantations in the United States on the eve of the Civil War.
>
> (Fogel, 1989: 24, cited in Cooke, 2003: 1897)

Thus the ante-bellum period in the American South was an important period for the establishment of managerial practice and authority. Cooke points out that a range of managerial practices were systematically developed and employed in the plantations in the American South. He writes: "[T]here was a substantial and growing group of people using what are now seen as management practices who were known as managers, running ante-bellum plantations (Cooke, 2003: 1911). Moreover, Cooke argues that "[w]hite supremacist racism underpinned the creation of the managerial identity". He continues: "Racism was used to justify the assumption of this right to manage. ... Black people were categorized as the moral and intellectual inferiors to whites, suitable only for drudgery, and beseeching management" (2003: 1911). For Cooke, Frederick W. Taylor's negative view of the co-workers is embedded in such supremacist ideas, depicting the manager as some kind of intellectually and morally superior being. Cooke summarizes the argument like this:

> The industrial discipline which emerged on the plantations was not disconnected temporally, spatially or in substance from that which emerged in other parts of the US economy. The imprint of slavery in contemporary management can be seen in the ongoing dominance from that time of the very idea of the manager with a right to manage. It can also be seen in the specific management ideas and practices now known as classical management and scientific management which were collated and re-presented with these labels within living memory of the abolition of US slavery.
>
> (2003: 1913)

However, the establishment of modern management practices and procedures was not without social costs in Europe either. Pollard (1965), examining the case of Britain from the beginning of the Industrial Revolution up to 1830, argued that workers were, on the one hand, treated as if they obeyed the simplest behaviourist principles of stimuli and response and, on the other hand, they were disciplined by religious teaching to follow rules and to abandon old customs. Pollard argue that the social costs for this transformation of society were "needlessly high":

> The task was finally accomplished, though at a needlessly high cost, and a society of peasants, craftsmen and versatile workers became a society of modern industrial workers: but it is doubtful whether, within the context of the present structure of society and industry, the dilemmas of its beginning have been resolved even today.

> (Pollard, 1965: 208)

In his conclusion, Pollard further emphasizes the significant cultural changes brought by managerial capitalism:

> [T]he view of the majority [of the employers] were bounded by the realization that they were dealing with a recalcitrant, hostile working force whose morale, whose habits of work and whose culture had to be broken in order to fit them for a form of employment in which they had to become obedient servants of the machine, of its owners and of crude monetary incentives. What was necessary, according to this view, was a reform of 'character' on the part of every single workman, since their previous character did not fit the new industrial system.

> (Pollard, 1965: 255–256)

While the professional co-worker in a premodern organization largely decided for him or herself what was a legitimate amount of output or work pace, in the new regime, the managers were expected to monitor the co-workers' activities. This new category of the manager was a category that entered the historical scene rather recently. Chandler (1977: 3) writes: "[A]s late as the 1840s there were no middle managers in the United States – that is, there were no managers who supervised the work of the other managers and in turn reported to senior executives who themselves were salaried managers." In Britain, Pollard (1965) found that managers were more of an effect of capitalism than its driver. Consequently, managers as a social category emerged slowly: "[A] managerial class as such was slow to develop and even by 1830 could hardly be said to be in existence, though well-defined classes of managers had emerged in various specific industries" (Pollard, 1965: 250). Shenhav (1999: 2) points at the struggles and controversies the use of "salaried managers" caused before being made legitimate: "Salaried managers eventually did become a quintessential part of modern organizations, but this coming to power was plagued by conflicts and rather fierce confrontation with capitalist owners as well as with labour unions and unorganised workers." The new systematic form of organization thereby implied new forms of management control and managerial practices previously unattended to (see also Veblen, 1904, and Berle and Means, 1991, for an extended argument). Chandler (1977: 1) talks about the emergence of managerial capitalism based on management at a distance and bureaucratic organization as the "visible hand" of management: "In many sectors of the economy the visible hand of management replaced what Adam Smith referred to as the invisible hand of the market forces. . . . The rise of modern business enterprise in the United States, therefore, brought with it managerial capitalism".

Parallel to the bureaucratization of administrative work in the state administration and in major companies, another major shift in management thinking took place around the turn of the twentieth century. The scientific management movement was emerging from the American Society for Mechanical Engineers (ASME), taking great interest in the day-to-day management procedures in companies. Still, similar to the growth of bureaucracies as an effect of a higher level of education, the interest for systematic management knowledge had its root in the increased number of engineers in American society. Jacoby (1985) reports that, between 1880 and 1920, the number of engineers grew from about 7,000 to 135,000 in the USA. The engineers brought with them a scientific mindset and a certain curiosity for social improvements and new forms of arrangement of manufacturing activities.

While there was little uniformity in the work routines and practices in factories prior to the emergence of what F.W. Taylor would dub "scientific management", the engineering expertise was focused on standardizing and restructuring manufacturing functions. This specialized group of engineers were the carriers of the credo of standardization and the driving force behind the "efficiency craze" in the period after 1910. Guillén (1994: 45) dates the start of the American movement to the famous Eastern Rate Case of 1910–1911, where the lawyer and Democratic reformer, Louis D. Brandeis, representing business associations from all over the American East Coast, argued that wages could be raised if scientific principles were implemented in the railroad companies. The restructuring of companies became one of the principal concerns for managers during the period. Taylor's colleague and follower, Henry Gantt, even argued that "a system of management based on these methods [scientific management] is just as much a part of our assets as plant, or equipment" (Gantt, 1919: 236; original emphasis removed). In addition, Gantt envisaged "[a] self-perpetuating system of management based on the efficient utilization of scientific knowledge" (Gantt, 1919: 249; original emphasis removed). Speaking in those terms, Gantt was anticipating the forerunners of resource-based view strategy theorists (see Barney, 1991) such as Philip Selznick (1957) and Edith Penrose (1959), portraying the firm as a set of material, social and intangible resources – "a firm is basically a collection of resources", as Penrose (1959: 77) put it – and conceived of a "management system" as being a firm-specific resource. Barley and Kunda write:

Although at times more nuanced than critics admit, scientific management's rhetoric revolved around three tenets; (1) an unshakeable belief in the unity and morality of scientific reasoning, (2) the axiom that all people are primarily rational, and (3) the supposition that all people view work as an economic endeavor. Drawing on these premises, Taylor argued that when placed in jobs appropriate to their abilities and when fairly paid, even the least-skilled worker could immediately recognize the superiority of rationality optimized work procedures.

(Barley and Kunda, 1992: 371)

In other words, scientific management imposed an overtly rationalistic and, in many ways, instrumental view of human beings and work (Guillén, 1994). Shenhav lists some of the implication from a more systematic management regime:

The institutionalization of management systems had several ramifications. First, it legitimized the engineers as managers and as propagators of managerial curricula in business schools. A new class of technocrats was crowned. Its gospel gradually spread to include an administrative view of society whose practices eventually became a worldwide ideology. Second, it has succeeded in cleaving a sharp compartmentalization between politics and economics, blurring the fact that economic logic is politically and ideologically weighted. The institutionalization of management systems gave objective and universal status to value-laden assumptions such as economic maximization, efficiency, and standardization.

(1999: 3)

Similar to the consequences of bureaucracies, the application of scientific methodologies in the pursuit of "one of the best ways of working" had the latent function of displacing nepotism. Jacoby (1985) argues that, prior to the engineering revolution – a concept that might sound grandiloquent but still is adequate – foremen reigned in the factory shops and could treat the workmen very much as they wanted. As a consequence, the foreman was one of the most hated and despised figures of the early years of the industrialized society. Taylor and his scientific-management principles gradually undermined the position of the foreman who, in the scientific-management regime, was downgraded to leading manual work in the factory shop while decision-making authority was given to the engineers and located in specialized departments. Notwithstanding the emphasis on professionalization of the engineers' work, practitioners were not overtly enthusiastic in their reception of the new ideas. Shenhav (1995: 565) writes:

Despite this blossoming of "organizations as systems" in the engineering literature and in professional circles, in practice, many employers were apprehensive about adopting a systems approach. Shop owners, particularly those with smaller shops, viewed systematization as a strategy employed by engineers to expand their professional territory. To them, systems were costly and superfluous.

As Guillén shows, Taylor's ideas where received very differently in the USA, the UK, Spain and Germany, and was often met with scepticism or even hostility, especially among the British elites who disregarded the "dehumanizing" effects of scientific management. The engineers became the carriers of the effectiveness credo and spokesmen of Taylorist principles that were, in fact, often implemented and applied under other labels, such as the successful Bedaux system advocated by Charles Eugène Bedaux in his book, *The Bedaux Efficiency Course for Industrial Application*, first published in 1917. Guillén (1994: 56-57) writes:

> While avoiding the negative stigma attached to anything represented under the name of Taylorism, many employees and managers used the Bedaux System to introduce scientific management through the back door. Unlike Taylor's, the Bedaux System could be implemented without revamping the entire management practices of the firm, a feature that employers welcomed.

Even scholars such as Thorstein Veblen were highly sceptical about the engineers' ambition to standardize and make everything systematic. Veblen (1904: 10) remarks in a sarcastic tone: "What is not completely standardized calls for too much of craftmanlike skill, reflection, and individual elaboration, and is therefore not available for economical use in the process." Later on, he continues: "The working population is required to be standardized, moveable, and interchangeable in much the same impersonal manner as the raw or half-wrought materials of industry" (Veblen, 1904: 326). At the beginning of the 1930s, some fifty years of unrestricted rationalization orchestrated by the engineers became a source of critique: "Engineers were criticized for having created a 'machine civilization': a hyper-mechanized society characterized by monotonous jobs, alienated workers, lack of spirit, lack of aesthetic, and dehumanization (e.g. Chase, 1929). The general feeling was that mechanization and systematization had gone too far" (Shenhav, 1999: 46).

What is noteworthy about the rationalization movement and the scientific management movement – a movement with obscure and modest origins at the turn of the twentieth century, but twenty years later had become a highly respected and praised movement within industry and the modern society – is that it rested on what Barley and Kunda (1992) calls "rational control"; that is, it based its suggestions on measurement of the work activities rather than normative ideas about industry. For Barley and Kunda (1992), management thinking has changed from rational to normative ideologies, each new era being a response to the shortcomings of the preceding paradigm (see Table 2.1).

Table 2.1 Management ideologies, 1870–1992

The succession of managerial ideologies since 1870		
Ideology	*Era of ascent*	*Tenor*
Industrial betterment	1870–1900	Normative
Scientific management	1900–1923	Rational
Welfare capitalism/human relations	1923–1955	Normative
Systems rationalism	1955–1980	Rational
Organization culture	1980–present	Normative

Source: adapted from Barley and Kunda (1992: 364).

While the scientific-management movement imposed a veritable battery of measuring techniques and tools for structuring manufacturing activities, its succeeding management ideology, human relations, was more concerned with the role and position of people at work. Although management writers such as Mary Parker Follett (1941) had addressed such issues in the 1920s, it was not until Elton Mayo was affiliated with Harvard University that such issues started to become more widely acknowledged. Mayo's research was financed by the Rockefeller Foundation and was given the assignment of finding means to ease the labour conflicts and the poor relations between capitalists and workers (Guillén, 1994; O'Conner, 1999). The emphasis on group dynamics and other forms of social and emotional aspects of work was one of the distinguishing features of Human Relations (Roethlisberger and Dickson, 1943; Mayo, 1946; Homans, 1951). Rather than focusing single-handedly on output, the work process itself became a key concern. What probably is the single most discussed and examined case study in management writing, that of the Western Electric Hawthorne plant conducted by Roethlisberger and Dickson (1943), set the research agenda for legions of organization psychologists, industrial sociologists and management researchers for decades to come. One of the latent functions of the Human Relations school was its role in the shift from what Michael Burawoy calls "despotic" to "hegemonic" factory regimes, wherein "workers must be persuaded to cooperate with management" (Burawoy, 1985: 126). Burawoy continues: "Their [workers'] interests must be coordinated with those of management. The *despotic regimes* of early capitalism, in which coercion prevails over consent, must be replaced with *hegemonic regimes*, in which consent prevails" (see also Barker, 1993; Jacques, 1996). While Taylor and his followers such as Henry Gantt (1919), in championing the scientific-management thinking, cared little about the attitudes and beliefs of the workers (with Frank and Lillian Gilbreth as clear exceptions to the rule, see Gilbreth, 1911; Gilbreth and Gilbreth, 1919), Human Relations made such issues a concern for management. Townley (1993) writes:

Where the workforce was largely undifferentiated in early factory organization, there was little knowledge of, or interest in, the individual. As classification systems were put into place, greater differentiation arose generally based on observable factors such as skill, age, performance, behaviour, and so forth. Later, the mind, or psyche, became identified as the key to gaining knowledge of performance. . . . New dimensions of subjectivity were introduced that helped bridge the external world of conduct and the internal world of the individual.

(Townley, 1993: 534)

Shenhav's (1995) review of the engineering literature during the period 1879–1932 supports Townley's argument:

A closer examination of the *American Machinist* [an engineering journal] reveals that the percentage of items associated with industrial psychology was ten times larger during 1913–1920 than in the earlier period, 1879–1912. As for *Engineering Magazine*, there were no items on industrial psychology prior to 1916. In 1916, the percentage was approximately 2 percent and rose to 22 percent in 1917 and to 35 percent in 1918.

(Shenhav, 1995: 577)

Shenhav (1995) refers to this period of increased interest for industrial psychology as the progressive period (1900–1917) because engineers were aiming to take a lead in transforming industry into a modern project, based on scientific principles, systematic methods and social equality (manifested in welfare legislation and antitrust laws and unionism). Recalling Bendix (1956), emphasis on bureaucracies as forms of organization wherein the attitudes of workers became a component of the management system, there is little wonder that the mental set-up of the worker became a long-term engagement in management thinking. Even though Barley and Kunda (1992) portray the Human Relations school as being representative of a normative ideology, it was still adhering to the principles of scientific research methods. In contrast to the scientific-management movement that grew from within the professional societies and associations of the abounding managerial class of engineers, the Human Relations school was perhaps the first significant first business-school contribution to systematic management knowledge. The academic affiliation of human relations not only enabled a quicker reception and recognition in the industry, but also contributed to a more systematic research on management practice. The interwar period was a period of emergence of a management discipline comprising the inception of business schools, academic journals and professional management consultants: *The Management Review* was founded in 1918; the *Harvard Business Review* in 1922; the American Management Association in 1925 (Thrift, 1998: 171). Consulting firms like Arthur D. Little and McKinsey were founded at the end of the First World War and on into the 1920s. Management thinking became increasingly *institutionalized*.

The emergence of modern management

After the Second World War, a new wave of rationalist ideology pervaded management thinking. Barley and Kunda (1992) refer to this thinking as "systems rationalism", dominating the period 1955 to 1980. Again, similar to the scientific management movement, the efficiency of companies became a major concern: "All systems rationalists regardless of discipline peddled programmatic techniques or universal principles that would enable managers to plan, forecast, and act more effectively. Accordingly, each camp draw moral, if not technical inspiration from scientific management" (Barley and Kunda, 1992: 379). The postwar period brought a veritable explosion of management research and new subdisciplines sharing the interest for ways to make things easier, better and more productive. European universities and an increasingly tighter network of conferences, journals and research communities adopted the American business school model and its research practices, and other research-based resources were constructed. Management became a scientific discipline in its own right, independent from neighbouring disciplines such as economics and sociology. The period after 1980 was, according to Barley and Kunda (1992), characterized by an interest for organization culture. As a consequence of the impressive performance of Japanese manufacturing companies posing a real challenge to American industry, organization culture became a major source of reflection and systematic inquiry throughout the 1980s and into the early 1990s. Czarniawska and Genell (1992) characterize this period as being dominated by ideological control:

> For a couple of centuries the industrial world was managed by a combination of supervision and accounting. But after that the scope for supervision started to explode, as companies left the homestead and spread all over the world. In the 1980s this development was met by an attempt at ideological control – referred to as the establishment of "organizational cultures". Now, however, a decade or so later, it has become clear that, short of brainwashing, it is hard to exert ideological control in non-totalitarian societies, and that cultures or indeed any kind of institutional order all develop slowly and change unwillingly. Not for the first time in history, engineering is coming to the aid of management, and standards of all kinds are used to support accounting, restricted up to then to financial matters.
>
> (Czarniawska and Genell, 2002: 471)

Czarniawska and Genell (2002) emphasize that culture was increasingly regarded as a rather blunt tool for wielding control. Instead, in the early 1990s, the notion of auditing was promoted as a new means of controlling organizations (see, for example, Power, 1994). In addition to the gradual loss of interest in organization culture, during 1990s the pluralism – or, as some would put it (for example, Pfeffer, 1993; Starbuck, 2003b), in somewhat negative terms, *fragmentation* – of management studies was accentuated in management studies, while new theoretical fields such as gender studies, critical management studies and postmodern and postcolonial theory were increasingly acknowledged as legitimate and relevant theoretical orientations (Calás and Smircich, 1999; Prasad, 2003; Linstead, 2004). Barley and Kunda's (1992) analysis of the evolution of management thinking suggests that surges of normative and rational ideologies are co-varying with various broader social, cultural and economic changes; there is, then, no linear progression from one kind of ideology to another, but the pattern demonstrates more fluxing and fluid changes. Barley and Kunda (1992) argue:

> Rather than having progressed steadily from coercive to rational and then to normative conceptions of control, managerial ideology may have been elaborated in surges of rhetoric that alternately celebrated normative and rational forms of control. Moreover, an interplay between broad cultural and economic forces may have underwritten these alternations. Specifically, deeply rooted but opposing images of Gemeinschaft and Gesellschaft appear to have constrained the collective imagination of the managerial community by dichotomizing the range of acceptable images of organizing.
>
> (Barley and Kunda, 1992: 392)

Management literature and management consulting have also constituted an industry in themselves and, the industry appears to be continuously growing. Jackson (2001: 4) argues that, in 1974, the management industry had a turnover of 11.4 billion USD in the US and 15.2 billion USD in the rest of the world. By 1997, those figures had more than doubled to 25 billion USD in the US and 50 billion USD in the rest of the world. In the publishing industry, similar figures are available:

> In 1991 McGraw Hill published 25 [business] titles; in 1996 it published 110. Marketing budgets at the esteemed ... Harvard Business School Press is estimated to have almost doubled in the last four years. In the UK alone 2,931 business titles were published in 1996, compared with a paltry 771 in 1975.
>
> (Crainer, 1997: 38, cited in Thrift, 1998: 174)

The demand for what we here call "systematic management knowledge" appears to be insatiable.

Bureaucracy and modernity

Even though the idea of bureaucracy is inextricably entangled with the modern society, several historians and anthropologists point to the presence of bureaucratic procedures and bureaucratic organizations in premodern and even tribal societies (de Landa, 1997: 32). Gluckman (1965) argues that the slave trade in the colonialist period was made effective because of close collaboration with African societies, organizing the slave-trade business in a bureaucratic form.

The French historian, Marc Bloch (1962: 422ff), writes that the earliest forms of systematic bureaucracy in Europe outside the great churches and the papal court date from the feudal period in the eleventh and twelfth centuries. However, prior to that, the most advanced human cultures had developed forms of systematic administration and routines for juridical matters, schooling, and the political and religious systems. Nevertheless, the emergence of modern bureaucracy is dependent upon the ability to write, to store, share and reproduce information, in short the ability to establish, in Kittler's (1990) words, a certain "discourse network". Jack Goody (1986) examines bureaucratic organization in premodern societies and emphasizes the practice of writing as the single most important skill preceding the emergence of the bureaucratic state: "[W]riting is critical in the development of bureaucratic states, even though relatively complex forms of government is possible without it. ... Writing was not essential to the development of the state but of a certain type of state, the bureaucratic state" (Goody, 1986: 91–92). Bloch (1962) also emphasizes the skill of writing and the emergence of a social elite in the feudal society as important drivers towards bureaucratization. The "bureaucratic state", then, is a state marked by its ability to exploit forms of writing. In addition to writing, Kallinikos (2004) argues that the bureaucratic organization is dependent on new ideas regarding individualism and individual freedom and rights embodied by the bourgeois ethos:

> Bureaucracy and modernity are ... inextricably bound up with one another. Bureaucracy is the organization form of modernity. It is closely associated with the overall cultural orientations of modern man, the social mobility that coincided with the gradual dissolution of premodern stratification, and the burgeoning bourgeoisie ideals of individual freedom and justice, which it helped itself to embed.
>
> (Kallinikos, 2004: 22)

According to Karl Marx and Friedrich Engels (1970), the bourgeoisie is the only successful revolutionary class, a class that has successfully transformed society on the basis of their values and modus operandi. For Kallinikos (2004), the bourgeoisie advanced social values that paved the way for the hierarchical and specialized organization that we name "bureaucracy". For instance, the very idea of separating social life (work) and family life and personal interests lies at the very heart of these values:

> The emergence of the bureaucratic form of organization was predicated on a major anthropological innovation (that is, a new way of conceiving humanity and institutionally embedding it) that we have tended to take for granted these days, namely, the clear and institutionally supported separation of work from the rest of people's lives. The conception of work as a distinct sphere of social life, sufficiently demarcated vis-à-vis other social spheres, has had a decisive significance for constitution of the modern workplace.
>
> (Kallinikos, 2003: 614)

Michael Reed speaks of the emergence of bureaucracy in terms similar to Kallinikos's, namely as the dominance of instrumental rationality over traditional modes of thinking: "Bureaucratic organizations were seen as the primary institutional expressed of the cognitive dominance of instrumental rationality in modern societies" (Reed, 1992: 2). He continues:

> The triumph of bureaucracy signaled the overwhelming cognitive power and technical superiority of an inner organizational logic and mechanism which eradicated the ineluctable conflict between foundational values and beliefs that had been the hallmark of traditional societies.
>
> (1992: 41)

Above all, bureaucracy separated office from social position and social class, and implied a professionalization of the state administration including the demands for formal education and training and other formal *individual* qualifications. Bendix (1971) writes:

> As long as government administration was in the hands of a social elite or a group of political partisans which had privileged access to office and conducted the "public" business as a species of private prerogative, administrative reforms were aimed at equalizing access, diminishing arbitrariness, and reducing private profiteering. The separation of office and incumbent, appointment by merit, the contractual regulation of appointment and promotion, fixed monetary salaries, and other related measures can be understood as *preventing* the intrusion of kinship relations, property interests, and political partisanship upon the conduct of the public business.
>
> (Bendix, 1971: 144)

With bureaucracy, the modern worldview is, for the first time, manifested in a proper organization form.

The effects of bureaucracy in the modern society have been grist for the mill for numerous historians, economists, sociologists and even artists and writers. Classic works such as Franz Kafka's *The Process* and Charlie Chaplin's *Modern Times* have been regarded as accounts of the consequences of a far-driven specialization and a too-low-degree of transparency in organizations. At the beginning of the new millennium, most people are aware of the supposedly negative effects of a bureaucratized society. What is problematic in this rather strongly accentuated negative view of bureaucracy is that its positive consequences are either taken for granted and thus naturalized, or are simply ignored. For instance, management historians such as Sanford Jacoby (1985) have shown that the recruitment of workers underwent a strong professionalization during the end of the nineteenth century and implied the emergence of a personnel function in manufacturing organizations. Jacoby (1985) examines the more systematic recruitment procedures that evolved in the early twentieth century, emphasizing transparency, systematic procedures and formal contracting as a form of bureaucratization of the personnel function. The long-term consequences for productivity and the individual's social security cannot be underrated. However, it is rare that such obvious social accomplishments are credited to the bureaucratic organization form per se. In most cases, the bureaucratic organization form is treated as the *infrastructure* (Bowker and Leight Star, 1999) of such accomplishments, and is therefore not sufficiently acknowledged as a major vehicle for social modernization and the implementation of democratic values.

Bendix (1956) examined another only modestly recognized effect of the bureaucratic organization. Bendix argues that, prior to the bureaucratization of activities, individual clerks and workers were held responsible for their own activities and their output. When the bureaucratic organization form is implemented, the responsibility for activities and output are, Bendix argues, shifted from the individual to management, and this shift implied that new factors such as emotional and social factors affecting output are taken into account: "With bureaucratization the importance of professional skills and administrative expertise increases, as does the difficulty of implementing the principles of accountability" (Bendix, 1971: 147). In the new regime, based on functional specialization and rule-governed activities, the individual's perception of his or her work becomes a source of interest; work is no longer the sole concern for individual co-workers but becomes a managerial concern, thereby giving rise to a number of activities and research objectives aiming at shedding some light on how individual beliefs and attitudes affect work and its output. In other words, bureaucracy gave relevance to a whole range of managerial research questions; issues of motivation, emotionality, the individual's perception of work, and so forth, became part of the research agenda for the entire post-Second World War period. While the Taylorist management regime strictly emphasized the extrinsic motivation of the workers – that is, the monetary rewards for the work – the bureaucratic organization was based on the ability to understand the intrinsic motivation of the workers, a field of interest that Taylor did not think of as being of central importance. On the contrary, if intrinsic motivation had been an issue, the scientific management principles would have been poorly implemented in Taylor's view.

In summary, the movement from an organization regime characterized by individual influence, nepotism and rules of thumb to a specialized organization form aiming at promoting transparency, professionalism, systematic inquiries and a number of other democratic and essentially bourgeois values, represent a decisive step in the progress of the modern society. The importance of a bureaucratic organization form in this movement cannot be underrated. Thus, seen from the perspective of the individual citizen, the bureaucratized society is by no means in itself a deeply concerning condition. In order to understand the bureauphobia in academic research, we need to return to Max Weber's initial account of the bureaucratic organization form.

Weber's view of bureaucracy

Max Weber stands out as a foundational figure in modern social thought. During his career, Weber held chairs in three different disciplines: in sociology (in Freiburg), in economics (in Heidelberg) and in philosophy (in Munich). Weber spoke not only English, French and Spanish, but also mastered Russian and Hebrew. His position as one of the most influential social thinkers to date is largely uncontested and his work demonstrates a remarkable breadth: juridical matters, theology, economics, history and philosophy are included in his oeuvre. However, one of his most widely recognized contributions to the social sciences is his work on bureaucracy. For instance, for Blau and Scott (1963: 27), Weber's principles of bureaucracy are "undoubtedly the most important general state-ments on formal organization". Bendix (1971: 130) argues a propos Weber's analysis of bureaucracy that "none of the critics of Weber's analysis has yet dis-pensed with his definition". Weber observed the emergence of a bureaucratic state apparatus in the German state and concluded that this new regime represen-ted a new mode of administration. Weber speaks of the emergence of bureau-cracy as the effect of accumulation of wealth in the contemporary society:

> The growing demands on culture ... are determined, though to a varying extent, by the growing wealth of the most influential strata in the state. To this extent increasing bureaucratisation is a function of the increasing pos-session of goods used for consumption, and of an increasingly sophisticated technique of fashioning external life – a technique which corresponds to the opportunities provided by such wealth. This reacts with the standard of living and makes for an increasingly subjective indispensability of organ-ized, collective, inter-local, and thus bureaucratic, provision for the most varied wants, which previously were either unknown, or were satisfied locally or by private economy.
>
> (Weber, 1948: 213)

The bottom line, then, is that, in a Marxist formulation, bureaucracy is the estab-lishment of a value-neutral state-control apparatus aimed at safeguarding the accumulation of private capital. This leads us to one of the central principles in Weber's bureaucracy model, the insistence on *Wertfreiheit*, the absence of per-sonal interests and objectives. Weber (1999: 100) writes: "Ideally the adminis-tration proceeds *sine ira et studio*, not allowing personal motives or temper influence conduct, free of arbitrariness and unpredictability". Since the bureau-cracy should not rest on traditional or charismatic rationalities, but must strictly adhere to predefined rules and regulations, "[b]ureaucracy represents the purest type of legal domination" for Weber (1999: 100). This legal domination is mani-fested in the ten rules of bureaucracy that Weber formulated:

1 They [Bureaucrats] are personally free and subject to authority only with respect to their impersonal official obligations.

2   They are organized in a clearly defined hierarchy of offices.
3   Each office has a clearly sphere of competence in the legal sense.
4   The office is filled by free contractual relationships. Thus, in principle, there is free circulation.
5   Candidates are selected on the basis of technical qualifications.
6   They are remunerated by fixed salaries in money, for the most part with a right to pensions. ... The salary scale is graded according to rank in the hierarchy; but in addition to this criterion, the responsibility of the position and the requirements of the incumbent's social status may be taken into account.
7   The office is treated as the sole, or at least the primary, occupation of the incumbent.
8   It constituted a career. There is a system of promotion according to seniority or to achievement, or both. Promotion is dependent on the judgement of superiors.
9   The official works entirely separate from ownership of the means of administration and without appropriation of his position.
10 He is subject to strict and systematic discipline and control in the conduct of the office.

(Weber, 1978: 220–221)

The consequences from these predefined working procedures was that bureaucracy was able to provide specialized and predictable activities:

> Bureaucracy offers above all the optimum possibility for carrying through the principle of specializing administrative functions according to purely objective considerations. Individual performances are allocated to functionaries who have specialized training and who by constant practice learn more and more. The "objective" discharge of business primarily means a discharge of business according to calculable rules and "without regard for persons".
>
> (Weber, 1948: 215)

Weber's most important work, *Wirtschaft und Gesellschaft* (*Economy and Society*) provides a long list of concepts characterizing the bureaucratic organization. Many of these concepts are complicated to translate into English (we here follow Höpfl's translations, 2006: 10). The bureaucracy has *Herrschaft* ("authority") over what it administrates; the administrators have strict domains of *Kompetenzen* (delimited "jurisdiction") and have *Fachwissen* (professional qualifications and knowledge) derived from *Kontorwissenschaft* ("administrative science"); the organization of the bureaucracy is *straff* ("taut", "tight", "ram-rod-straight"); the bureaucracy controls *Machtmittel* ("instruments of power") and *Verwaltungsmittel* ("means of administration") to carry out its assignments; a specific attention is paid to the *Akten* ("the keeping of records"). For Weber, the bureaucratic organization form is much more effective than the traditional "collegiate" forms of administration. Weber argues:

The decisive reason for the advance of bureaucratic organization has always been its purely technical superiority over any other form of organization. The fully developed bureaucratic mechanism compares with other organizations exactly as does the machine with the non-mechanical modes of production. Precision, speed, unambiguity, knowledge of the files, continuity, discretion, strict subordination, reduction of friction and of material and personal costs – these are raised to the optimum point in the strictly bureaucratic administration, and especially in its monocratic form. As compared with all collegiate, honorific, and avocational forms of administration, trained bureaucracy is superior on all these points. And as far as complicated tasks are concerned, paid bureaucratic work is not only more precise but, in the last analysis, it is often cheaper than even formally unremunerated honorific service.

(Weber, 1948: 214)

Taken together, the bureaucratic organization form is capable of serving a society increasingly dependent on coordination and infrastructure with a range of services. For Weber, bureaucracy is an indispensable organization form in contemporary society, and the bureaucrats themselves are "carriers" (*Träger*) of the democratic values of transparency and predictability. However, Weber has a rather strong reputation for presenting a somewhat gloomy image of modern life, in terms of it being an iron cage administered by narrow-minded specialists demonstrating little empathy and interest stretching outside the individual domain of expertise. Therefore, Weber was not only enthusiastic about the bureaucratic organization but also pointed to a series of potential dysfunctions and flaws in the model. One of the negative effects of bureaucracy is its strong emphasis on "rationalist" thinking, a mode of thinking emphasizing utility and functionalist solutions to perceived problems:

Naturally, bureaucracy promotes a 'rationalist' way of life, but the concept of rationalism allows for widely differing contents. Quite generally, one can say that the bureaucratisation of all domination very strongly furthers the development of 'rational matter-of-factness' and the personality type of the professional expert.

(Weber, 1948: 240)

This makes the bureaucrat susceptible to a sort of rigid "factism" wherein only brute facts are worthy of taking into account. Weber's worries about the influence of this mode of thinking have given birth to an entire genre portraying bureaucrats as lifeless and stodgy administrators representing a "bureaucratic personality", more concerned about their own rules and regulations and the organization's own objectives than the practical effects of their work. Needless to say, this rationalist outlook is by no means solely representative of the bureaucratic organization form but, rather, is one of the dominant modes of thinking in the modern contemporary society.

The other major concern for Weber regarding bureaucracy was agency and the operating procedures of the bureaucrats. Weber points at the problems associated with keeping bureaucratic procedures transparent for all stakeholders: "Every bureaucracy seeks to increase the superiority of the professionally informed by keeping their knowledge and intentions secret. Bureaucratic administration always tends to be administration of 'secret sessions': in so far as it can, it hides its knowledge and action from criticism" (Weber, 1948: 232). This idea was empirically supported by the study of Robert Michels (1962) who studied the German socialist party and found that all organizations obey to what he calls "the iron law of oligarchy", that is, the tendency that power and decision-making authority become centralized to the top of the organization. Even though the intentions from the outset are to operate on the basis of democratic decision-making, in due time a smaller number of individuals may be influential and control decision-making and the access to resources. Weber's second problem is, similarly to the first problem, not only a problem in bureaucratic organizations but is also of great importance for all sorts of organized activities. However, bureaucratic organizations aimed at dealing with public matters are for this very reason more susceptible to criticism than other organizations. Weber thought of bureaucracies as being not only a solution to the problem, but also essentially a part of the problem, of modern society; society is not only a matter of the organization and administration of uncontested facts, but is equally a social accomplishment in terms of making sense out of ambiguous and/or even elusive elements and conditions, and a rationalist ethos may prove to be incapable of dealing with this condition. As a consequence, we see from Weber's work, one needs to maintain a sceptic's view of society's institutions.

In the middle of the first decade of the new millennium, Weber's position remains debated. Lounsbury and Carberry (2005) reviewed all articles published in *Administrative Science Quarterly* from 1956–2002 and found that the citation patterns indicate a gradual marginalization of Weber in organization theory. Weber, whom Lounsbury and Carberry (2005) regard one of the "founding fathers of organization theory", has been "increasingly cited in a ceremonial way" over the time period. In the title of their article, the authors do not hesitate to speak of "Weber's fall from grace" in organization theory. However, they emphasize that Weber, in many cases, serves as an indirect source of influence (for instance, in the new institution theory) but without being explicitly acknowledged. In contrast to this view, Walton (2005) suggests that the bureaucratic model of control conceptualized by Weber is a persistent theme in organization theory. Walton even argues that this particular model of control is a generic and generalizable model for all types of organizations. Höpfl (2006) argues that Weber's writing on bureaucracy is sketching an ideal type that is rarely if ever found in social life; bureaucracy, then, is one of many possible *species* derived from one single *genus*, that of administration. As a consequence, it is complicated, Höpfl argues, to speak of "post-bureaucracy" or "post-bureaucratic organizations" because the very concept of bureaucracy is fluid and indeterminate: "[w]ithout a clear conception of bureaucracy, post-bureaucracy is indistinguishable" (2006: 18).

Like all influential thinkers and writers within a specific field of interest, Weber's position and influence remain debated and contested. What is an interesting implication from the analyses of Lounsbury and Carberry's (2005), Walton's (2005) and Höpfl's contributions is that Weber is here placed in opposing positions: on the one hand, Weber is marginalized, while on the other hand, the relevance of his theories is recognized. Weber's importance for organization theory is therefore still open for debate.

Classic bureaucracy studies

Talcott Parsons, the chair in sociology at Harvard University and the great proponent of functionalist sociology (Parsons, 1991), introduced Weber's thinking to a North American readership. Parsons was the greatest influence in the field of sociology in the 1950s and 1960s and his translation of parts of *Economy and Society* became a standard reference for American sociologists. Robert Merton, also at Harvard, represented another methodological orientation to Parsons and advocated "middle range theories", that is, theories that aims at explaining not society as a whole but parts of it, local conditions and specific problems and concerns. In one of Merton's classic papers, he examined bureaucracy and claimed that the bureaucratic organization form suffers from "dysfunctions" (Merton, 1957). Several of Merton's students, such as Alvin Gouldner and Peter Blau, made this statement a point of departure for their research. But Merton's negative image of bureaucracy was by no means the first sceptical account of this particular organization form.

In the 1940s, Ludwig von Mises, an economist representing the liberal Austrian economics orientation, published an ardent critique of bureaucracy. Von Mises opens his book with the following statement: "The terms *bureaucrat, bureaucratic,* and *bureaucracy* are clearly invectives. Nobody calls himself a bureaucrat or his own methods of management bureaucratic" (von Mises, 1944: 1). For von Mises, bureaucracy is an embodiment of market failure, the erection of a hierarchy within what was supposed to serve as an open market. Pledging allegiance to his market liberalism, von Mises claims that "the trend toward bureaucratic rigidity is not inherent in the evolution of business. It is an outcome of government meddling with business" (1944: 12). Business activities should not be organized in bureaucracies, von Mises argues. This master idea was actually challenged as early as the 1920s when companies like General Motors developed large bureaucratic organizations (Sloan, 1964). For von Mises, however, state interventions in the market are the primary motor for the emergence of bureaucracies. Von Mises also addresses one of the persistent themes in the bureaucracy literature, that of "the bureaucratization of the mind" (von Mises 1944: 81ff). According to von Mises, the petty bureaucrat is incapable of escaping the inevitable corruption of the organization form per se: "It [bureaucracy] kills ambition, destroys initiative and the incentive to do more than the minimum required. It makes the bureaucrat look at instructions, not at material and real success" (von Mises, 1944: 56). In this respect, von Mises are siding with the greatest name of the Austrian school of economics: Joseph Schumpeter. In his classic work, *Capitalism, Socialism and Democracy* (1943), Schumpeter writes:

> The bureaucratic method of transacting business and the moral atmosphere it spread doubtless often exert a depressing influence on the most active minds. Mainly, this is due to the difficulty, inherent in the bureaucratic machine, of reconciling individual initiative with the mechanics of its working. Often the machine gives little scope for initiative and much scope for vicious attempts at smothering it. From this a sense of frustration and of futility may result which in turn indices a habit of mind that revels in blighting criticism of the efforts of others. This need not be so; many bureaucracies gain on closer acquaintance with their work. But it is difficult to avoid and there is no simple recipe for doing so.
>
> (Schumpeter, 1943: 207)

For von Mises (1944), bureaucracy is a monstrous form of organization, unable to deliver the benefits its proponents are suggesting and effectively ruining the market opportunities for smaller companies and entrepreneurs. In contrast to this far-reaching liberal critique of the state interventions embodied in the bureaucratic organization form, Karl Polanyi's classic, *The Great Transformation*, emphasizes the influence of the institutions governed and monitored by the state. The liberal view of the market is, for Polanyi, one great utopia unable to remain viable without the supporting infrastructure provided by the state (see also Bourdieu's analysis of the French housing market, 2005). "Pure market economies" such as those advocated by Von Mises (1944), therefore, are not capable of organizing all economic activities (see, for example, Perrow's analysis of the American railways, 2002). Therefore, von Mises's criticism of the bureaucratic organization form as posing a threat to effective market activities may be somewhat misguided. Nevertheless, the critique of the kind formulated by Von Mises (1944) and Merton (1957) served as what Michel Foucault (1972) calls "the field of emergence" for the bureaucracy studies of the 1950s and 1960s. The war economies provided a laboratory for developing and managing large-scale organizations and projects such as the Manhattan project developing the atomic bomb. These experiences showed that it was possible to monitor large organizations and that large-scale organizations were not, by definition, inefficient but, rather, proved to be a worthwhile way to organize complex activities.

Alvin Gouldner (1954) studied what he called processes of bureaucratization in a Midwest gypsum plant. The gypsum plant was divided into a mining division and the factory processing the natural resources. The miners and the so-called "surface men" were organized in different types of work organizations demonstrating different company cultures. When the old manager, called "Old

Doug", retired, a new manager named Vincent Peele was appointed to the manager position. Old Doug was popular among the workers and he followed his principle of "leniency" where the workers were not too closely monitored and where they could always get a "second chance" if they had been caught ignoring the company rules. However, Peele started to monitor work hours in greater detail and quickly abandoned Old Doug's principle of leniency. The workers responded with a critique of the new managerial policy, and as the relationship between Peele and his workers eventually deteriorated, a wildcat strike ended the worsening relations within the gypsum plant (accounted for in Gouldner, 1954).

Among other things, Gouldner's study examined the notion of nostalgia in organizations. He wrote: "Almost to a man, workers in the plant were in the spell of a backward looking reverie. They overflowed with stories which highlighted the differences between the two managers, the lenience of Doug and the strictness of Peele" (1954: 80). For Gouldner, Peele's management implies a bureaucratization of the plant. The "flexible application to rules" dominating Old Doug's management was displaced by more detailed job descriptions. While the miners were capable of escaping a substantial part of Peele's directives because of their strong professional culture and specific work conditions, the workers in the gypsum plant were affected more directly. In the great organization changes initiated by Peele, a number of complementary "patterns of bureaucracy" were developed, Gouldner (1954) argues. First, Gouldner speaks of "mock bureaucracies" in those cases where rules are implemented but ignored by virtually everyone because such rules are not reinforced by various forms of instituted behaviours or punishment procedures. For instance, Peele implemented a non-smoking policy in the factory that most people de facto ignored, using a variety of arguments. Second, Gouldner speaks of "representative bureaucracies" in those cases where decisions and policies are supported by the co-workers and when decisions are supported by widely shared ideals and beliefs. For instance, the safety rules that were enacted and implemented were supported by all workers and were consequently adhered to. Finally, Gouldner uses the concept of "punishment-centered bureaucracies" to denote all those practices and procedures employed to make co-workers follow rules and regulations. In the case of the gypsum plant, all these three divergent patterns were observed and entangled during Peele's regime.

For Gouldner, bureaucratization and bureaucracy are not of necessity and by definition bad things, displaying dysfunctions, but are instead more or less applicable in different settings. A bureaucracy may work very effectively but may also, in other cases, work less smoothly. For instance, Peele's directives were less attended to among the miners because their work was already highly determined by a variety of instituted rules and specific practices jointly agreed upon by the miners themselves. The nature of their work, including the risks the job implied and their strong professional culture and identity, made them less prone to follow the directives from management. Gouldner therefore represents a tempered view of bureaucracy, not strongly determined by a range of political and ideological assumptions and beliefs, but very much dependent on local conditions and practices.

Blau's study, *The Dynamics of Bureaucracy* (1963), is another classic study from one of Robert Merton's students representing a rather positive view of the bureaucratic organization form. Blau's study is, in many respects, an application of the functionalist methodology favoured by the Parsonians at Harvard; Blau assumes that there are "dysfunctions" in large organizations and aims at showing that bureaucracies are capable of dealing with these dysfunctions. Blau presents two case studies: one of a work employment agency in the East of the USA and one of a federal control agency in Washington, DC. In the first study, Blau points at how the day-to-day work is structured in accordance with a variety of administrative rules and regulations. Blau also shows how certain bureaucratic practices are producing negative effects. For instance, the monitoring of how many jobs each manager is capable of providing is regarded as a source of stress. At the same time, Blau argues that the co-workers are demonstrating the highest degree of satisfaction when they can offer a job to a client and help somebody back into an employment position. On the other hand, conflicts between clients and the co-workers are the most cumbersome parts of the job. Blau speaks of these conflicts as the "social costs" of the employment agency. One of the methods to deal with these social costs is to let off steam through joking about the clients. In these cases, the bureaucratic procedures are complemented by what Hochschild (1983) would call "emotional labour", working to keep one's emotional responses to stressful experiences under control.

In the other study of the federal control agency, Blau identifies a series of rules, norms and beliefs guiding the everyday work in the agency. Social status and the relationship between co-workers are of great importance for the work. As a consequence, there are levels of output that the co-worker needs to meet. One must neither deliver too much, nor too little, but stay within a certain range of performance. Second, one norm states that one must not work overtime without compensation because the social status of the profession may be threatened unless additional work is compensated for. Third, perhaps the most strongly articulated rule is not to report any attempt at bribery to the supervisor. Even though the co-workers were strongly opposed to bribery because it may affect the social status of the work negatively, they did not want to make their work appear as being susceptible to such external influences. Hence this norm about not reporting such events.

In Blau's two cases studies, a number of mechanisms and practices mediating the influences from the external environment were identified. For Blau, bureaucracies are by no means self-enclosed organization units incapable of responding to external changes and conditions. Instead, bureaucracies are capable of establishing local rules and practices that mediate the discrepancies between, on the one hand, the "book of rules" of the bureaucracy and, on the other hand, the demands for flexibility from the outside. Individual bureaucrats are therefore demonstrating intelligent and thoughtful responses to these two systems they are operating within. For Blau, this is an indication of the *dynamics* of a bureaucracy; that is, their ability to adapt to external conditions while adhering to bureaucratic principles and rules.

While Gouldner (1954a) and Blau (1963) are rather positive towards the bureaucratic organization form, the third classic study, Michel Crozier's (1964) study of two French workplaces is much more critical. Again, Merton's idea regarding dysfunctions of bureaucracies are cited, and Crozier really does his best to convince the reader of the shortcomings of a French state-owned tobacco company and French state administration agency. While Goulder and Blau speak of psychological issues such as nostalgia and – albeit *avant la lettre* – emotional management, Crozier makes references to the Human Relations school as a source of influence. Crozier's main argument is that bureaucracies are incapable of providing meaningful job assignments and career prospects, and that this inability leads to internal politics and struggles to extend the individual domain of influence in the organization. Crozier writes:

> Each group fights to preserve and enlarge the area upon which it has some discretion, attempts to limit its dependence upon other groups and to accept interdependence only insofar as it is a safeguard against another and more feared one, and finally prefers retreatism if there is no other choice but submission.
>
> (1964: 156)

Moreover, Crozier talks about "vicious circles" (with reference to Gouldner) in bureaucracies. Narrowly defined work assignments, poor communication between individuals and little external influences are, for Crozier, the vices of bureaucracy. Internal politics and what Crozier calls a "self-reinforcing equilibrium", self-perpetuating positions that the organization cannot escape from, may be established in the organization. The consequence is an organization riddled by internal conflicts, low degree of work satisfaction and poor performance. Crozier also contributes to the establishment of the image of the "bureaucratic personality" – Guillén (1994: 281) speaks of the *Homo Hierarchicus* – the petty administrator embodying a series of bureaucratic shortcomings. "He [*sic*] is a legislator . . . rather than a discoverer," Crozier (1964: 201) contends.

Crozier's study is a paradigmatic work in terms of debunking bureaucracy as a form or organization incapable of fulfilling its role in society. The study is also referenced in most texts pointing at the shortcomings of bureaucracies. However, even though Crozier's text is empirically grounded in two French organizations, it is at times complicated for the reader to see whether Crozier is critical of the French administration per se, the bureaucratic organization form as such, or if he is concerned about the work-life experiences of people employed by such organizations. "[I]t is striking," Albrow writes, "how much Crozier's analysis reflects his own dissatisfaction with French organizational structure rather than registers the complaints of the participants in the situation" (1970: 90). Regardless of whether one shows sympathy with Crozier's analysis, his work remains one of the central works in a longstanding tradition of bureaucracy critique. However, Gouldner, Blau and Crozier's work shares the characteristic of de-familiarizing the view of bureaucracy as what is once and for all determined by the rules and regulations established by faceless bureaucrats; bureaucracies are not totalitarian organizations but are, rather, like all forms of organization, dependent on the compliance of a variety of social actors and stakeholders to function properly. Casey (2002: 76–77) writes: "Blau (1955), Crozier (1964) and Gouldner (1954), showed that organizations, despite their formal adherence to bureaucratic rationalities and legitimation are really unstable, weakly coherent, fragile ensembles of compromises between constant sources of pressures, constraints and contestation." The liberal view of the bureaucracy as posing a threat to the open, democratic society is, then, little supported by empirical evidence. If bureaucracies are a real threat to such markets, it is because of the influence of certain groups, not because of a particular organization form as such.

Bureaucracy critics

While the classic bureaucracy studies of the 1950s and 1960s examined the practical functioning of bureaucracies and pointed at the practical implications of bureaucratic procedures, in the more recent literature addressing the notion of bureaucracy as largely playing the role of the *supplement*, that is, what is always already default, failing to become something different than an outmoded and misconceived organization form. The studies of the 1950s and 1960s explored bureaucracies in order to learn to know how they operated in practice; later on, researchers seem to assume that they already know how bureaucracies work and, instead, they move on to offer advice on how to remedy these supposedly preexisting dysfunctions. Bureaucracies, then, are moving from being what is *potentially ineffective* to what is always already enacted as a social problem. The discursive production of the "ineffective bureaucracy" is one of the major effects of the longstanding tradition of bureaucracy studies in organization theory. In this section, some of the arguments in this bureaucracy critique discourse will be examined.

Starbuck testifies to the perennial issue of bureaucracy critique in organization theory:

> From the 1860s to the 1960s, two themes have dominated organization-theoretic writing. One theme was "bureaucracies has defects". The earliest organizational writings by sociologists and economists focus on governmental bureaucracies and they paid much attention to how bureaucratic governments affect societies. They expressed particular concern about bureaucracies' propensity to ignore its environments. The second theme was "How can organizations operate more effectively?" The earliest organizational writings by consultants and former managers discuss factories and other businesses, and they concentrated on identifying structural

properties that influence organizations' productivity and responsiveness to top managers.

(Starbuck, 2003a: 161)

"Bureaucratic organization loses its technical power and moral authority because it is unable to cope with the new demands and pressures that dramatic economic, technological and cultural transformation entails," Reed (2001: 140) writes, thereby subscribing to a long-standing theme in the bureaucracy critique, that of bureaucracies being incapable of responding to external changes. Such negative accounts are abundant in the literature on bureaucracy. In addition to the liberal critique of bureaucracy, in this section critiques formulated by Marxists, feminists and innovation-management researchers will be examined.

The Marxist critique

From a Marxist perspective, advocated by, for instance Clawson (1980), bureaucracy is the outcome of the struggle over the control of the means of production: "[W]hat capital did (specifically including Taylorism and the rise of bureaucracy) is hardly comprehensible except as a response to workers' success in resisting previous capitalist attempts at control." For Clawson, bureaucracy is not primarily, as in the Weberian view, the inevitable movement towards more rational forms of social organization but is, instead, inextricably bound up with a series of managerial innovations in the latter half of the nineteenth century. Bureaucracy, Taylor's scientific management, the professionalization of the management role, and institutional effects including the founding of the first business schools, such as Wharton Business School at the University of Pennsylvania in 1881, are, for Clawson, a number of events springing from the same well, that of struggle between labourers and capitalists. Still, Clawson acknowledges Weber's compelling analysis:

> What makes Weber's argument so powerful is that it is essentially classless: bureaucracy advances not so much because people fight for it, as because it is the only way. In important ways, bureaucracy is to everyone's advantage, since it is technically superior and allows the work to be done better with the use of fewer resources. At the same time, bureaucracy has deadening and chilling effects, which also seems to apply to everyone equally.
>
> (Clawson, 1980: 17)

In terms of actual practices in the workplace, Clawson defines bureaucracy in terms of decision-making authority assigned to different groups of workers: "A key factor that distinguishes bureaucratic from nonbureaucratic systems is whether production decisions are made by the members of the work crew or by full-time officials who themselves do no production" (Clawson, 1980: 84). In bureaucratic organizations, experts and specialists are held responsible for the planning of the operation, while in the non-bureaucratic form, it is the labourers themselves making such decisions. Clawson (1980: 166) also points at the use of foreman and elite groups among the workers as favoured groups within the American industrial bureaucracy: "['W]orkers' control' meant that a minority of workers – comparatively high paid, white, male, born in America – controlled work for themselves, and also for a larger number of lower paid, less skilled, largely immigrant workers." In this Marxist analysis, bureaucracy is yet another tool in the hands of the capitalists, ceaselessly preventing workers from maintaining their jurisdiction. Bureaucracy, therefore is not, as Weber suggests, a value-neutral manifestation of instrumental rationality but must be examined within the field of tension between different social groups, and primarily between labourers and capitalists, but also subgroups such as professional managers and foremen pursuing their own idiosyncratic interests and agendas. Today, at the beginning of the new millennium, when traditional Marxist analysis emphasizing direct confrontations and struggles over control over the means of production is largely out of fashion, the notion of bureaucracy is rarely examined in such terms. Marxist and so-called post-marxist analyses emphasizes more subtle means for control and intangible resources, such as ideology (see, for example, Laclau and Mouffe, 1985). Therefore, the main stream of critique of bureaucracy derives from either neo-liberal economics or humanist orientations such as the Human Relations school (Roethlisberger and Dickson, 1943; Mayo, 1946; Homans, 1951). However, Marxist analysis points at a number of interesting connections between a variety of managerial practices and methods developed in the latter half of the nineteenth and the beginning of the twentieth century. Bureaucratization of industry and administration are here by no means treated as isolated events but, rather, are examined in an integrated historical context.

The feminist critique

In feminist analyses of bureaucracy, "masculine" norms of rationality, hierarchy and professionalism have been claimed to exclude other human faculties such as emotionality and feminine concerns for egalitarian modes of working (Ashcraft, 2001: 1302; Billing, 2005; Savage and Witz, 1992). In a classic critique of bureaucracy, Ferguson (1984: ix) claims that "the power structures of bureaucratic capitalist society" are "a primary source of the oppression of women and men". Bureaucracy, here, is a means of control in the hands of capitalist and patriarchal elites. Similarly to the fiercest critics of bureaucracy, Ferguson does not hesitate to make her point as explicit as possible: "Put simply, bureaucracies have a tremendous capacity to hurt people, to manipulate, twist and damage human possibility" (Ferguson, 1984: xii). Ferguson argues that bureaucracy institutes impersonal work-role positions wherein there is little room for personal development and meaningful human interaction. Bureaucracies are rationally managed and faceless machines, not recognizing the human needs of the employees. For Ferguson, bureaucracies are manifested rationalist social arrangements and therefore represent masculine ideologies and norms; yet, bureaucracies tend to degrade both men and women equally. Ferguson argues that employees in bureaucracies are subsumed under bureaucratic ideologies similarly to the submission of women under patriarchy. Therefore, both men and women undergo a "feminization" in bureaucracies, that is, they are treated as passive objects incapable of agency. Ferguson writes: "The requirements of depersonalisation in bureaucratic relations mean that individuals are isolated from one another and meaningful social interaction is replaced by formal associ-ation" (Ferguson, 1984: 13).

Ferguson's radical critique draws on a number of predominant themes in the bureaucracy literature: the emphasis on depersonalization, rule-governed activities, the hierarchical chain of commands and other "bureaucratic dysfunctions" are examined through a feminist perspective. Ferguson's analysis stands out as one of the most ardent critiques of bureaucratic organizations in contemporary society.

In a more specific analysis, Martin *et al.* (1998) point to the lack of recogni-tion of emotionality in bureaucracies. They say that emotions have been a "largely de-emphasised, marginalized, or ignored" quality of human beings in organization theory (1998: 429). In cases where emotions are acknowledged as being valuable for organizations, it is primarily supposedly that "masculine" emotions are recognized: "Some emotions, such as anger and competitiveness, are generally condoned in bureaucratic organizations, while others such as sadness, fear, some forms of sexual attraction, and vulnerability are taboo" (Martin *et al.*, 1998: 434). The suppression of feelings are troublesome to femi-nist scholars because, as Martin *et al.* say: "women are more likely than men to engage in self-disclosure, express a wider range of emotions, and seek ways to acknowledge the inseparability of work and personal lives without letting work concerns take priority over family needs" (1998: 433). This partial and highly selective recognition of emotionality is referred to as an ethos of what Mumby and Putnam (1992) call "bounded emotionality"; some emotions are legitimate and may be displayed without causing any strong reactions, while others cannot. Martin *et al.*'s (1998) critique is therefore centred on the narrow range of human competencies that are mobilized in bureaucracies.

In another study of a non-profit organization, called "SAFE", helping bat-tered women and children, Ashcraft (2001) speaks of "feminist-bureaucratic hybrids" in cases where "hierarchical and egalitarian modes of power" merge. SAFE is a voluntary organization managed by women explicitly aiming at developing a new form of bureaucratic arrangement. Ashcraft here speaks of "organized dissonance" because alternative perspectives and ideas were articu-lated among the SAFE members and because there was no autocratic leadership cadre present in the organization. For Ashcraft, the organized dissonance model was facing a few challenges but its merits were also substantial. First, the egalit-arian system "counteracted hierarchy", thus enabling a less centralized organi-zation providing much space for various communities within the firm. Second, emotions were made a legitimate and valued resource in the organization, thus undermining the "bounded emotionality" ideal identified by Martin *et al.* (1998). Taken together, Ashcraft argues that the feminist–bureaucratic hybrid represent a new form of bureaucratic organization dealing with some of the shortcomings of the conventional bureaucratic form.

In summary, feminist critiques of bureaucracy include a variety of perspectives and approaches. In general, the view of bureaucracy is that it represents an outmoded form of organization incapable of hosting intelligent and emotional co-workers because the bureaucratic form cannot take into account a broader range of human competencies than those being specified in work descriptions and instructions. Therefore, some feminists suggest modifications of, or even hybrid forms of, bureaucracy more capable of responding to human needs and effectively taking advantage of human potentialities.

Bureaucracy and innovation

One particular field within the bureaucracy literature deals with the innovative and creative capacities of bureaucracies. While most analysts and writers have argued on the basis of a priori reasoning that bureaucracies are probably poor arenas for innovators, some authors report empirical studies on this matter. Thompson (1969) examines the relationship between innovation and the bureaucratic organization form. He defines innovation accordingly: "By innovation I mean the generation, acceptance, and implementation of new ideas, processes, and products or services. Innovation, therefore, implies the capacity to change and adapt" (1969: 5). Since innovation implies variety, creativity, new modes of thinking, and cross-functional collaboration, and an additional set of capabilities and practices, bureaucracies are, Thompson agues, poor innovators: "Innovation is more risky for the bureaucrat than for the entrepreneur."

When firms are bureaucratized, uncertainty and conflicts are controlled by the imposed bureaucratic order, arranging the activities into specialist fields and clear domains of responsibility. Thompson states: "Other things being equal, the less bureaucratized (monocratic) the organization, the more conflict and uncertainty and the more innovation" (1969: 17). Among other things, one of the drawbacks with the bureaucratic organization is its sole reliance on what in motivation theory is called "extrinsic motivation", that is, motivation that is derived from outside the individual, such as salary, bonuses, forms of formal rewards, and so forth. For Thompson, innovation is very much based on "intrinsic motivation", motivation that is derived from the individual's personal interests and aspirations; for instance, the scientist's will to know how a particular process can be examined in scientific terms. Thompson explains: "The extrinsic reward system, administered by the hierarchy of authority, stimulates conformity rather than innovation ... creativity is promoted, for the most part, by an internal commitment, by intrinsic rewards" (Thompson, 1969: 18–19). Even though Thompson largely avoids a polemic tone vis-à-vis the bureaucratic organization, he is still overtly negative about its innovative capacities. Rather than recognizing innovative work in large bureaucracies (for example, IBM in the 1950s), Thompson suggests that the notion of professionalism needs to be further developed in bureaucracies:

Professionalism ... is an alternative to bureaucracy (or the market) as a social control. As a system of control it is pluralistic and collegiate rather than monocratic and hierarchical. The rewards it offers are professional recognition for increasing competence (professional growth) and the intrinsic satisfaction associated with professional work.

(Thompson, 1969: 93)

Dyer and Dyer (1965), in another monograph contribution to the literature, essentially portray bureaucracies as an organization form incapable of innovating. They provide a series of accounts from both the literature and practising managers making claims that bureaucracy is an organization form more or less in opposition with the very idea of innovation and creativity. The bureaucrat is narrow-minded and focused on details, while the "creative individual" (1965: 41ff) is defying the virtues of rank, order and predictability praised by the bureaucrat. Still, they suggest that creativity is possible in bureaucratic organizations when overcoming some of the rigidities of bureaucracy. In chapter 8 of their book, they present "four rules for minimizing the dilemma between bureaucracy and creativity": (1) "Recognize the type of organization – bureaucratic or creative – and adjust your leadership–followership patterns accordingly"; (2) "Don't suppress information"; (3) "Provide for many interchanges among people"; (4) "Let the second team watch – and also play" (1965: 41–42).

Kuhn's edited volume (1993) includes a variety of contributions pointing at the problems associated with making bureaucracies creative. Throughout the book, there are numerous derogatory remarks on the bureaucratic organization form. For instance, Schumann (1993: 111) claims: "Large organizations are traditionally noninnovative. Yet there is nothing in largeness that prohibits creativity and innovation." Schumann argues that it is the routinization of practices so central to bureaucracy that is wielding a negative influence on creativity (1993: 114). However, empirical research – Schumann's (1993) contribution is a conceptual paper – suggests that routines are more flexible and adaptive than is generally believed (Feldman, 2000). The paper of Kuzmetsky (1993: 3–4) offers numerous remarks of the following kind: "The word 'bureaucrat' conjures up in the general public mind slow-moving, unresponsive, stick-to-the-letter-of-regulations-and-procedures employers in large-scale government agencies and departments, large corporations, and academic and educational institutions." Kozmetsky, then, does not portray bureaucracies as arenas where innovation and creativity are played out and are given a central role. Moreover, the anthology edited by Kuhn (1993) presents a number of different techniques, tools and, practices, for instance, market-orientation methods, "ordinal time series analysis", leadership skills and "artificial intelligence and expert systems", that are claimed to help bureaucratic organizations become creative and innovative. There is, however, little attempt at critically reflecting on the predominant assumption in the field, that of bureaucracies as being naturally incapable of being creative and innovative.

Bushe and Shani (1991) discuss what they call "parallel learning structures" as a method to overcome bureaucratic inertia. Even though the subtitle of their study speaks of how to make bureaucracies innovative, there is, in fact, little said at all about bureaucracies per se. Instead, the notion of bureaucracy is again playing the role of the supplement, that is, embodying all the organizational dys-functions that the "parallel learning structure" is claimed to handle (see Bushe and Shani, 1991: 120). In their foreword, Bushe and Shani make the following declaration: "[A]s we go into the 1990s, bureaucracies are still going strong. OD [Organization Development] oriented managers and consultants tend to be at odds with bureaucracies: We don't like them, and we don't really know how to handle them" (1991: xiii). Again, innovation and creativity are conceptually excluded from bureaucracy. The differences between the "parallel learning structure" and the "rigid bureaucracy" are displayed in Table 2.2.

Table 2.2 Bureaucracy vs. "parallel learning structure organization"

Rigid bureaucracy	Parallel learning structure
Normative assumptions	
Subordinates naturally dislike and avoid work	Subordinates naturally want to be involved in their work and will volunteer for greater involvement
Subordinates are motivated through extrinsic threats and rewards	Subordinates are motivated through recognition and the opportunity for greater involvement
Make systems idiot-proof	Make systems that allow for individual creative contributions
Subordinates should only be seen working and not heard	Subordinates should be encouraged to give ideas and opinions
There are experts for everything, and only they know what's important	Everyone knows something important about their work
Procedures	
Break down tasks into simple, repetitive actions	Grapple with whole tasks
One person, one job	Whole group, whole task
One person supervises many	Leadership emerges and is distributed throughout the group
Decisions are made by authorities	Decisions are made by group consensus
Enforce rules and standards	Question rules and standards
In summary	
Manage people through tasks	Manage tasks through people

Source: adapted from Bushe and Shani, 1991: 120.

In Table 2.2, it is evident that the bureaucracy – here complemented by the word "rigid" for the sake of clarity – is serving as the supplement to other forms of organizations (displaying a "parallel learning structure"), and that bureaucracy is regarded as the "degree zero" of innovation. Unfortunately, Bushe and Shani (1991) do not provide any solid evidence for this derogatory view of bureaucracy, but are instead assuming that bureaucracies are incapable of innovating. Such a critical view is shared by Reis and Betton (1990: 21), who conclude their paper with a clear rejection of bureaucracy as an arena for innovation:

> The hierarchical, bureaucratic structure characteristic of U.S. organizations is both inappropriate and ineffective in a dynamic environment where individual creativity and innovation must also be viewed as the consequence of the sociotechnical transformation system in organizations. Bureaucracy has impeded the full flow of creative effort in organization.

One of the few explicit empirical studies of innovation in bureaucracy, Gerald Britan's (1981) ethnography of the Experimental Technology Incentives Program (ETIP) at the Department of Commerce in the US federal administration, points to a number of political implications for the lack of success, rather than seeing the organization form per se as the main impediment for innovation in bureaucratic organizations – in this case a public administration. Britan concludes:

> Government agencies cannot make "rational decisions" about the kinds of ends that should be pursued. These are determined through political processes, in the largest sense. Even when agencies must interpret or redefine policy goals, this does not result from scientific research so much as from bureaucratic pressure, professional culture, or constituency interests.
>
> (Britan, 1981: 141; see also Goodsell, 2004: 64)

A similar conclusion is made by Hoggett (2005: 170), pointing to the complexity of decision-making in public administration:

> Rather than slavish adherence to rule-governed procedures the objective of bureaucracy is founded upon the use of judgment in complex, ambiguous, and contested environments that constitute the everyday lived reality of the civil servant, health service professional or local government official.

Hoggett continues: "It is not bureaucracy per se which is responsible for instrumentalism or hierarchy" (2005: 170).

In summary, the literature on bureaucracy and innovation not only dissociate bureaucracy and innovation as opposing terms, more or less incapable of forming a synthesis, but they also largely ignore innovative and creative work in bureaucracies as a legitimate and fruitful domain of investigation. Sweeping derogatory remarks are presented without any reference to empirical studies or even anecdotal evidence. Instead, bureaucracy is, once and for all, removed from innovative and creative activities.

Bureaucratization

One specific domain of interest has been the process called "bureaucratization", that is, the establishment of bureaucratic procedures and rules in an organization. Today, bureaucratization has attained a slightly negative tone, suggesting that organizations are becoming more bureaucratic just for the sake of it. However, as Albrow (1970) points out, the meaning of the term has not always been negative:

> In the 1920s it was quite normal to speak of a bureaucratization of the firm, meaning the introduction of systematic administration and the growth of the number of purely administrative employees. ... If the firm itself is viewed as a bureaucracy then we can conceive of the bureaucratization of society in terms of an increase in the number of and size of its organizations.
>
> (Albrow, 1970: 104–105)

Prior to the twentieth century, in the early modern period, bureaucratization denoted the development of a modern state apparatus. Bendix (1971) writes:

> The term "bureaucratization" serves to designate these patterns of social change, which can be traced to the royal households of medieval Europe, to the eventual employment of university-trained jurists as administrators, to the civilian transformation of military controllers on the Continent, and to the civil-service reforms in England and the United States in the nineteenth century. These several changes were related to other social trends, especially the development of the universities, the money economy, the legal system, and representative institutions.
>
> (Bendix, 1971: 133)

Albeit originally being a part of the modernization of European society, the notion of bureaucratization today represents the process of formalizing practices in organizations, thereby anchoring them in written rules and formal procedures. Stinchcombe (1959) contrasts what he calls the "bureaucratic administration" in manufacturing firms and the "craft administration" in construction companies. In construction companies, the workers were responsible for making decisions on the basis of their competence, while in the "bureaucratic administration", experts and specialists were responsible for much of the planning work. Stinchcombe therefore defines bureaucratization in terms of formalized communication:

> Bureaucratization of administration may be defined as a relatively permanent structuring of communications channels between continuously functioning officials. This permanent structuring of channels of legitimate

communications, channels defined by the permanent official status of the originator of the communication and of its receiver, permits the development of routine methods of processing information upward and authoritative communication downward. That is, it permits administration on the basis of files and the economic employment of clerical workers.

(1959: 176)

Roy (1981) examined the process of the bureaucratization of a State Department in the USA and defined bureaucratization in terms of "three related trends": "(1) growth in size, (2) appointment and promotion of the basis of merit, and (3) organizational differentiation" (Roy, 1981: 424). In the Weberian model of bureaucracy, bureaucracies are serving as important vehicles for democratization, i.e. they are supposed to take into account the interests of all stakeholders. In Roy's study, specific interests were given more attention that others and Roy therefore concludes that bureaucratization does not always, of necessity, imply a more fair or value-neutral administration:

The findings challenge the notion that a bureaucratic, universalistic orientation necessarily opens up an organization to a wider set of interests than does a particularistic organization. Although universalistic criteria may open up broader opportunities for many groups, they do not assure allocation of equal costs and benefits for all groups

(Roy, 1981: 420)

Maniha (1975: 182) speaks of bureaucratization in terms of an increased emphasis on formal record-keeping: "A bureaucratising organization is, among other things, a record-keeping, report-writing organization." Maniha's (1975) study of the St Louis Police Department suggests that even though the police department enacted a policy where all kinds of ethnic groups should be represented in the workforce, there was still an overrepresentation of certain groups among the policemen. For instance, the Irish community of St Louis were overrepresented in comparison to the German community. Maniha (1975: 189) concludes: "[t]here was ... a definite preference for certain ethnic groups in recruitment." In Edward Arian's (1971) study of bureaucratization in a somewhat different setting, that of the Philadelphia symphonic orchestra – an orchestra in which Arian himself was a member for more than twenty years – the negative consequences of bureaucratization are emphasized. For Arian, bureaucracy is the problem rather than the solution to perceived problems. He sketches the development of the orchestra from being based on artistic freedom and creativity under the leadership of the legendary director Leopold Stokowski in the period of 1915–1935 to an increasingly systematic and standardized workplace wherein the musicians experience a substantial degree of stress and alienation and express their dissatisfaction over the limited recognition of their work. In the new bureaucratized regime, the performance schedule is tight and the repertoire becomes increasingly conservative. Arian claims that the outcome of the bureaucratization represents "a divorce from the performance culture from the creative culture" (1971: 122). He concludes:

> [T]he same bureaucratic policies which have up to now enabled it to survive have at the same time been exacting a heavy cost in artistic, social and individual terms which are accounted for in Weber's theory. These costs now pose a real threat to the future existence of the orchestra.
>
> (1971: 120–121)

Again, bureaucracy is double-sided; on the one hand, it enables effective administration and transparent activities while, on the other hand, it eliminates the creativity from the operations and, instead, establishes a mass-performance regime. Arian's study thus envisages bureaucracy as inherently in opposition to creativity rather than supporting it. The studies of Roy (1981), Maniha (1975) and Arian (1971) suggest that an increased degree of bureaucratization does not, of necessity, lead to value-neutral choices and decisions in bureaucracies. In another, more positive account of bureaucratization, Howe examines social work in the UK and the identification of dysfunctional families through the implementation of certain guidelines for the social-work practices. He writes:

> The depth and detail of social work assessments has increased under the direction of these central guides. As a consequence the level and extent of surveillance of families identified "at risk" has grown considerably. Indeed, it may be that no other group of the population is subject to so much officially guided scrutiny.
>
> (1992: 501)

Even though the effects of bureaucratization were positive, Howe also points to the increase in workload for the social workers:

> In order to ensure the full and proper running of these protective systems, a vast array of guides, procedures and checklists was created. Practices could no longer be left to the discretion of child care workers; their responses were increasingly prescribed by the manuals and guides.
>
> (Howe, 1992: 504)

Howe concludes: "The implementation, maintenance and co-ordination of these complex and demanding systems required advanced administrative and managerial skills" (1992: 504–505). In Howe's study, bureaucratization leads to positive outcomes, but at the cost of more administrative work and new demands on the social workers. As opposed to Roy (1981) and Maniha's (1975) research, bureaucratization is not failing to achieve its goals, but, still, the costs of increased administrative procedures need to be taken into account. The effects of bureaucratization are therefore not evident beforehand.

Dismantling the bureaucratic subject: the case of middle-management

Perhaps the most significant position available in a bureaucracy is that of middle-manager. Its hierarchy and functional specialization characterize the bureaucratic organization. In such an organization form, the middle-manager plays a decisive role in what organization psychologist Rensis Likert calls the "linch-pin model", that is, as being the intermediary function between top management and the level of operations. The first thing to notice is that, in comparison with the literature on leadership, the writing on middle-management is meagre. The middle-manager remains relatively unexplored and is therefore located in a marginal, almost subaltern, position in organizations. In addition, the labour process theory tradition within sociology and organization theory exploring the day-to-day work "on the shopfloor" (see, for example, Homans, 1950; Lupton, 1963; Blauner, 1964; Burawoy, 1979; Collinson, 1992; Delbridge, 1998) has little to say about middle-managers and foremen except in terms of being the embodiment and carriers of managerial control and surveillance, in many cases the direct antagonists of the workers. In the general critique of the bureaucratic organization form, the middle-manager has been portrayed as on the way out and representing an endangered species in an age of de-layering and flexible, organic organization forms. For instance, a passage from Floyd and Woolridge (1994: 47) may be representative of this view of the middle-manager:

> Are middle managers becoming the dinosaurs of the business world? They once dominated the corporate landscape with salaries and perks that were the envy (and career goal) of every MBA. Now, like prehistoric reptiles, these behemoths of bureaucracy appear likely to succumb to a hostile environment.

Barley and Kunda (2006: 55) examine what they call "itinerant professionalism", a form of professionalism based on temporal contracting emerging in post-industrial times. The emergence of itinerant professionalism is a tendency in opposition to the hierarchical organization and has been preceded by a reduction of middle-managers: "Since the mid-1980s corporations have systematically reduced the number of middle managers they employ, often eliminating entire layers of hierarchy, which shortens a firm's chain of command." Dopson and Stewart address this negative image of middle-managers in the organization theory literature:

> Few people have anything encouraging so say about middle management ... most people portray the middle manager as a frustrated, disillusioned individual caught in the middle of a hierarchy impotent and with no real hope of career progression. The work is dreary, the careers are frustrating and information technology, some writers argue, will make the role yet more routine, uninteresting and unimportant.
>
> (Dopson and Stewart, 1990: 3)

In many cases, middle-management is envisaged as a group failing to serve as accountable actors and is, instead, susceptible to top-management decisions. Linstead and Thomas write:

> [E]xisting research on the "state" of middle management suggested that middle managers are reduced to little more than structurally and environmentally determined phenomena in this literature. ... Managers are portrayed as univocal and homogeneous entities that are passive victims rather than active agents constructing, resisting and challenging the subjectivities offered them.
>
> (2002: 3; see also Thomas and Linstead, 2002)

In addition, middle-managers are often pinpointed as a group who are disgruntled by their career opportunities and their inability to influence day-to-day work life (Sims, 2003). For instance, Newell and Dopson (1996: 9) reference an empirical study: "[B]artolome and Evans in their study of 532 male middle managers found that half of them were dissatisfied with the way in which they were investing time and energy in their professional, rather than their private lives." In other words, there is a reasonably shared view of middle-managers as being a subject-position experiencing severe concerns and challenges. Moreover, such a subject-position is largely bound up with the bureaucratic form.

Nevertheless, middle-management are assigned specific roles and functions. Pinnoneault and Kraemer write:

> In essence, middle managers operationlize, detail, further refine, and disseminate information about objectives, policies, and structural changes formulated at the top of the hierarchy. Middle managers mediate between top and operations level managers by communicating and interpreting policies downward to operations managers, and by monitoring and aggregating detailed information from operations upward in a form useful to top managers.
>
> (1997: 666)

However, the middle-manager has comparatively little room for playing such a role because they are operating under a bureaucratic regime preventing entrepreneurial and creative actions. In Della Rocca's (1993: 57) formulation:

> What distinguishes a middle manager from a business executive is his lack of autonomy in decision making as to the deployment of resources. The middle manager's is thus an intermediate, vicarious job devoid of entrepreneurial and managerial responsibility. His autonomy is regulated and prescribed by the division and organization of labor within the company.

In other words, the middle-manager has few opportunities to take action, in many cases because there are no resources available:

Sometimes, senior managers expect middle managers to take charge of a process but give them very little real authority. Without the freedom to experiment, middle managers quickly become frustrated and cynical about top management's intent. "Slack" has become a dirty word, but the flexibility, experimentation, and learning which is the goal of horizontal organization does require resources.

(Floyd and Woolridge, 1994: 54)

Ogbonna and Wilkinson (2003) studied a major cultural-change programme in one of Britain's leading grocery chain stores. The culture-change programme aimed at improving "co-operation", "trust", "continuous learning and development", "constant listening and appraising" and "workforce involvement" while, in fact it led, Ogbonna and Wilkinson argue, to more surveillance, direct control, the threat of sanction and perceived career insecurity. Middle-managers were thus assigned a narrower range of duties and faced "a greatly reduced scope for strategic decision making" (Ogbonna and Wilkinson, 2003: 1173). Ogbonna and Wilkinson here speak of a "proletarization" of middle-management: again, middle-managers are portrayed as victims of managerial initiatives rather than active agents.

In bureaucratic organizations, of necessity incapable of instituting entrepreneurial behaviour according to critics, the middle-manager is the principal carrier of the bureaucratic malaise, that is, its failure to adapt and innovate. The work of the middle-manager is constrained by a dense network of rules and regulations and a limited access to resources, thereby making the middle-manager a frustrated and cynical agent failing to take action. The supplementarity of bureaucracy is manifested in the middle-management literature in terms of portraying the bureaucratic form that is always already the only possible explanation for the unfavourable position of the middle-manager. Rather than invoking exogenous forces and conditions, it is again the bureaucratic organization form as such that is to blame.

Even though bureaucracy and one of its principal subject-positions, the middle-manager, are both envisaged as, of necessity, failing to maintain productive relationships with the external environment, there is a body of literature that provides a more affirmative view of middle-managers. Here, a positive account of a middle-manager's work is regarded a research contribution per se. For instance, Floyd and Woolridge (1994) argue – in an otherwise critical paper – drawing on a full-feathered iconoclast like Tom Peters, that in the de-bureaucratized or post-bureaucratic organization, everyone is expected to think and act like a middle-manager:

While the resulting bureaucratic hierarchy may no longer fit today's demand for flexibility, wholesale elimination of the middle management role may be short-sighted. Some suggest middle managers are a dying breed, but Tom Peters writes [in his *Thriving on Chaos*] that everyone is becoming a middle manager. This outlook is grounded in his customer- and change-oriented view of organization. There will be fewer layers and fewer managers overall, but the strategic roles of middle managers are likely to become more, rather than less, important in organizations of tomorrow.

(Floyd and Woolridge, 1994: 56)

There are more examples of how middle-management is portrayed in more-affirmative terms. King *et al.* (2001) argue that middle-managers play a central role in implementing strategic decisions on the shop-floor and that middle-management very much remain an untapped reserve in firms (see also Floyd and Woolridge, 1997, for a similar argument):

> Middle managers play an essential, but often unappreciated, role in success-ful strategy making. Middle managers' participation in strategy formulation is associated with improved firm performances, and their commitment is critical to successful strategy implementation.
>
> (King *et al.*, 2001: 98)

In a similar vein, Delmestri and Walgenbach (2005) argue on the basis of research on middle-management work in the UK, Italy and Germany that middle-managers play either the role of knowledge brokers (as in the UK case) or as technical experts capable of dealing with practical problem-solving. In the three cases, middle-managers thought of themselves as gate-keepers for top-management; they were responsible for dealing with the small and everyday work concerns, thereby preventing them from moving up the hierarchy and stealing valuable time from top-management. Other writers such as Nonaka and Takeushi (1995), drawing on Japanese management models emphasizing middle-management as of central importance for a firm's performance, suggest a "middle-up-down" strategy wherein middle-managers who have detailed control, yet are capable of seeing the broader picture, should have a say in the strategy formulation process. Similarly, Huy (2002) argues that middle-managers are capable of dealing with emotional responses among the co-workers in an organization change project and therefore play a central role in any change-management initiative.

In summary, middle-managers are relatively marginalized in terms of research interests and are, in many cases, portrayed in unnecessarily critical terms, but are in some cases examined as a central group for firm performance and the implementation of strategic decisions. In addition, there is reason to believe that the image of the future of middle-managers is too negatively slanted. Littler and Innes (2004) discuss a quantitative study of the Australian economy and argue that the "myth of middle management downsizing" needs to be abandoned. Large Australian organizations and firms are downsizing their activities, but the amount of middle-managers in the economy remains rather constant. Middle-managers who lose their positions are moving on to smaller companies and therefore the cadre of middle-managers remains at a stable number. Littler and Innes (2004) are therefore critical of the strong emphasis on the middle-manager as an endangered species of the organizational landscape.

Even the middle-manager and the bureaucratic organization form are once and for all cast as unfit to survive in the new business ecology, it is as if middle-managers in their darkest hour are being rediscovered in some quarters. Suddenly middle-managers are given some function and purpose. This literature aiming at a resurrection of the middle-manager is therefore representing a puzzling genre; generations of cadres of middle-managers are, all of a sudden, identified as, contrary to conventional wisdom, actually able to play a fruitful role. In addition, the very notion of "middle-management" is being displaced by a variety of concepts such as "teams leaders" or "projects managers" derived from the discourse of the post-bureaucratic organization. For instance, the American Project Management Institute announced that its membership rolls grew from 8,817 in 1992 to 60,000 in year 2000 to 90,000 in 2002 (Hodgson, 2004). The middle-manager one may suspect, is re-shaped and returned into the organization as a "project manager". "Project manager" may be a fashionable work title for the moment while "middle-manager" is not, but new management doctrines may easily introduce new job titles and subject positions (Foucault, 1970). In summary, the disregard for middle-managers is inextricably entangled with the long-standing critique on bureaucracy. Being associated with the bureaucratic organization model is, in many cases, entailing a marginal status.

Proponents of bureaucracy

The effectiveness of bureaucracy

While a vast majority of the writers addressing bureaucracy have scorned and criticized the bureaucratic organization form, there are also some researchers who have tried to defend it against its detractors. Perhaps the most ardent defence of bureaucracy is Goodsell's *The Case For Bureaucracy* (2004). Goodsell argues that the general treatment of bureaucracy by all sorts of researchers is overtly negative. Virtually all sorts of disciplines and political orientations can find something that they dislike about bureaucracy and the most heterogeneous groups can join hands in their mutual disregard for this particular organization form. Goodsell writes:

> Bureaucracy's reputation in the halls of academe, then, is quite bad – at least in the minds of many. It is castigated by economists, sociologists, psychologists, political scientists and even many scholars of public administration and public policy. Bureaucrats are portrayed as poor performers as well as budget maximizers, ant and megalops as well as empire builders; and merciless oppressors of their own kind as well as their clients, It is as a bureaucratic personality that they think, as an authoritarian army in mufti that they march, and as a Jesuitical priesthood that they mystify. Bureaucracy, institutionally, is said to sap the economy, endanger democracy,

suppress the individual, and be capable of embodying evil. It is denounced on the right by market champions and public-choice theorists and on the left by Marxists, critical theorists, and postmodernists. One side of the political spectrum finds bureaucracy a convenient target because it represents taxes, regulations and big government, the other sees it as representing elitism, injustice to the underprivileged, and social control.

(2004: 17)

Goodsell points out that both economists and sociologists have dismissed bureaucracy but for the two standard reasons, its lack of efficiency and quality of work-life concerns. When speaking of the sociologists' image of bureaucracy, Goodsell points out the persistent idea on the dysfunctional bureaucracy:

One of the favourite ideas of sociologists is that bureaucracies are destined to work against themselves, that is, to be 'dysfunctional'. Because of the inherent attributes of organizations following the Weberian model, it is said, bureaucracies inevitably acquire countereffective, 'pathological' behavioural patterns. One of the most important of these is obsessive conformity to rules, which creates a phenomenon called 'goal displacement' or placing the procedures required ahead of the ends being sought. Another diagnosis is persistent conflict between superiors and subordinates, which results in petty game-playing and eventual organizational breakdown. Still another perceived dysfunctionality is communication blocks that arise in the hierarchical chain of command. Bureaucracy is also perceived as inherently rigid and incapable of innovation.

(2004: 12–13)

Rather than accepting the idea about such dysfunctions offhand, Goodsell provides empirical evidence that such assumptions are grounded in folk psychology and taken-for-granted beliefs. Goodsell argues:

Numerous empirical studies strongly refute the concept of a unified, pervasive bureaucratic personality characterized by inflexibility, alienation, timidity, ruthlessness, uncaring haughtiness, and all the other ominous features cited by theorists ranging from Merton to Hummel. In fact, behaviours of these kinds do not even seem to exist as tendencies, let alone totalities.

(Goodsell, 2004: 101)

Another common critique of bureaucracy is that bureaucracies tend to grow uncontrolled and regardless of their social function. Goodsell argues that this critique is not supported by empirical evidence and, in cases where bureaucracies grow, like in the case of the US Postal Services, the amount of work actually has grown faster than the organization per se. Neither are bureaucracies as large and impersonal as people tend to think: "I found 30,000 out of the more than 80,000 local governments employ fewer than 25 people, three-quarters have fewer than 50 workers, and 85% fewer than 100" (Goodsell, 2004: 114). This is not to say that there are no large bureaucratic organizations. The City Administration in major American cities like New York, Chicago and Los Angeles may employ thousands of people, but such large-scale bureaucracies are, Goodsell claims, an exception rather than the rule.

Another popular belief is that the clients and customers of bureaucratic organizations are not pleased with the services provided and that any encounter with a bureaucracy is a frustrating and annoying experience. This persistent belief is not supported by empirical evidence:

> Broadly speaking, between two-thirds and three-fourths have reported their encounters with agencies as satisfactory. The American Customer Satisfaction Index, probably the most sophisticated measure of its kind, scores the federal government at 70 on a scale of 100, a level close to that attained by consumer production in the economy.
>
> (Goodsell, 2004: 139)

Goodsell manages to defend the bureaucratic organization form against its detractors on the basis of empirical evidence. Since the public sector is in many cases organized in accordance with bureaucratic principles, the bureaucratic organization form per se is criticized for the supposedly weaker efficiency of the public sector vis-à-vis market activities. Craig (1995), reporting a study of innovation in the Japanese brewing industry, argues against both critics of bureaucracy and several prominent innovation researchers that the bureaucratic organization form is actually capable of hosting innovative activities:

> [T]he bureaucratic machinery of an organization is not necessarily a blocker of innovation and change, but can be used effectively to promote it. Bureaucracy is one of the dirtiest words in business, signifying unresponsive, slow, and costly. Yet one of the most striking aspects of Japan's beer companies in the 1980s is their use of bureaucratic means such as formal working arrangements, systems, and procedures to achieve goals – innovation, responsiveness, and change – that are the exact opposite of what bureaucracy generally represents.
>
> (Craig, 1995: 32)

Craig (1995) claims that "innovation work" in fact includes less creative work than is generally supposed. Therefore, bureaucratic organizations are not, of necessity, poor innovators:

> [B]ureaucratic means are useful not only for overcoming specific organizational weaknesses, but also for providing stability and discipline to the product development process and the organization as a whole. While newness and raw creativity are often thought of as the key ingredients in new product development, as Von Hippel points out, "most innovation

projects in most firms do not involve great novelty". As important as novelty is the discipline provided by an organizational arrangement and procedures that guide and facilitate the efficient transformation of inputs and ideas into a marketed physical product ... product development is a purposeful, not a haphazard, activity.

(Craig, 1995: 33)

In Craig's account, bureaucracy is not of necessity in opposition to innovative work. Instead, the ability to provide "stability and discipline", that is, well-known bureaucratic virtues, becomes helpful when innovating. Courpasson (2000: 157) expresses this idea as follows: "Bureaucracy does not necessarily imply passivity, as Gouldner (1954) or Selznick (1949) demonstrated a long time ago; within bureaucracies, action is largely determined by the context of conformity. Bureaucracy is neither enslavement, nor permanent renegotiations about the rules of action."

Bureaucracies in the discourse on the enterprising self

Another body of texts defending bureaucracy take their starting point in the discourse on the "enterprising self", the image of the individual members of a society as an entrepreneurial and enterprising autonomous universe operating in an open market, competing with other autonomous entrepreneurs. This "Me, Inc." image of the self has been criticized by a number of authors. Richard Sennett's (1998) bestseller, *The Corrosion of Character*, argues that the demands on the individual in this age of enterprise are breaking down the traditional ways of living and undermining meaningful relationships between individuals in organizations. What Pierre Bourdieu has called the esprit de corps, the sense of belonging to a certain group or community, and the work ethos implied from this identification, is no longer a strong sentiment in organizations and companies. Since one knows that the company no longer cares for you unless you are capable of contributing to the firm's value-adding activities, no true sense of identification is being developed on the part of the co-workers. As a consequence, human beings are more or less assigned the role to serve as available resources in a quasi-market that cannot guarantee any long-term employment because there are no such possibilities for foresight in contemporary capitalism. For Sennett (1998), this movement from hierarchical organizations based on clear roles and identification with the employer is problematic because it undermines all sense of long-term commitment – a commitment that may go out of fashion in other domains of human lives as well. The traditional bureaucracy is here treated as representing a more decent form of capitalism, despite all of its real and potential flaws and shortcomings.

Speaking from a UK perspective, Paul du Gay (1996) articulates a similar line of argument. He emphasizes the similarities between the subject-position employee and the consumer. In a consumer society, the consumer is a central actor expected to make conscious and deliberate choices between a variety of available alternatives. Even though most consumers' choices are delimited for financial reasons, the ideology of the consumer society suggests a great degree of freedom of choice for the consumer. However, this freedom of choice is in many cases a chimera, a mere fabrication conjured by marketing practices and commercial campaigns. Du Gay argues that such a consumerist ideology is penetrating the employment market as well, that employees are expected to regard themselves as being in a position to freely chose what they want to become or to be. The labour market, then, is portrayed as some kind of smörgåsbord where the free and enterprising self can make his or her own choices of career, job or profession. This liberal image of the labour market is not mirroring true conditions in the market, du Gay (1996) says. The freedom of choice of career and job opportunities are by no means a prerogative of the multitude, and in an industry increasingly concerned with short-term financial performance, there are few chances of long-term relationships between employers and employees unless the adequate financial results are delivered. In du Gay's *In Praise of Bureaucracy* (2000b), the bureaucratic form is brought into discussion as an organization form that, rather than providing demeaning work assignments devoid of purpose and meaning, are capable of providing a certain social security in a deregulated labour market (see also Jones *et al.*, 2005, chapter 7). Du Gay thus follows Sennett in regarding bureaucracy as being potentially capable of providing meaningful work-life chances and an adequate degree of foresight. However, it is noteworthy that both Du Gay (2000b) and Sennett (1998) do not defend bureaucracy per se in terms of being a rational way of organizing certain activities and undertakings. Instead, bureaucracy is portrayed as a safe haven, a last resort where one may take cover and rest from the clamour and ordeal of the deregulated and competitive economy. Just like Crozier's (1964) critique of bureaucracy is complicated to separate from his general discontent with French administration, du Gay and Sennett's arguments in favour of bureaucracy are difficult to separate from their critique of the discourse of the enterprising self and contemporary capitalism at large. Du Gay and Sennett are thus primarily speaking *against* something via bureaucracy and not in favour of the capacities of bureaucracy as such.

Hynes and Prasad (1997) point to another important aspect of properly functioning bureaucracies, namely that of preventing accidents in both tightly and loosely coupled organization systems. Studying accidents in a Canadian mining company, they shows that weakly developed routines and standard operation procedures gradually undermined the respect for safety concerns in the mining company. Similar to the disregard for the smoking prohibition in the gypsum factory studied by Alvin Gouldner's (1954), the management of the mining company and its employees thought of rules and regulations in terms of "bureaucratic paraphernalia" that could be neglected without risk. Gouldner speaks of "mock-bureaucracy" in cases where enacted rules are poorly followed or directly ignored, that is, when enacted rules are not embedded in predominant institutions and cultures in the organizations (see also Jermier *et al.*, 1992). Besides the poor functioning of the safety regulations in the mining company,

Hynes and Prasad (1997) emphasize a number of contextual factors contributing to the establishment of a mock-bureaucracy there; for instance, the weak monitoring of the mining activities from relevant authorities and the hassle facing miners complaining about the absence of safety regulations. In summary, bureaucratic procedures are establishing boundaries between legitimate and illegitimate practices that may be regarded helpful ex post facto, even though they may be criticized, and even ridiculed, prior to any major accidents. A "de-bureaucratization" may thus imply unpredicted risks in many industries.

The rehabilitation of bureaucracy

Blau (1956) writes: "Bureaucracy ... can be defined as organization that maximizes efficiency in administration, whatever its formal characteristics, or as an institutionalized method of organizing social conduct in the interests of administrative efficiency" (Blau, 1956: 60). Here, bureaucracy is what *maximizes* efficiency rather than the opposite. In many cases, bureaucracy is portrayed in the literature as either good or bad. However, a fruitful rehabilitation of bureaucracy needs to move beyond such a binary structure of thinking, and the strength and weaknesses need to be examined. Adler and Borys (1996) try to overcome a binary form of thinking and speak of "coercive" and "enabling" bureaucracies. Coercive bureaucracies are bureaucracies that restrain the individual co-worker's work-life and impose a number of procedures and practices that prevent his or her work. The coercive bureaucracy is the Crozierian bureaucracy wherein there are few chances of finding a meaningful work opportunity within the large-scale structure. On the other hand, the enabling bureaucracy is the organization that provides the adequate support and service for the individual to effectively carry out one's work. The enabling bureaucracy is based on the virtues of transparency, predictability, value-free engagement, fair treatment of all clients and a number of other bureaucratic values. Adler and Borys (1996) show that bureaucracy can be, like any other organization form, useful as well as harmful, good and bad, and so forth. In this more temperate view of bureaucracy, new ideas and perspectives are being provided, enabling new images of bureaucracy to emerge. Such rehabilitation of bureaucracy is very much needed in the organization theory and management studies literature.

Summary and conclusions

In this chapter, the notion of bureaucracy is examined as being both what emerges and is continuously re-formulated in a discourse and as a specific organization form. It is not always the case that the discursive production of concepts and beliefs associated with such concepts are mirroring empirical conditions in society. In the case of bureaucracy there is a discrepancy between the disregard of bureaucracy and the strong reliance on bureaucratic organization forms in all domains of society. On the one hand, bureaucracy is dismissed as fundamentally flawed and perverted, and, on the other hand, it is the most broadly implemented form of social organization. One of the reasons for this most critical view of the hierarchical and functionalist form is that there is a strong orientation in contemporary society towards more fluid and fluxing epistemologies, a variety of perspectives on subjectivity, social institutions, and history as being what is always in a state of becoming, on the move, in flux. While the worldview of, say, a person in medieval times, was essentially stable and predictable, and captured by the religious scriptures which, in turn, were interpreted on the basis of Aristotelian metaphysics,[4] the contemporary age is an age where continuous change is praised as being responsible for liberating human beings from established structures and institutions. Not only are the contemporary times an age where people tend to perceive the world around them as moving and changing, theories suggesting such views are also fashionable. A variety of natural scientists, social scientists, philosophers and other professional groups subscribe to different theories and epistemologies assuming change over stability, discontinuity over continuity, fluidity over entities. In this episteme (Foucault, 1970) organization forms such as bureaucracy become unfashionable or even illegitimate because they are conceptualized as being opposed to such continuous change and movement. As Paul Virilio (2002) points out, one may distinguish between the "tactical war", the "war of siege" where fortifications and rampant play a central role, and the "strategic war", the "war of movement" aiming at destruction through the uses of bombs and missiles. The tactical war is the pre-modern or medieval war; the strategic war the modern war, the war wherein speed plays a central role. In the medieval war, things slow down and antagonist build fortresses to defend their domains. In the modern war, things speed up and become fluid and moving. The bureaucracy represents the premodern emphasis on stability and "fortification" and the forms of "post-bureaucratic organization" are based on an ideology of speed, of what Virilio calls "dromology". In the next chapter, fluid epistemologies are examined and the organization forms adhering to this mode of thinking are discussed.

3 Affirming the fluid

Debating post-bureaucratic organizations

Introduction

In this chapter, the predominant critical view of bureaucracy is examined in terms of a movement from the favouring of what may be called an epistemology of solids to what can be named an epistemology of fluids or fluidity as the most privileged mode of thinking (Bauman, 2000; Urry, 2003; Thrift, 2005). In this chapter, the notion of what will be called "epistemology of fluids" will be discusses as the favoured view of society at the beginning of the new millennium. While the previous chapter examined the writing on bureaucracy in the organization theory literature, this chapter will discuss the ontological and epistemological roots for the general disregard of the hierarchy vis-à-vis the market (Williamson, 1975), and discuss the concept of post-bureaucratic organization. The philosophical foundations for what will be referred to as an "epistemology of fluids" is of pre-Socratic origin and is today represented by a variety of discourses including complexity theory, poststructuralist thinking and feminist theory. These different epistemological positions and meta-theoretical perspectives have also influenced, or are intersecting with, a number of theoretical debates regarding specific organization forms. In this chapter the virtual organization, the project organization form, the network organization, and what some researchers have called the "post-bureaucratic organization" will be examined. These different theoretical – or "practico-theoretical" – constructs are more or less loosely coupled with underlying epistemological discussions; in some cases explicitly, in some cases without full recognition. However, taken together, a variety of discourses in the social sciences have pointed to the need for exploring more fluid and fluxing images of organizations and the underlying ontological and epistemological assumptions serving as the foundation for such theoretical elaborations.

Epistemology of fluids

Introduction

The notion of the fluid or fluidity will here be used as a root metaphor for all processes of becoming that transcend the ideas of unity, coherence and solids.

The notion of the fluid thus contains a series of related notions, concepts and models that all share the quality of being in opposition with unity and coherence. Another important concept is the philosophical notion of "becoming". Becomings are the things-in-the-making, the transitions, "coalitions" (Michaels, 2000), and events that construct new subjectivities and assemblages (see Grosz, 1999). Although the notion of becoming is of pre-Socratic origin (employed by Heracleitus), and was later used by Plato in his metaphysical dialogue, *Timaeus* (Plato, 1977: 68), it remains a most contested concept. In this chapter, it will be used as a general model for processes unfolding and changes outside of teleology and finalism – becoming is here fundamentally anti-Aristotelian in terms of rejecting entelechism and finality. In contemporary thinking, the process philosophy of Henri Bergson (1998), Alfred North Whitehead (1978) and William James (1912, 1996) has reinstated the notions of process and becoming in the philosophical debate. For instance, William James (1996: 253), commenting on Bergson's thinking, points to the need for a vocabulary apprehending what is intrinsically fluid and changing:

> The essence of life is its continuously changing character; but our concepts are all discontinuous and fixed, and the only mode of making them coincide with life is by arbitrarily supposing positions of arrests therein. With such arrests our concepts may be made congruent.

"What really *exists* is not things," James (1996: 263) contends, "but things in the making." This shift from being to becoming, from existence to "in-the-making", is the important contribution of process philosophy to an epistemology of fluids.

Even though the interest in process philosophy has grown over the last ten years (see, for example, Wood and Ferlie, 2003; Wood, 2005), in the mainstream research on organization and management practice, a Cartesian–Newtonian ontology of stable matter is adhered to. In this section, a number of alternative fluid epistemologies will be examined. These different discourses or streams of thinking are by no means compartmentalized but, rather, are codependent and entangled in terms of deriving from similar sources and influences. It is nevertheless useful to think of them as different fields of research since they are emphasizing different aspects of organization and managerial practice.

Complexity theory

Complexity theory serves as a label for a number of theories, ideas and research programmes that are derived from scientific disciplines such as biology, mathematics, chemistry and physics (Rescher, 1996; Prigogine, 1997; Cilliers, 1998; Marion, 1999). Etymologically, the concept of "complex" derives from "*plexus*, that which is woven, but also from *plicare*, a fold" (Brown, 1999: 1). The complex is integrated and entangled, yet capable of unfolding, that is, proving to demonstrate new emerging qualities. This rather heterogeneous body of theories share a critical view of the Cartesian–Newtonian model of physical systems (Heisenberg, 1958; Whitehead, 1978). As Dupré points out, modern science has been largely operating within this metaphysical tradition: "The metaphysics of modern science, as also of much of modern Western philosophy, has generally been taken to posit a deterministic, fully law-governed, and potentially fully intelligible structure that pervades the material universe" (Dupré, 1993: 2). This Cartesian–Newtonian ontology is no longer uncontested. Concepts such as "emergence" (Holland, 1998; Bergmann Lichtenstein, 2000), "dissipative structures" (Prigogine and Stengers, 1984; Prigogine, 1997) and "autopoesis" (Maturana and Varela, 1980; Luhmann, 1990), have become popular when theorizing social and natural systems as differing from the mechanical models suggested in Newtonian physics. While Newton thought of astral bodies as being determined by mechanical laws and linear causality, the emerging paradigm of complexity theory does not assume such rigid causality. For instance, the notion of emergence is based on the idea that all evolving systems are (to borrow a concept of Freud's, later used by Althusser) "overdetermined", that is, they are based on a multiplicity of intersecting causes rather than one single cause. As a consequence, social and natural systems are always emerging from a number of sources, thereby making it more complicated to estimate the next phase in the development of an emergent system.

Dissipative structures conceptualized by Nobel Prize winner and physicist Ilya Prigogine operate in accordance with a non-linear logic. For Prigogine, a dissipative structure is a semi-stable configuration that does not respond to external pressures and manipulations in a linear manner. The dissipative structure can, for instance, absorb significant external pressure in certain stable positions, while it can be radically altered by only minor influences in other positions. When a dissipative structure is close to what Prigogine calls a "bifurcation point", the dissipative structure is seemingly stable but vulnerable to external influences. When being affected on the verge of a bifurcation point, a dissipative structure may then alter its structure entirely. Autopoetic systems constitute the basis for their own reproduction: they are self-regulating, enclosed structures whose mechanisms are interconnected and mutually dependent. Taken together, neither emerging structures, dissipative structures, or autopoetic models are based on a Cartesian–Newtonian mechanical framework wherein all causes are linear and are derived from one single source. Complex systems theories enable an analysis of social systems, in this case organizations, as being multiplicities whose causes and effects are always dependent on a variety of influences. Making use of concepts such as emergence, dissipative structures and bifurcation points, and autopoesis provide alternative images of social organizational systems departing from mechanical explanations and ontologies. Cilliers (2005) summarizes complexity theory in a set of propositions:

1 Complex systems are open systems.
2 They operate under conditions not in equilibrium.

3 Complex systems consist of many components. The components themselves are often simple (or can be treated as such).

4 The output of components is a function of their inputs. At least some of these functions must be non-linear.

5 The state of the system is determined by the values of the inputs and outputs.

6 Interactions are defined by actual input–output relations and they are dynamic (the strength of the interactions changes over time).

7 Components, on average, interact with many others. There are often multiple routes possible between components, mediated in different ways.

8 Some sequences of interaction will provide feedback routes, whether long or short.

9 Complex systems display behaviour that results from the *interaction* between components and not from characteristics inherent to the components themselves. This is sometimes called "emergence".

10 Asymmetrical structure (temporal, spatial and functional organization) is developed, maintained and adapted in complex systems through internal dynamic processes. Structure is maintained even though the components themselves are exchanged or renewed.

11 Complex systems display behaviour over a divergent range of timescales. This is necessary in order for the system to cope with its environment. It must adapt to changes in the environment quickly, but it can only sustain itself if at least part of the system changes at a slower rate than changes in the environment. This part is seen as the "memory" of the system.

12 More than one description of a complex system is possible. Different descriptions will decompose the system in different ways. Different descriptions may also have different degrees of complexity.

(Cilliers, 2005: 257)

Cilliers (2005) emphasizes that complex systems are not to be mistaken for intrinsically fickle ones. Most of the time, complex systems are, in fact, "robust": "Complex systems are not balanced on a knife's edge between chaos and order. They have mostly robust structured, which change over time and enable the system to respond to different circumstances" (Cilliers, 2005: 264). One of the consequences of the adherence to a complexity theory perspective is that one needs to avoid what Cilliers (2005: 256) calls "self-confident or assertive positions" and instead take a "modest position", a position similar to what Vattimo (1992) names "weak thought". Such a modest position implies what Nietzsche (1967: 267, §481) called "perspectivism" (see also Heidegger, 1987: 102), and Harding (1998) speaks of as a "standpoint epistemology", that is, an awareness of one's standpoint vis-à-vis the object of study and the active choice of perspective. Cilliers (2005: 259) writes:

There is no stepping outside of complexity (we are finite beings), thus there is no framework for frameworks. We *choose* our frameworks. This choice need not be arbitrary in any way, but it means that the status of the framework (and the framework itself) will have to be continually revised. Our knowledge of complex systems is always provisional. We have to be modest about all claims we make about such knowledge.

Taken together, complexity theory implies a new epistemology calling into question the modern worldview. It is affirmative of what is fluxing and fluid, operating in non-linearity and what is complex.

The emergence of an organization theory based on complexity theory has enabled alternative modes of theorizing organization (Tsoukas, 1998; Maguire and McKelvey, 1999; Black and Edwards, 2000). A few applications of complexity theory include studies of organizational transformation (MacIntosh and Maclean, 1999), corporate strategy (Stacey, 1995; Brown and Eisenhardt, 1998), organization culture (Frank and Fahrbach, 1999) and organization design (Levinthal and Warglien, 1999). One of the key contributions of the emerging complexity theory paradigm is the departure from linear models (Anderson, 1999; Morel and Ramanujam, 1999). Tsoukas (1998: 229) writes: "Chaos theory highlights the impossibility of long-term prediction for non-linear systems, since the task of prediction would require knowledge of initial conditions of impossibly high accuracy." Another highly influential theoretical perspective is Niklas Luhmann's autopoetic theory of society (1995) drawing on Maturana and Varela's theory of autopoetic systems in biology. For Luhmann, society is based on communication; there is no society unless there is communication. Communication is composed of three interrelated components or events: "information", "utterance" and "understanding". The act of communication is bringing together these three components into a functional unity. Since communication is producing a need for further communication, regardless of whether it is successful or not, society is evolving as a continual process of communication. This production of communication is modelled on an autopoetic model wherein communication is decoupled from individual human interests and constitutes its own operational register. In a similar manner, Luhmann (2003) examines the organization as the social formation defined on the basis of its ability of making decisions.

Altogether, complexity theory has been used as a source of influence for a variety of organization research activities aiming at moving beyond the taken-for-granted view of organization as based on stability and timeless structures. Even though the highly advanced theories derived from the natural sciences (e.g. chemistry, mathematics, biology, physics) have proven to be complicated to employ when examining social formations on the meso and micro levels, the complexity theory framework has served as a domain wherein new and fruitful metaphors have been developed. The general will to contribute with fluid epistemologies not assuming linearity and simple causality as the dominant model has enriched the field of organization theory and management studies.

Poststructuralist and postmodern thinking

Poststructuralist and postmodern thinking refers to a loosely coupled framework of texts, in many cases representing a Continental tradition of thinking, that addresses a series of topics such as the status of the subject, the Western epistemological tradition, and the status and function of language. Philosophers and thinkers such as Jacques Derrida, Gilles Deleuze, Jean-François Lyotard and Michel Foucault are often portrayed as poststructuralist writers. However, it is noteworthy that all of these writers resist this type of labelling and regard this an Anglo-American closure of a literature that is highly heterogeneous. A series of concepts such as "différance", "intertextuality", "discourse", "différend", "deterritorialization", and so forth, are introduced in poststructuralist works, all pointing to the fluid, transient, contingent and conditional nature of being, language, subjectivity and social practice. The scope of this book does not allow for a detailed introduction to the poststructuralist vocabulary, but there are a number of useful introduction books to the field (for example, Best and Kellner, 1991; Linstead, 2004). The main contribution from the poststructuralist tradition of thinking is the critique of what Derrida (1976) calls "logocentrism" and Heidegger (1959) refers to as "the metaphysics of presence", the idea that being is essentially stable and does not obey to principles of movement, change and becoming. Best and Kellner (1997) emphasize the consequences of adhering to a poststructuralist epistemology:

> [P]ostmodern science turns more toward probability and statistical regularities and away from absolute certainty; it rejects notions of fixed, immutable orders and absolute truths in favor of conceptions of evolving complexity and probability; it breaks away from mechanism and machine metaphors and affirms organism and biological models, and thus shifts from a self-contained and immutable universe to an open, self-organizing, dynamic cosmos that is constantly changing and evolving.
>
> (Best and Kellner, 1997: 224)

Deleuze emphasizes the rejection of "fixed and immutable orders" (Best and Kellner, 1997) and claims that all entities are multiplicities, are composed of many parts, both actual and virtual: "Philosophy is the theory of multiplicities, each of which is composed of actual and virtual elements. Purely actual objects do not exist. Every actual surrounds itself with a cloud of virtual images" (Deleuze and Parnet, 2002: 148). Similarly, Michel Serres writes: "[T]he thing is nothing else but a centre of relations, crossroads or passages" (Serres, 1982: 39).

For Best and Kellner (1997), poststructuralist and postmodernist thinking implies that social science needs to change its perspectives to aspects previously unattended to. New stories, new voices and new perspectives are brought into the discussion. Robert Chia (2004), drawing on a process philosophy tradition of thinking represented by Bergson and Whitehead rather than poststructuralist theory, discusses this assumption about stability as a privileged state as one of the major impediments for the advancement for organization theory:

> [T]he stabilities and regularities that we find in social reality must be understood as islands of artificially constructed order in a sea of ceaseless change. The image of how such apparent stability is achieved is best captured by the idea of two trains traveling on parallel tracks in the same direction and the same speed. For the passengers in each of the two trains, the other train is effectively stationary. This clearly *exceptional* situation is what allows the travelers in the two trains to hold out their hands to one another or talk to each other, since they are 'stationary' in this special sense. Our mistake in academic theorising has been to take this eminently 'stationary' situation as the rule rather than an exception and to then weave our systems of comprehension around it. What the principle of relativity and quantum theory reasserts is the primacy of flux, change, movement and spatio-temporal interpenetration. Things, entities and apparently solid substances are but temporal coalesce of matter-energy, and the actual world is a ceaseless process involving the *becoming* of such even-entities.
>
> (Chia, 2004: 181)

For Chia (2004), an organization is not a solid entity, a thing, but instead a transient and temporal accomplishment and is therefore in a state of constant change and modification. Chia and King (1998: 475) argue, drawing on Whitehead's process philosophy, that organization is "an entity" produced in the course of action: "Organization ... is this heterogeneous process of 'event-clustering' through which patterns of regularities emerge, are established, and the formation of an 'entity' attained." The dominant mode of thinking, an epistemology of solids in the Platonist and Newtonian traditions, is serving as an obstacle for a more elaborate view of organization. Chia (2004: 182) continues:

> [A] decentred approach to the analysis of organization and management would open up entirely new avenues of enquiry, in that it would eschew simple causal explanations for a far more complex and dispersed as well as historically informed understanding of how events take shape, develop and realize themselves in the unpredictable flux of life.

In a similar manner, Clegg *et al.* (2005) argue that organization is what emerges on the verge of chaos and the fluid, in the intersections where the predictable and the unstructured meet: "Organization is the knot, the fold, where order and disorder meet. It is the very process of transgressing the boundaries between the old and the new, the stable and the unstable" (Clegg *et al.*, 2005: 154). Exemplifying the notion of organization learning, Clegg *et al.* (2005) point to the role of learning as overcoming the boundary between inside and outside, order and disorder:

Learning implies the transgression of boundaries between inside and outside, and between order and disorder – even between what is and is not considered learning. It occurs in the space inbetween, in the grey area, where the border are breached, where definitions are unstable.

(Clegg *et al.*, 2005: 157)

They conclude:

[O]rganization learning and becoming are brought together to understand learning not as a discrete and identifiable practice or suite of tools, but rather as a process through which an organization exists. Learning is thus a form of dis-organization that connects with and can destabilize the desire of a unified, timeless and static idea of organization.

(Clegg *et al.*, 2005: 161).

Another example of research recognizing the fluid constitution of organization can be located within the research on knowledge management. Patriotta (2003) examined the use of knowledge in organizations – the specific case studied being a new plant in southern Italy for the Italian automotive company FIAT – as what is intrinsically fluid and evolving and what therefore must be fixed and made manageable by making agreement as to what is credible and useful knowledge. Patriotta (2003) speaks of the process of turning "knowledge in the making" into widely shared and applicable knowledge in terms of the "institutionalization" of knowledge. This institutionalization is largely dependent on what Patriotta calls "the articulation of knowledge":

Through articulation, knowledge is represented and made visible. In fact, articulation can be defined as the act of making knowledge manifest. Controversies recede into the background and legitimate knowledge is sealed into organizational black boxes: organizations create knowledge that can be fitted into purposeful devices. The organization is formally represented and reduced to an abstraction. Only now can we see knowledge lies precisely in this apparent paradox of making manifest while hiding ... as a result of institutionalisation, knowledge is inscribed into a system of norms, practices and conventions, and incorporated into stable structures. Knowledge becomes canonical, factual, definite and certain. Institutionalization implies a process of epistemological closure similar to the closure of black boxes.

(Patriotta, 2003: 181)

"Reaching epistemological closure" is therefore one of the most important accomplishment in a community of "knowledge workers". Since knowledge is always what is contested and under negotiation prior to such closure, Patriotta (2003) speaks of "knowledge in the making", that is, a fluid image of knowledge, as his position. Here, we move from "a static, commodified definition of knowledge" and instead emphasize the "becoming" of the organization knowledge system (Patriotta, 2003: 199). For Patriotta, analyses of knowledge need to take into the account the very processes within which knowledge is sheltered from criticism through being fixed and agreed upon: knowledge is what is emerging when continuous flows of know-how are turned into discrete elements. Therefore an epistemology of fluids is applicable when examining the use of knowledge in organizations.

In Chia's (2004), Clegg *et al.*'s (2005) and Patriotta's (2003) view of organization, fluidity and flows are determinate ontological conditions affecting practices of organizing. While previous organizational forms have assumed hierarchical and semi-stable arrangements, the new forms of organization and its underlying epistemologies need to be conceived of in processual terms. The poststructuralist epistemology is affirming movement, fluids, changes and becoming, and adhering to such epistemology of fluids implies a radical shift in perspective on organizations.

Feminist theory

"Feminist theory" is an umbrella term capturing a variety of different and, at times, even opposing perspectives (Prasad, 2005: 123). In this section, a poststructuralist or "post-feminist" epistemology will be presented. In this view, the line of demarcation between sex and gender is a fluid and permeable one, making it possible to examine them from a number of perspectives (Borgerson and Rehn, 2004; Linstead and Brewis, 2004). Lines of demarcation and binary structures are never wholly self-enclosed and emerging as a natural necessity but, rather, are socially and culturally embedded and derived. Therefore, examining the assumptions on the relations between sex and gender need, for some feminist thinkers, to start from a detailed ontological and epistemological re-evaluation of the dominant phallogocentric tradition of thinking. For Susan Bordo (1996), masculine thinking is indebted to the Cartesian split between mind and body, the thinking (*res cogitans*) and the extended substance (*res extensa*). The Cartesian ontology and epistemology emphasize solids as the elementary forms of matter. For Bordo, the Cartesian mode of thinking has been widely embraced in contemporary technoscience and society. Here, the solids dominate over the fluid, the rational over the emotional, mind over matter and embodiment. Thus, Cartesian thinking constitutes what can be called a "hegemony of solids" excluding notions of fluidity and movement (see also Gatens, 1996). Luce Irigaray, French feminist philosopher and psychoanalyst, writes: "Solid mechanisms and rationality have maintained a relationship of very long standing, on against which fluid have never stopped arguing" (Irigaray, 1985: 113). She adds: "[F]luid is always a relation of excess or lack vis-à-vis unity" (Irigaray, 1985: 113). Elsewhere, Irigaray writes:

> In the pre-Socratics, we observe the casting out – or at least the framing – of fluids by solids: the world-*cosmos* surrounded by the shell in Empedocles, the world-thought closed off in a circle by Parmenides. Occidental logic

appeals to and is based on the mechanics of solids. Fluids always overflow reason, the ratio, exceed by measure, plunge back into undifferentiation: they are the universe of myths and magic, of darkness resistant to the light of the philosophers who approach it only to enclose it within the confines of their thought. Forgetting that, without fluid, there would be no unity, since fluid always remains *between* solid substances in order to join them together, to reunite them. Without fluid intervention, no discourse could hold together. However, the operation of fluids is not expressed as a condition of the truth of the coherence of the *logos*. That would unveil its unstable edifice, in shifting foundations.

(2002: 233)

Rosi Braidotti's (1994, 2002) discussion on what she calls the "nomadic subject" is another specific analytical framework drawing on the notion of the fluid. Braidotti is explicitly referring to Gilles Deleuze as the main influence for her concept of the nomad subject (Braidotti, 1994). For Braidotti (2002), it is important that a theory of the subject, affirmative of the fluid, is capable of breaking with the incumbent vocabulary of the ontology of solids:

To attack linearity and binary thinking in a style that remains linear and binary itself would indeed be a contradiction in terms. This is why the poststructuralist generation has worked so hard to innovate the form and style, as well as the content, of their philosophy.

(Braidotti, 2002: 8)

The act of writing the fluid is thus of central interest. Without an elaborated terminology, tropes and expressions, there are few opportunities to formulate what is aimed at escaping received wisdom and taken for granted ideas. Braidotti thus wants to develop both a nomadic mode of thinking and to construct the "figuration" of the nomadic subject. On the first objective, she writes:

The nomadic and rhizomatic mode of critical theory aims to account for processes, not fixed points. This means going in between different discursive fields, passing through diverse spheres of intellectual discourse. Theory today happens "in transit", moving on, passing through, creating connections where things were previously disconnected or seemed unrelated, where there seemed to be "nothing to see". In transit, moving, displacing also implies the effort to move on to the invention of new ways of relating, of building footbridges between notions.

(Braidotti, 2002: 173)

Nomadic thinking is what aims at capturing that which is "in-between", in movement, in transit, in short, what is becoming. It seeks to go beyond the "fixed points", the solids, and instead think what is "processual". Braidotti's second objective, the figuration of the nomadic subject, is introduced: "The nomad is my own figuration of a situated, postmodern, culturally differentiated understanding of the subject in general and of the feminist subject in particular" (Braidotti, 1994: 4). Braidotti continues: "The nomad is a transgressive identity, whose transitory nature is precisely the reason why s/he can make connections at all. Nomadic politics is a matter of bonding, of coalition, of interconnections" (1994: 35). She explains her position further:

> Nomadic embodied subjects are characterized by their mobility, changeability, and transitory nature. Their power of thinking is not the expression of in-depth interiority, or the enactment of transcendental models: it is a tendency, a predisposition that expresses the outward-bound nature of the subject.
>
> (Braidotti, 2002: 70)

In a more recent publication, Braidotti (2006: 62) makes reference to legal studies scholar Kimberley Crenshaw's concept of "intersectionality" denoting a methodology to examine "the multi-layered structure of identity within each singular subject". That is, each subject-position is not unified and unitary but is instead composed of a series of identities and affiliations. Braidotti provides an illustration to the concept of intersectionality:

> It is absolutely the case that one is not a muslim on Tuesday and a European on Wednesday, a woman on Monday, black on Sunday and lesbian on Thursday afternoon. These variables coexist in time. They also intersect, coincide or clash; they are seldom synchronized. The point is that one's consciousness of oneself does not always coincide with all variables all the time. One may, for a period of time, coincide with some of the categories, but seldom with them all.
>
> (Braidotti, 2006: 94)

The nomadic subject is a figuration of the subject, a subject-position, that escapes what Whitehead (1925) calls the "fallacy of misplaced concreteness" that the humanist subject succumbs to; it is a "non-unitary subjectivity" (Braidotti, 2006: 4) that is dispersed and fragmented, yet "functional, coherent and accountable". Here the subject is not the autonomous and coherent cognitive universe (see Sampson, 1989) masterfully controlling and monitoring his or her own social reality, but is instead a fluid construct produced within a multiplicity of forces and interests within the social fabric. The nomad subject is always transitory and transgressive; it is never founded on itself but is always affected and informed by external forces. In an ontology of solids (e.g. Cartesianism), there are no possibilities for conceiving of an open-ended subject because the subject is constituted as a solid per se. In an epistemology of fluids, there are many opportunities for open-endedness because the fluid is always in opposition to unity. A masculine ideology of solids is displaced with a feminist ideology of becoming and fluidity.

Summary and conclusions

Moving from an epistemology of solids to an epistemology of fluids implies that certain perspectives, metaphors and images of organizations are more easily recognized. In an epistemology of solids, organizations are regarded as hierarchical structures made manifest and immutable by material resources such as machinery, office equipment, and information and communication technologies, and socially constructed resources such as norms, values and cultures (see, for example, Czarniawska-Joerges, 1992: 186). Organizations are then "put in place" and are thereafter located in a fixed time–space. In this view, an organization is an entity, a fixed and enclosed body of processes and resources maintaining its form through various mechanisms. In an epistemology of fluids, in contrast, an organization is never a fixed and enclosed entity but is, instead, regarded as the outcome from a process of organizing wherein different activities, resources and external influences are continuously brought together in the course of progress. In this view, organization is an outcome from the process of organizing rather than the point of departure; organizations recursively emerge where structure and action jointly constitute and shape one another. Adhering to an epistemology of fluids therefore underscores the importance of thinking in terms of *becoming* rather than *being* (Chia, 1996; Clegg *et al.*, 2005), that is, in terms of being-in-the-making (Patriotta, 2003) rather than being at hand. In the next section, a number of different theoretical perspectives on organization which more or less explicitly recognize an epistemology of fluids will be reviewed.

Fluid organization forms

In this section, the general tendency to recognize fluid and transient social arrangements in social theory is examined in terms of various organizational configurations. Such configurations are not easily translated into neat taxonomies but we will address virtual organizations, projects organizations, network organizations, and what more generally has been referred to as post-bureaucratic organizations.

Virtual organizations

The notion of virtuality has been discussed in the organization theory literature recently. Even though the notion of virtuality is philosophically complicated (Deleuze, 1988; Lévy, 1998; Hayles, 1999; Ansell Pearson, 2002; de Landa, 2002; Massumi, 2002; Shields, 2003), in the organization theory literature, the notion of virtual organizations denotes a variety of qualities and characteristics (Schultze and Orlikowski, 2001). The concept of virtual organization is used to denote organizations that are in one way or another "spatialized", that is, distributed between individuals, departments, functions, geographical domains and so forth. For instance, to Poster (2001: 102), "virtual companies" are companies "[w]hose location in space is increasingly difficult to determine". Alexander (1997) discusses the virtual organization as a firm without "physical proximity" between its employees, and with organizational units that do not formally own their resources but lease tangible resources such as office space and adequate technology. One of the standard examples of virtual organizations is the Italian fashion house, Benetton, famous for outsourcing most of its activities such as design, production and marketing. Other examples of virtual organizations are the computer manufacturer, Dell (Fitzpatrick and Burke, 2000) and the sportswear company, Nike (Black and Edwards, 2000).

The literature on virtual organizations offers a number of different views of what the virtual organization is, but no common shared definition is strictly adhered to. Paul Jackson (1999: 7), speaking about "virtual working" rather than the virtual organization, writes:

> There is often little agreement as to what the "virtual" in virtual working actually stands for, and in using this new language, many vendors, writers and consultants bring with them some simplistic and flawed assumptions about organizations and the human being at work.

"The virtues of going virtual are often asserted without an exact definition of the meaning of a virtual organization," Boudreau *et al.* (1998: 121) write (see also Robey *et al.*, 2003: 115, for a critical view of the virtual organization literature).

Boudreau *et al.* (1998) identify three characteristics of the virtual organization. First, virtual organizations are based on alliances with other firms: "The central feature of the virtual organizations is their dependence on a federation of alliances and partnerships with other companies. A virtual organization operates as a federated collection of enterprises tied together through contractual and other means" (Boudreau *et al.*, 1998: 121). Second, the parts of a virtual organization are relatively autonomous: "A second characteristic of a virtual organization is its relative spatial and temporal independence. No organization operates completely independent of space or time, but virtual organizations are able to overcome vast spatial and temporal barriers by linking together geographically remote resources" (Boudreau *et al.*, 1998: 122). Third, virtual organizations are designed to enable flexibility: "Parts of virtual organization may be formed, disbanded and reformed to respond to rapidly changing business needs. Flexibility is an important asset for transnational companies because opportunities in global markets are constantly shifting" (Boudreau *et al.*, 1998: 123). In addition, the use of information technology is presented as a common feature for virtual organizations: "Virtual organizations would simply not exist without the advanced information technologies that links their parts together" (Boudreau *et al.*, 1998: 123).

Black and Edwards (2000) emphasize virtual organizations as flexible and fluid organizational configurations and explicitly draw on a complexity theory framework to make sense out of the emergence of such organizational forms. Here, Nike is introduced as "one of the first organizations that took advantage of advanced communication and logistic technology to create a global network of organizations to produce athletic shoes instead of keeping all the work inside the organization" (Black and Edwards, 2000: 572). In a similar manner, Allcorn (1997) speaks about the need for maintaining "a fluid state that promotes learning, reflexiveness, innovation and growth" in virtual organizations. For Jackson (1999:1), "[v]irtual working is bound up with attempts to find ever more flexible and adaptive business structure. It addresses the need to break with old, bureaucratic ways of working, and to allow for rapid innovation and product development." Jackson (1999) identifies five "images and perspectives" on what he calls virtual working: (1) virtual working as information processing; (2) virtual working as heightened flexibility; (3) virtual working as disembodiment; (4) virtual working as boundary-erosion; (5) virtual working as electronic commerce (Jackson, 1999: 7ff). Cascio (2000), Davenport and Pearlson (1998), Venkatraman and Henderson (1998) and Maznevsky and Chudoba (2000) examine the practical managerial effects from virtual work, for instance how communication, motivation and corporate culture should be managed in "virtual work teams". In these accounts, the virtual organization implies the extension of organizational space into home offices, hotels and mobile offices in cars, in short "a variety of mobile and remote work environments" (Davenport and Pearlson, 1998: 53), effectively supported by a number of technologies such as laptop computers, high-speed modems, fax machines, pagers and cellular phones. Even though the "virtual workplace" is equipped with a number of technologies, Davenport and Pearlson (1998: 64) conclude that some managers "[a]re findings it much more difficult to manage in the virtual environment than they had originally thought. At Xerox, for example, some sales managers have moved back into their offices after deciding that the virtual office was not a workable arrangement for them".

Handy (1997) discusses trust in virtual organization but offers no straightforward definition of the virtual organization. Instead, Handy (1997: 92) says, in a rather sweeping formulation, that virtual organizations "feed on information, ideas, and intelligence" (see also Knights *et al.*, 2001, for a different treatment of trust in virtual organizations). For Kotorov: "*virtualization* implies the vanishing of the formal and spatial boundaries of firms" (2001: 55, emphasis in the original). Robey *et al.* (2003) argue that the virtual organization needs to "intertwine" what they refer to as "the virtual" with "the material". The virtual denotes information and communication technology based workspaces while tangible resources such as desks, chairs and office space represent the material. In Robey *et al.*'s (2003) view, the virtual is opposed to the material; the virtual is not "really real" but is a computer-simulated image of the real, what is immediately given. Only an effective "intertwinement" of these two levels enables an effective organization. Schultze and Orlikowski (2001: 55) identify five metaphors for the virtual organization used in the field: virtual organization as *platform*, as *space*, as *bits* (derived from computer science terminology), as *community* and, finally, as *network*. The virtual organization is here examined from complementary or even incommensurable views. In these different accounts on the virtual organization, a few recurring common themes emerges: flexibility in form (Allcorn, 1997; Fitzpatrick and Burke, 2000; Hedberg *et al.*, 2000), joint cooperations across firm boundaries and even the dissolution of firm boundaries (Boudreau *et al.*, 1998; Lansing, 2001), and the use of information and communication technology and other forms of technology (e.g. Brown and Lightfoot, 2002; McGail, 2002; Mason *et al.*, 2002) are frequently examined. Most of the literature affirms the idea of the virtual organization.

In one of the few critical papers on virtual organizations, Hughes *et al.*, (2001: 49–50) write: "'Virtual' organizational arrangements consists of networks of workers and organizational units linked by information and communication technologies (ICTs), which will flexibly coordinate their activities, and combine their skills and resources in order to achieve common goals." Although Hughes *et al.* (2001) take an explicit critical stance towards the guru theory version of the virtual organization, and present an ethnographic study of an organization change programme in a retail bank, they fail to critically examine the notion of the virtual. In their conclusion, they argue that the "virtualization" of the bank implied little more than "business as usual" (Hughes *et al.*, 2001: 62). Nevertheless, they take on the standard formulation of the virtual organization and discuss the use of information and communication technologies to set up "specialized functional centres" and "distribute decision support" in the bank.

In summary, the virtual organization is a distributed organization form mediated by various forms of information and communication technologies. Rather than being simply located in one place, the virtual organization is a fluid and permeable construct marked by its flexibility and ability to cover geographical territories and the overcoming of the difference between near and far. The virtual organization is based on the discourse of "death of distance" and seeks to integrate various organization members that are distributed over large areas.

Projectified organizations

Another, recently conceived organization model or configuration based on an epistemology of fluids is the projectified organization (Midler, 1995) wherein the organization is treated as a bundle of interrelated or autonomous projects being coordinated by a relatively small line organization. Several writers speak of the projectified organization as being at "the front-wave of post-bureaucracy" (McSweeney, 2006: 29). While the bureaucracy is put forth as the *atemporal* organization par excellence, the projectified organization is envisaged as its *temporal* counterpart (Hobday, 2000; Söderlund, 2004). While bureaucracies are controlled by rules, standard operation procedures, and clearly separated responsibilities and roles very much detached from a temporal perspective – bureaucracies are essentially designed to last forever – the projectified organization is managed through a tight focus on time; time is, in fact, the very basis for the "project organization". Since temporality is given pre-eminence in the projectified organization, the notions of becoming and the fluid are more closely associated with the projectified organization than with the bureaucratic form.

The ontology of a bureaucracy is based on solids and enclosed entities while the ontology of the projectified organization, in practice as well in theory, takes an affirmative view of the fluid.

Projects are always open-ended (although intended to operate on certain grounds), contingent (rather than being isolated from external influences) and complex (rather than being unified and void of paradoxes). The very idea of the project is to organize a multiplicity of competencies within one single structure in order to deal with complex problems or challenges. Projects are therefore at the very heart of attempting to deal with great complexities. According to what Ashby (1956) calls "the law of requisite variety", a theory emerging from the cybernetic programme (Wiener, 1948), a system must always be more complex than the system it aims to control. Thus, complex project objectives demand a certain degree of complexity in competencies. Project organizations are set up to deal with specific and highly specialized tasks that a functionally organized organization fails to deal with under short time constraints. The strength of the project organization thus lies in its ability to mobilize specific resources in a short-term perspective and to effectively undertake one work assignment at the time. In terms of the morphology of the firm, an organization is then no longer a hierarchical structure but is instead a portfolio or a bundle of interrelated or individual projects, constituting a field of competence within an organization. Rather than being functionally organized, in the project-based organization, the different functions are located within each project. This organization of competencies provides good opportunities for dealing with a series of individual tasks but implies a problem in terms of integration of central competencies and skills. Empirical evidence suggests that the project organization needs to be supported by managerial mechanisms enabling a sharing of learning and experiences between projects (Roth, 2003). Without structured and predetermined points of mutual learning, each project evolves as an autonomous body detached from other projects (Bresnen *et al.*, 2004; Scarbrough *et al.*, 2004). The long-term consequences are that various bodies of expertise may become fragmented because there is no critical mass of expertise integrating itself.

Another problem facing the projectified organization is the demands for a professionalization of the project-management work, that is, the institutionalization of certain work practices and procedures structuring the project management work. In their study of a project management model at the telecom company, Ericsson, Räisänen and Linde (2004) found that the project manager's work is structured in accordance with a series of rules and standards: "PMMs [Project Management Models] are tied to a variety of technocratic planning, execution and reporting tools to ensure that projects are run rationally according to set budgets, goals, and time schedules" (Räisänen and Linde, 2004: 103). Project managers, then, are no longer free to make his or her own choices and decisions but, instead, the work is closely tied to a number of specified standard operating procedures. Räisänen and Linde conclude: "In multi-project organizations today, projects are no longer the exceptional, unique and innovative work form of a new work order. Instead, project management is being subjected to the forces of organization rationalization, resulting in a bureaucratization of projectified activities" (2004: 117). Hodgson (2004) also uses the notion of bureaucratization to portray the same movement within the field of project management. Needless to say, for Hodgson, bureaucratization is a bad thing, delimiting the project manager's ability to achieve the project goals. Hodgson writes:

> Project management can be seen as an essentially bureaucratic system of control, based on principles of visibility, predictability and accountability, and operationalized through the adherence to formalized procedures and constant written reporting mechanisms. At the same time, however, project management draws upon the central rhetoric of empowerment, autonomy and self-reliance central to post-bureaucratic organizational discourse.
>
> (2004: 88)

Hodgson concludes: "[W]hat distinguishes project management as of particular relevance to 21st-century organizations is its rediscovery of a very 19th-century preoccupation with comprehensive planning, linked to a belief in the necessity of tight managerial control" (2004: 86). Clegg and Courpasson (2004) discuss project organizations as a hybrid organization form comprising both "modern" bureaucratic forms of control, including routines, rules and direct control and "post-modern" forms of control such as what Clegg and Courpasson calls "reputational control" wherein the project manager's reputation, his or her credibility within the social system, is always at stake, "calculative control", the close monitoring of all activities in the project work and, finally, "professional control" wherein the project-manager role is becoming increasingly predetermined and scripted into sequences of actions that need to be undertaken. For Clegg and Courpasson, project-management work and the project organization form does not represent a radical break from bureaucratic control and the bureaucratic organization form but is, instead, an example of a modification and reformulation of previous forms of managerial control.

For Räisänen and Linde (2004), Hodgson (2004), and Clegg and Courpasson (2004) project management is based on the ideal of fluidity and flexibility, but in its context of application, for instance the new product development organization, conventional beliefs and taken-for-granted ideas on how management should be organized penetrate the project-management practice and structure the project-management process in accordance with what Hodgson (2004) calls a "bureaucratic model". Again the disregard for bureaucracy is articulated and regarded as a mistaken influence within a particular practice. However, the papers of Räisänen and Linde (2004) and Hodgson (2004) point to the uneasiness an epistemology of fluids gives rise to; we know a bit about how to manage organizations that are stable and hierarchical, but managing networks, projects, virtual teams and other forms of "non-solid" or "porous" organization, we have only a limited experience with. This shortage of experience may explain the significant increase in membership in project-management associations such as PMI (Project Management Institute). The ambiguities in practices are, as

Hodgson (2004) points out, compensated for with stricter managerial routines and the legitimacy provided by major international professional associations. Managing fluid organizations is, after all, a rather recent phenomenon.

Network organizations

The network organization is also examined in the organization theory and management literature. The network organization or the structure of network organizations has been examined in terms of their emergence and growth (Hite and Hesterly, 2001), as having a strategic capability to create sustainable competitive advantage (Gulati *et al.*, 2000; Oliver, 2004), and as an arena for joint knowledge-creation and sharing and organization learning (Augier and Thanning Vendelø, 1999; Gulati, 1999; Seufert *et al.*, 1999; Dyer and Nobeoka, 2000). When science-based innovation, demanding significant research resources, becomes a more important factor in certain industries, for instance the biotechnology sector, individual firms may no longer be capable of mobilizing the demanded resources. Instead, such firms are participating in forms of organization networks enabling a more effective exploitation of available resources. In other words, economy of scale is achieved through the joint investment and sharing of resources across firm boundaries. Powell *et al.* (1996) studied network organizations in the pharmaceutical industry and identified the shortcomings of the bureaucratic organization form in terms of innovating on its own:

> Knowledge creation occurs in the context of a community, one that is fluid and evolving rather than tightly bound or static. The canonical formal organization, with its bureaucratic rigidities, is a poor vehicle for learning. Sources of innovation do not reside exclusively within firms; instead, they are commonly found in the interstices between firms, universities, research laboratories, suppliers, and customers.
>
> (Powell *et al.*, 1996: 118)

The successful innovating firm, then, is closely associated with a number of knowledge-intensive organizations of various kinds. Powell *et al.* (1996: 116) continue: "A key finding from a diverse set of studies is that the R&D intensity or level of technological sophistication of industries is positively correlated with the intensity and number of alliances in those sectors." The long-term success and innovativeness of an industry, then, is correlated with its ability to orchestrate a fruitful interaction between organizations and communities. Not only do such collaborations enable the mutual sharing of know-how, the external influences actually reinforce the firm's internal resources:

> Our concept of networks of learning highlights two key observations: (1) interorganizational collaborations are not simply a means to compensate for the lack of internal skills, (2) nor should they be viewed as a series of

discrete transactions. A firm's value and ability as a collaborator is related to its internal assets, but at the same time, collaborations further develop and strengthen those internal competencies. Firms deepen their ability to collaborate not just by managing relations dyadically, but by instantiating and refining routines for synergistic partnering.

(Powell *et al.*, 1996: 119)

In another paper, Powell (1998) concludes:

Rather than seeking to monopolize the returns from innovative activity and forming exclusive relationships with only a narrow set of organizations, successful firms position themselves as the hubs at the centre of overlapping networks, simulating rewarding research collaborations among the various organizations to which they are aligned, and profiting from having multiple projects in various stages of development.

(Powell, 1998: 230)

In terms of an epistemology of fluids, know-how and expertise are no longer simply a matter for the focal firm but, rather, is what is jointly exploited, created and shared within clusters or networks of organizations. Knowledge resources are constantly overflowing the juridical boundaries between firms and cannot be kept within closed walls. Knowledge is not simply located in specific places but is fundamentally dislocated and channelled in various directions. The innovative industry is capable of exploiting this flow of knowledge and distributes it in directions that enables it to contribute to innovation processes to the largest possible extent.

Post-bureaucratic organization

Besides the research on virtual organizations, project organizations and network organizations, there are a number of studies of what may be called, with a joint label, "post-bureaucratic organizations". The notion of post-bureaucratic organizations is by no means new, but was used by Maniha (1975) and, before that, Warren Bennis (1970). Bendix (1971: 142) talks of the governmental administrative apparatus of the former East European communist countries as being "post-bureaucratic". With the prefix "post", the post-bureaucratic here denotes a variety of organization forms that, in various respects, are deviating from the Weberian bureaucratic model. Heckscher and Donnellon (1994) and Maravelias (2003) studied the Swedish insurance company, Skandia, and emphasized specific human-resource management practices within post-bureaucratic organizations. Rather than employing various conventional managerial means for control of the workers, Skandia used what Maravelias (2003) calls "trust-based control" of the employees. Since there were few fixed rules of conduct and standardized practices, it was essentially up to the employees to decide for themselves what was to be regarded as an adequate workload. As a consequence, many co-workers at Skandia worked long hours because they simply did not know how to draw a line of demarcation between an adequate workload and excessive work. The movement from one mode of control to another in the post-bureaucratic organization therefore implies a new degree of ambiguity in work-life. Maravelias argues:

> The case shows that on the other side of those characteristics the managerial discourse refers to as freedom and emancipation we find uncertainty, potential distrust and unclear responsibilities which drive individuals to work harder and pay closer attention to their own and their colleagues' behavior. However, individuals did not appear to be forced to subordinate to implicit roles commissioned to a direct system of instituted norms and values – a particular organization culture – as the critical discourse suggests. In fact, the term subordination did not seem to apply; what drove the individuals to work harder and smarter was not a pressure to subordinate to a distinct culture, but a lack of any clear system to subordinate to.
>
> (Maravelias, 2003: 557)

In a study of a consultancy firm, Robertson and Swan (2003) found evidence of a similar condition wherein the consultants praised individual freedom, yet became "enslaved" under the absence of rules: "The strong values associated with individual freedom, autonomy and ambiguity were constructed and sustained by consultants themselves and, at the same time, enslaved them to behave in ways that were ultimately beneficial for the firm" (Robertson and Swan, 2003: 850). The Skandia co-workers and the consultants were not asked to work a specific number of hours but were, on the contrary, given a choice to make on their own. This paradoxical conclusion, that the absence of management procedures leads to more work rather than less, is of interest when trying to understand the human-resource practices of post-bureaucratic organizations. Maravelias concludes:

> [P]ost-bureaucracy is not simply bureaucracy dressed in a new and subtler disguise. It is controlled by a decentralized principle of power, which is only marginally disseminated from an organizational center; it is immanent within the networks of practice it sets in motion. In this respect we may conclude that post-bureaucracy emerges as, simultaneously, more totalitarian and more democratic than bureaucracy: more totalitarian because it lacks clear boundaries, it is continually present, and seeks to subordinate aspects of instrumental role-playing; more democratic, because these incessant expansionist powers follow an inclusive not exclusive logic. That is, in contrast to bureaucracy that excludes those individual characteristics, which fall outside of its instrumental schemes, post-bureaucracy, in its urge to harness aspects of the 'free spheres' of individuals' lives, does not obliterate these 'other' forces it faces, it opens itself to them and includes them in the networks of practice.
>
> (2003: 562)

Maravelias's conclusion is supported by other studies. Du Gay (1996) is speaking about "auto-surveillance" as a form of self-monitoring where co-workers are expected to be in charge of their work operations and performance, and Barker (1993) is talking about a "concertive system of control" wherein it is essentially the co-workers, the peers, who are supposed to maintain the control over the operations. Barker (1993: 412) contrasts this model with "bureaucratic control":

> Under bureaucratic control, employees might ensure that they come to work on time because the employee handbook prescribed it and the supervisor had the legal right to demands it, but in the concertive system, employees might come to work on time because their peers now have the authority to demand the workers' willing compliance.

If nothing else, the post-bureaucratic organization implies a new regime of management control.

Besides the concept of bureaucratic organizations, some authors have been using the term "boundaryless organizations" (Ashkenas *et al.*, 1995) to capture organization forms that have permeable and open boundaries. This open-system model of organizations is supposed to function as a seamless web of suppliers and end-producers and is representative of another form of post-bureaucratic organization, again very much in opposition to the supposedly closed quality of the bureaucratic organization form.

Summary and conclusion

A number of different organization conceptualizations are adhering, more or less explicitly, to what we have here called an epistemology of fluids. The virtual organization emphasizes its technological embeddedness and the "tele-presence" of managerial practices within extended territories. The projectified organization is theoretically derived from a temporal model and is distinguished vis-à-vis other organization forms on the basis of its focus on temporality. The network organization transcends the single organization form and instead emphasizes the co-evolution and joint collaboration of a number of organizations, thus sketching a specific ecology wherein a variety of organizations share a joint interest. Finally, the post-bureaucratic organization is perhaps the least unified construct, comprising a number of practices and tendencies that are only loosely coupled but that share the characteristics of replacing instrumental and direct control with novel forms of discipline and self-monitoring, essentially different from the predominant forms of control in the bureaucratic model. These different organization models recognize a change in perspective, from organizations as being stable or semi-stable entities, more or less simply located and obeying certain machine-like laws, to a perspective on organizations as emerging through processes of organizing wherein heterogeneous materials (tangible and intangible, physical and symbolic, embodied and cognitive) are mobilized and put into use. In this latter model, organization is always more or less subject to external influences and, therefore, evolves in a more fluid manner than the classic organization model assumes. In summary, fluid epistemologies have gained greater influence in organization theory since at least the end of the 1980s. While concepts such as the "complex organization" (e.g. Etzioni, 1964) or the "formal organization" (Blau and Scott, 1963) prevailed during the post-Second World War period, until at least the end of the 1980s, today a multiplicity of alternative organization models are suggested in the organization theory and management literature. Such fluid epistemologies are more or less regarded as being in opposition to the bureaucratic organization form, and therefore it is of interest to review this literature in order to understand the disregard of bureaucracy.

The post-bureaucratic organization: the sceptic's view

Although there is a substantial literature suggesting that bureaucracies are on their way out and will be replaced by various new organizations forms, some researchers are critical of this view and demonstrate that such might not necessarily be the case. Courpasson and Reed (2004) take a most sceptical stance towards the "the demise of bureaucracy" thesis and the emergence of "the post-bureaucratic organization", locating this narrative within the "discourse of endings" (see also McSweeney, 2006), favoured in iconoclastic management writing:

> The putative "demise of bureaucracy", as well as the phoenix-like emergence of the "post-bureaucratic or network organization" out of its ashes, is a crucial, indeed an axiomatic, component of this discourse of endings. It anticipates, if not predicts, the disintegration, or more accurately implosion, of Weber's "iron cage" of bureaucratic domination and control under the multi-layered and disjunctive pressures exerted by globalization, entrepreneurialism and informationalism.
>
> (Courpasson and Reed, 2004: 5–6)

Equally critical, Thompson and Alvesson (2005: 93) debunk the post-bureaucracy literature and claim that "the territories covered by post-bureaucratic claims are huge and encompass virtually every change undertaken by organizations in the past two decades. However, much of this literature is conceptual and fails to provide adequate empirical support". Thompson and Alvesson (2005: 96) continue to say that the claims made about post-bureaucracy are "not matched by a similar depth or scope of empirical support" but instead the discussion is "speculative and insufficiently specific" and that the construct of "the post-bureaucratic organization" is riddled with ambiguities. Reed (2005) argues that the discourse on post-bureaucratic organization is representative of a narrative of human development influenced by an Enlightenment enthusiasm over social progress and human refinement:

In many respects, the post-bureaucratic/network organization thesis offers us a highly optimistic scenario of the developmental trajectory that social and organizational change will follow over the coming decades. . . . It insists that most, if not all, of the core structural features (specialized division of labour; extended authority hierarchies; exclusive organizational domains and boundaries) and operating principles (non-inclusivity, differentiation, standardization, formalization) characteristic of bureaucratic organization will disappear in the fluid and mobile world of the network organization.

(Reed, 2005: 128)

Salaman (2005), who centres his critique on the bureaucracy/post-bureaucracy dichotomy, emphasizes the continuity between the two ideal-typical organization forms and points at the reliance on rule-governed control in the two forms:

The competent manager, like the bureaucratic manager, is exposed to rules. It is true they are different sorts of rules [in bureaucratic and post-bureaucratic organizations]: output not input, internal not external, post-action not pre-action; descriptive not prescriptive. *But they remain rules nevertheless –* rules which are clearly, precisely, and formally specified; rules which may be more insidious in that they hold the manager responsible for designing and managing her own behaviour in order to achieve outcomes consistent with the organization's purposes. If it is the existence of rules, centrally determined behaviour-controlling rules which is the essence of bureaucracy, then the new organization may be less non-bureaucratic than its advocates claim.

(Salaman, 2005: 162, emphasis added)

Rather than being "a move away" or "a negation" of bureaucracy, the management practices of the post-bureaucratic organization may, on the contrary, be the "final and perhaps most complete achievement" (Salamanm, 2005: 163) of the bureaucratic ethos. Contrary to the grandiose claims formulated on the demise of bureaucracy, much empirical evidence suggests that the bureaucratic organization form and its procedures are still in use. For instance, McSweeney (2006) points at what he calls the "industrialization of services" over the last ten years:

Studies of call centers and other service settings have identified a focus on standardization, often reinforced by high-surveillance technology, such that operatives experience "an assembly-line in the head" (Taylor and Bain, 1998). Multiple studies of employees involved in "emotional labour" in a variety of settings such as leisure parks, flight attendants, receptionists, and social workers point to a growth in rule-driven and standardized verbal and visual displays of "niceness" (Hochschild, 1983). Here again, we find substantial evidence for re-bureaucratization and little or nothing to support the belief that events are "flowing with an epochalist tide".

(McSweeney, 2006: 30)

Iedema (2003) takes the sceptic's view of the grand narrative of the "ending of bureaucracy". In a report on an empirical study of an Australian company, he says that post-bureaucracy rarely appears in a pure form (see also Salaman, 2005; Josserand *et al.*, 2006). Instead, many organizations have adopted what Iedema calls "a post-bureaucratic rhetoric" (2003: 2) while, at the same time, they retain "traditional structural hierarchies, expert and specialization boundaries, and procedures and processes whose intent is top-down control rather than bottom-up facilitation". Iedema says that this adherence to two opposing traditions is causing confusion among co-workers. He argues:

> Traditionally, bureaucracy set great store by rationality, accountability, hierarchy, and depersonalization . . . and each of these dimensions manifested as practices to do with rule-setting and rule-following. Post-bureaucracy, by contrast, is the pursuit of rhetorical, structural and social-interactive change away from top-down rules. In this sense, it is a rarefied space where spontaneity, initiative, involvement, enthusiasm and pragmatic decision-making converge.
>
> (Iedema, 2003: 2–3)

The idea that there is no clear line of demarcation between bureaucracy and post-bureaucracy is empirically supported by Colin Hales (2002) who speaks of what he calls "Bureaucracy-lite". "Bureaucracy-lite" do not depart from the conventional bureaucratic organization form but, rather, is a reformulation of some of its practices, adapting them to new social conditions. Hales (2002) identifies two parameters for the post-bureaucratic organization: (1) organization form, and (2) management practice. He also argues that the post-bureaucratic, internal network organization is characterized by "[t]he *absence* of a rigid division of labour, hierarchy and rules" (2002: 54). In this type of organization, the management role is being altered:

> [T]he distinct, traditional role of "manager" as someone who is individually responsible for the planning, coordination and control of the work staff under their specific command, within the constraints set by policy and regulations, is, supposedly, disappearing. "Managers" in the traditional sense are replaced by a particular brand of professional "knowledge worker" charged with a more general, less constrained entrepreneurial or leadership role.
>
> (Hales, 2002: 55)

Hales (2002) presents four case studies: a hotel chain in Zimbabwe, a manufacturing company in Malaysia and two public organizations in the UK, using them to explore the new modes of organizing. Hales points at the consistency between conventional bureaucracy and the "new" organization forms in terms of emphasizing rules and "output control": "[M]uch of the evidence of variations in organization forms suggests not alternatives *to* but alternative *versions* of bureaucratic organization" (2002: 62). He continues to examine the implications for management practice and finds that there is, in fact, little new under the sun; instead, managers' "'[r]esponsibility' continues to be defined by a system of hierarchical relationships and rules". Hales points at the preferences of the middle-managers for what Giddens (1990) calls "ontological certainty" as being what is conserving management practice; since managers have to deal with ambiguity, uncertainty and disagreement in their work, they have to "negotiate" their role in the organization. In such "negotiations", managers tend to "gravitate toward those activities which *are* conventionally understood as 'managing', and hence conform, wittingly or unwittingly, to certain taken-for-granted expectations about what managers should do" (Hales, 2002: 62). In the face of uncertainty and ambiguities, managers resort to what is well-known and familiar, namely management practices that are firmly established as legitimate practices within the company, industry or profession. Hales concludes: "Managers continue to be preoccupied with routine, day-to-day monitoring and maintenance of work processes, managing staff and processing information, to the exclusion of instigating change, developing staff and seeking new business opportunities" (2002: 64).

In Hales's account, there is a disjunction between post-bureaucratic rhetoric and actual managerial and organizational practices. Rather than breaking with the bureaucratic organization form, the new forms of organization are, in Hales's parlance, "bureaucracy-lite", that is, the continuation of the same means of organizing but somewhat reformulated to suit the new times (2002). Kärreman *et al.* (2002) express similar ideas in their study of a consultancy firm and a pharmaceutical company. These two firms are what Kärreman *et al.* (2002) call, after Starbuck (1992), "knowledge-intensive firms" (KIFs). In the general management literature, KIFs are assumed to be some kind of avant-garde organizations wherein new forms of organizing and managerial practices will be developed and established to eventually be spread elsewhere. However, the researchers found, somewhat surprisingly, that the consultancy firm (referred to with the pseudonym "Beta") was very much organized like a conventional bureaucracy:

> [B]eta departs quite dramatically from the conventional wisdom of how KIFs are supposed to be organized. Strikingly, Beta appears to operate in a way that shares more features with the traditional bureaucracy form than with conventional images of KIFs. Beta is distinguished by an emphasis on hierarchy, formalization of work procedures, predictability in work outputs, and interchangeability of parts (i.e., individuals).
>
> (Kärreman *et al.*, 2002: 76)

Still, Beta employed a bureaucratic organization form to support the co-workers rather than control them. Therefore, Kärreman *et al.* (2002) use Courpasson's (2000) notion of "soft bureaucracies" (see also Jermier *et al.*, 1992; Kärreman and Alvesson, 2004; Robertson and Swan, 2004, for the use of the term) or "selective bureaucracies" in cases where a "bureaucratic mindset" helped to guide the activities. Here, the bureaucratic procedures served more as a vehicle for "shared understanding" than as a "protocol for prescribed behaviour" (Kärreman *et al.*, 2002: 79). In the pharmaceutical company, the discovery research process in the new drug-development activities were formalized and subject to increased control. "It used to be more brain and less mass production," one manager claimed, deploring the movement towards new laboratory practices (cited in Kärreman *et al.*, 2002: 82). A managerial terminology thus penetrated the laboratory domains and imposed new modes of control and regulation:

> [M]uch managerial talk is clearly based on the assumption that it is possible to formalize, and subsequently more consciously manage, the research – hence, the objective to create a standard model supposedly implemented by managers in all research sites throughout the corporation. The R&D processes are now also usually coined "management processes" of various kinds, thereby signifying and elevating the managerial aspects in the research processes.
>
> (Kärreman *et al.*, 2002: 84)

Similarly to Hales's (2002) discussion of ambiguity as an immanent quality of managerial work, Kärreman *et al.* (2002) argue that the same kinds of ambiguities are possible to observe in knowledge-intensive firms. Complex tasks, complex environments and complex organizational patterns produce situations wherein ambiguity and uncertainty are "endemic". To handle these ambiguities, bureaucratic procedures are adhered to in order to achieve a sense of "closure, control, and predictability in organizations and work relations" (Kärreman *et al.*, 2002: 87–88). This coping with uncertainty through bureaucratic means is named "selective bureaucracy".

Courpasson speaks of "soft bureaucracies" in organizations wherein much responsibility for everyday routine work is delegated while strategic decision-making remains centralized:

> [T]he concept of "soft bureaucracy" tries to express the emergence of a political centralization of organizations, in line with the development of decentralized ways of conducting their activities: jobs and responsibilities have become more decentralized, but political decisions more centralized. That is why we think that soft bureaucracies are an efficient way of governing decentralized organizations which need to establish a certain coherence.
>
> (Courpasson, 2000: 155)

Jermier *et al.* (1992) use the concept of soft bureaucracy in their study of the informal culture of an American police department in a crime-ridden town in southern USA. The police officers did not subscribe to the formal "crime-fighting" rhetoric of the police department but were, instead, divided into no less that five different groups that, in their own individual ways, contributed to the police work. For Jermier *et al.* (1992), the soft bureaucracy, then, is the informal, cultural and practice-based organization operating parallel to the formal bureaucratic model:

> The image of the *soft bureaucracy*, an organization with a rigid exterior appearance symbolizing what key stakeholders expect but with a loosely-coupled set of interior practices ... or of an *action-generating system*, an organization churning independently of the problem it will later claim oriented its actions ... captures the emphasis Organizational Symbolists place on informal organization and emergent subcultures.
>
> (Jermier *et al.*, 1992: 189)

Here, the soft bureaucracy is similar to what Gouldner (1954) called a "mock-bureaucracy" (see also Hynes and Prasad, 1997), a register of formal directives, rules and rhetoric representing the "ceremonial, command bureaucracy model" (Jermier *et al.*, 1992: 189), only loosely coupled with actual practices. In a study of public-sector work in the UK, Farrell and Morris (2003) spoke of the "neo-bureaucratic state" wherein bureaucracy is, similar to Courpasson's (2000) "soft bureaucracy", simultaneously centralized and decentralized. Farrell and Morris (2003) are critical of the movement towards the "marketization" and contracting-out in the new public management and rational-choice ideology:

> We have argued that far from witnessing the post-bureaucratic state we have seen the emergence of a neo-bureaucratic state. To use Rhodes's (1997a) term, public administration has itself been "hollowed-out" with the locus of bureaucracy taken away from the middle layers and pushed to the top (the centre) and the bottom (the periphery). ... Ideologically informed, this neo-bureaucratic state has not functioned as intended: it has arguably increased bureaucracy; its real impact on accountability is questionable; it has made modest inroads into organizational efficiency and increasing 'consumers choice'.
>
> (Farrell and Morris, 2003: 149)

They continue:

> What we are seeing ... is that market mechanisms have not worked: they have provided greater public choice in the main and have increased bureaucracy, albeit a bipolarised bureaucracy with anarchic forms at the decentralized level and a bloated centralized cadre desperately trying to control the anarchy.
>
> (2003: 150)

For Farrell and Morris (2003), new public management remains anchored in a market ideology that we will address in greater detail shortly. As a consequence, the neo-bureaucratic state becomes a mixture of old forms of bureaucratic control and new post-bureaucratic forms of control including agency and self-monitoring of the activities.

Somewhat paradoxically and in opposition to what is said in much of the recent popular-management literature, knowledge-intensive firms and other supposedly "post-bureaucratic organizations" are not fully breaking with the bureaucratic organization form but are, instead, drawing on such ready-made arrangements to give stability to a world in flux. Both Hales (2002) and Kärreman *et al.* (2002) demonstrate that the "inescapable and overdue demise of bureaucracy" (Hales, 2002: 64) is poorly supported by empirical evidence and that there is ample evidence of firms developing alternative versions of bureaucracy rather than departing from it. In addition, the nature of managerial work and knowledge-intensive work are riddled with ambiguities and possibilities for negotiated orders and, consequently, there is a great need for the emotional and cognitive stability provided by the bureaucratic organization form. In summary, the discourse on the post-bureaucratic organization need to be examined *cum grano salis* and with a healthy degree of scepticism; much of the "anti-bureaucracy" literature (Du Gay, 2005) rests on ideological rather empirical grounds.

The market ideology and the post-bureaucratic organization

In this section, the notion of the market is invoked as the embodiment *par préférence* of an epistemology of fluids. Various types of markets are what Knorr Cetina (2005) calls the "flow worlds", essentially loosely coupled with or even detached from underlying realities. In the dominating mindset, such social arrangements are effective means for balancing various social interests and concerns (Callon, 1998; Armstrong, 2001; Thrift, 2001). The argument is that the influence of a market ideology partially explains the enthusiasm for various forms of post-bureaucratic organization arrangements and the accompanying disregard of bureaucracy.

In the following, when we speak of an ideology of the post-bureaucratic organization or even the post-bureaucratic organizational landscape (see Ahrne, 1990), we use the definition of Louis Althusser (1984: 32), saying that "[I]deology is the system of the ideas and representations which dominate the mind of a man or a social group." The underlying idea is that management practice is, to use Foucault's concept, a "practico-theoretical field", deeply imbued with ideology (Barley and Kunda, 1992; Deetz, 1992; Armstrong, 2001; Holmberg and Strannegård, 2002). Shenhav (1999: 8) writes: "Managerial ideology should be considered not as a neutral endpoint without moral and political consequences, but as a means bearing a clear moral and political responsibility that requires constant scrutiny." Therefore, management thinking needs to be examined as a domain heavily influenced by predominant ideologies in society.

The different forms of fluid organizational configurations stress different features departing from the bureaucratic organization form. The virtual organization model stresses the geographical distribution of the organization, the project organization stresses the cross-functional nature of project teams, while the network organization highlights the central role of collaboration within industries, and the more diverse post-bureaucratic organization model considers a number of new practices and routines that differ from the bureaucratic model.

In addition, the public sector is restructured in accordance with a new manager-ial regime labelled "New Public Management" wherein managerial principles and techniques from private enterprises are implemented and executed. Changes include the construction of quasi-markets within the public sector, or the use of short-term contracting on an open market, replacing long-term agreements between public sector organizations (Ferlie *et al.*, 1996; Lane, 2000; Farrell and Morris, 2003; Hoggett, 2005; Newton, 2005). All of these different organization forms share a general belief in the market as being a more efficient mode of reg-ulation than the hierarchy. Bureaucracies, then, are treated as detached from markets, while new organization forms are supposedly more apt to respond to market influences. However, the notion of the market is a troubled one, strongly affected by various ideologically imbued assumptions and beliefs. In order to discuss the concepts of markets and hierarchies, one needs to have a proper theory of the market. Knorr Cetina and Bruegger (2002: 161) point at three dif-ferent images of the market:

> Current market theories conceptualize the market essentially in three ways: (1) as a price-setting mechanism consistent with equilibrium conditions, where individual decision-makers already in possession of the relevant information adjust their behaviour and output to a price at which supplies are exhausted and demands are satisfied ... (2) as a mode of coordination that contrasts with hierarchies and networks: while rules and authority con-stitute the central coordinating mechanism of hierarchies, and trust and cooperation that of networks, the mechanism operating in markets is price competition ... (3) as a form of action (exchange) embedded in social rela-tions ... the first concept corresponds to the neo-classical approach in eco-nomics, the second exemplifies the transaction cost approach and the third corresponds to the new economic sociology, whose premise is that social networks based on kinship, friendship and trust influences economic trans-actions and sustain economic relations.

The neo-classical approach to the market as a price-setting mechanism was adhered to by bureaucracy critics such as von Mises (1944); transaction cost theory, in the tradition of Ronald Coase (1991) and his follower Oliver Williamson (1975), has been a dominant model of organization in organization theory and especially in strategic management theory. Finally, economic soci-ology shares a number of assumptions with qualitatively oriented organization theory. In this view, the market is not a thing per se but, rather, is the arena in which different actors make deals on the basis of negotiations and shared inter-ests. This latter view does not assume that markets per se are capable of solving any economic problems but simply assumes that the market is one mechanism among others enabling economic and organizational activities. It is noteworthy that the neo-classical view of the market is a particularly fertile soil for bureau-cracy critique and a more general critique of the intervention of the state and other politically grounded organizations. In an epistemology of fluids, and especially in its neo-classical manifestations such as neo-liberal economics and policy, the stable and the hierarchical are often dismissed in terms of disrupting the flows of the economy, thereby reducing the liberating force inherent to the market. May (2002), discussing the discourse on what a variety of authors have called the "information society", is critical of this general ignorance of the importance of regulating societal institutions:

> Much of the analysis of the information society reifies the market by ignoring the crucial role of legal institutions in capitalist society. More importantly, given the dependence of the new economy on intellectual property rights, without strong state authority the economy of the information society would be unworkable.
>
> (May, 2002: 17)

For May, then, there is a dominant belief that the state and its institutions – often portrayed in the form of rigid bureaucracies – are detrimental to the fulfilment of the information society. Again, the arguments of Karl Polanyi (1944) regarding the shortcomings of market liberalism is applicable when examining the discourse on how information and communication technologies are claimed to "overturn" the world as we know it.

Wajcman and Martin (2002) account for another form of market-based discourse in the research on post-bureaucratic organization. In their research on how managers perceived their work-life chances and career prospects, they found that most of the interlocutors conceived of themselves as some kind of entrepreneurial, enterprising selves that obeyed the rules of the markets rather than the management regime. Wajcman and Martin discuss this outlook and mode of self-formation and what Michel Foucault calls subjectification [*assujetment*] as being based on a "market narrative":

> The dominant mode in which both men and women interviewees told their career stories was through what we call a *market narrative*, that is, a kind of individualized, neo-liberal account of market action and choice. This contrasts with an earlier bureaucratic narrative based upon commitment to the organization. In the first market narrative mode, managers placed themselves as "choosing selves". As buyers and consumers on markets, they pictured themselves as purchasing goods and services which best satisfies their needs and preferences.
>
> (2002: 992)

Benhabib (2002) emphasizes that the self, one's subject-formation, is dependent upon the "webs of interlocution" that the individual are "inserted into". Benhabib writes:

> To be and to become a self is to insert oneself into webs of interlocution; it is to know to answer when one is addressed and to know how to address

others. . . . Strictly speaking, we never really *insert* ourselves, but are rather *thrown* into these webs of interlocution, in the Heideggerian sense of "thrownness" as *Geworfenheit*: We are born into webs of interlocution or narrative, from familiar and gender narratives to linguistic ones and to the macronarratives of collective identity. We become aware of who we are by learning to become conversation partners in these narratives.

(Benhabib, 2002: 15)

While Wajcman and Martin (2002) speak of a "market narrative", Benhabib similarly talks of "corporate identities" to capture the dominant discourse shaping the subjectification: "I will use the term *corporate identities* to refer to group identities that are officially recognized by the state and its institutions" (Benhabib, 2002: 72). In a similar manner, du Gay (1996) talks about the image of an "enterprising self", an individual taking full responsibility for him or herself and their careers, closely connected to this type of "market narrative" attended to by Wajcman and Martin (2002) (see also Fournier, 1998; Sturdy, 1998; Du Gay, 2000b).

In a study of temporarily employed workers in Scandinavia, so-called "temps", Christina Garsten found a similar type of narrative. Garsten (2002) talks about the construct of a "market man", *homo mercaris*, that is, the subject grounding his or her identity in the ability to function effectively within a market setting, in short, having the ability to promote one's "employability" (see Adamson *et al.*, 1998). Garsten argues: "Market man is taught to think in terms of financial transactions, value him- or herself as a product of the market, and to take the idea of enterprise as a mode of action. Moreover, he or she is flexible, autonomous, self-reliant and disciplined" (2002: 247). For temporary workers, this may be, Garsten (2002) argues, to make a virtue out of a necessity. In fact, most temps claimed that they would appreciate the opportunity of a long-term contract with one employer rather than being forced to move to new workplaces every now and then (Pialoux and Beaud, 1999). Nevertheless, the ideology of the primacy of the market is firmly established and only occasionally criticized within various communities. Expressed differently, one may argue that the emphasis on the market as the principal arena for organizational activities and transactions, rather than within hierarchies, lies at the very heart of the image of the post-bureaucratic organization form. An epistemology of fluids demonstrates a more affirmative view of the image of the market as a field of intersecting forces and flows of information, capital and resources than that of the bureaucratic hierarchy and its emphasis on procedures and rules written in books and enacted behind closed doors. Since our age is an age of speed (Gleick, 1999; Virilio, 2004) and of flows and movements, what is perceived as being hierarchical and only slowly adapting to new external conditions is not exactly praised as being of great social value. However, as new formations of knowledge and new assumptions and beliefs emerge, new organization forms will be put forth and perceived as capable of dealing with new opportunities and threats. For the time being, the market-oriented and market-dependent organization is regarded as being of great social value and, therefore, the market stands out as the single most important mechanism for economic activities.

Accountability and the market narrative

A more specific implication of the discourse of the enterprising self is, as Iedema (2003) says, the emphasis on transparency and accountability in an organization's practices. The market logic, at least in its neo-classical form, pre-supposes that the agent is capable of making rational evaluations and decisions on the basis of available information. In the ideal market situation, one of the axiomatic principles of much economic theory – a proposition subject to harsh criticism in economic sociology – is that all information is immediately available for all agents within a field at all times. Such images of full transparency as an applicable solution to managerial problems are also, Iedema (2003) suggests, observable in practices in post-bureaucratic organizations. In his study of clinical practice in a hospital in Australia, Iedema speaks of an "accountability rhetoric": "This new accountability rhetoric comes with concepts like the measurement of clinical performance, benchmarking of outcomes and quality, integration of clinical decision-making with formal scientific evidence, and leadership on clinical practice improvement" (Iedema, 2003: 178).

This accountability rhetoric had material discursive effects on the healthcare organizations in terms of the establishment of new roles, practices and institutions in the hospital. Iedema (2003: 180) points to an "Institute of Clinical Excellence" being funded, and roles such as "Quality Coordinators" and "Pathway Officers" as examples of organizational innovations. Another example of the manifestation of transparency in clinical practice was the formulation of so-called "clinical pathways", defined as "[s]ystematically developed written statements of the agreed sequence of diagnostic and therapeutic processes which, in light of available evidence and stated resource constraints, are essential for achieving nominated outcome for specified clinical conditions" (Hindle and Degeling, 1999: 3, cited in Iedema, 2003: 181). Iedema argues that the clinical pathway brings together a range of aspects of the work, socialization processes and information management practices. The pathway not only accounts for the procedures of work but also for the "variances" of the procedure and how it can be altered when new evidence – scientific, organizational or financial – is brought into the discussion. In other words, the pathway is supposed to be a dynamic and flexible mapping of the work – a script enabling many alternative applications. Rather than being formulated by "Taylorist managers in distant boardrooms" (Iedema, 2003: 182), it is the practitioners themselves formulating the clinical pathways.

The clinical pathway is here the principal model for making the knowledge-intensive work of the practising clinician transparent and open to inspection and debate. The clinical pathway is therefore a useful vehicle for joint learning and agreement regarding how clinical practice is to be conceived of and carried out, and also a method for making embodied and cognitive skills visible. Similar to the market logic, clinical pathways are a means for structuring and even, in some cases, de-mystifying the everyday practice of specific expert groups in organizations. For Iedema, this tendency to aim at capturing and making practices visible is not unproblematic because it presupposes compliance to such inspection from the co-worker. Robertson and Swan (2004) show that a UK-based consultancy firm, Dynamic Consulting, changed its organization structure and its management control systems from a flexible adhocracy structure and entrepreneurial governance in the mid-1980s to what Robertson and Swan call a "soft bureaucracy" and more tight forms of formal and professional control at the beginning of the new millennium to cope more effectively with changes in the market. For Robertson and Swan (2004: 143–144), it is the "marketization" – a term also used by Farrell and Morris (2003) in their study of the public sector – of knowledge-intensive work that plays a pivotal role in the emergence of soft bureaucracy in Dynamic Consulting. In his praise of the rise of the "creative economy" and its foremost bearer – its, to use Weber's term, "culture carrier" [*Träger*] (Schroeder, 1992: 22) – the member of the emerging "creative class", Florida (2002: 37) writes: "[m]ore workers than ever control the means of production because it is inside their heads; they *are* the means of production." Iedema's (2003) and Robertson and Swan's (2004) analyses suggest that such a view of knowledge-intensive work and expertise cannot be accepted offhand. On the contrary, various managerial practices (techniques, methodologies, tools) aiming at making such embodied and, in Florida's account, cerebral "means of production" transparent are being formulated, designed and implemented in organizations. Such managerial practice obeys, at least partially, a market logic presupposing that there are possibilities for agreeing on legitimate quanta (Power, 2004), measures capturing what Feldman (2004: 693) calls "objective knowledge" embedded in "aperspectival objectivity". The post-bureaucratic organization, therefore, is what is constituted as a legitimate organization arrangement not as what is more predictable than the corresponding market activities (like the bureaucratic organization), but in terms of its ability to orchestrate social agreements on transparent and reasonably "objective" procedures for operating. *Homo mercaris* becomes used to thinking of his or her work as, in every instant, subject to evaluation in terms of performativity. Speaking in those terms, the line between inside and outside an organization becomes permeable and fluid; a market logic pervades both spheres.

Summary and conclusions

In this chapter, the discourse on bureaucracy presented in Chapter 2 has been contrasted against the examination of a variety of post-bureaucratic organization forms. Prior to the analysis of specific organizational configurations, an epistemology of fluids has been examined as being an underlying conceptual and theoretical framework supporting the belief that the general movement from hierarchies to markets is the single most important generic principle for organization forms.

While the epistemologies of fluids and the different images of organizations discussed in this chapter do not constitute a seamless web but, rather, are only loosely connected and weakly integrated – feminist theories of fluidity are, for instance, only modestly influential in the management literature (see, for example, Styhre, 2006) – it is complicated to claim that theories of the post-bureaucratic organization present a unified and coherent critique of bureaucracy. The discourse on the post-bureaucratic organization is instead just as hetero-geneous as Foucault (1972) suggests in his seminal analysis of what he called "discursive formations". Rather than being unified and one-dimensional, the dis-course is fraught with internal disruptions, voids and opposing arguments, yet brings forth certain axial principles and ideas pointing in specific directions. When comparing the discourse on bureaucracy and that of the post-bureaucratic organization, one may then see a gradual shift in focus from the hierarchical forms of organization embedded in a rationalist and instrumental mode of think-ing to a market-based and horizontal form of organization. In agreement with Miettinen and Virkkunen, drawing on Rheinberger (1997), one may conceive of the post-bureaucratic organization as an "epistemic object", an object of analysis not yet fully stabilized: "[o]bjects are not things with fixed qualities but are open-ended projections oriented to something that does not yet exist, or to what we do not yet know for sure" (2005: 438; see also Lynch and Woolgar, 1988; Knorr Cetina, 1999). Researchers, then, not only examine existing entities but also actively *invent* epistemic objects; for instance, "a molecule, a production system, a disease or a social problem" (Miettinen and Virkkunen, 2005: 438). An epistemic object is a multiplicity or assemblage that comprises many qual-ities and is therefore complicated to capture in one single model; it is therefore contested and debated within epistemic cultures and thought collectives (Fleck, 1979). In our case, the post-bureaucratic organization is partially a conceptual model, partially an empirically observable fact, partially an ideological con-struct, and partially a great many other things: it is both actual and virtual. The facticity of the post-bureaucratic organization is therefore contested, but it still serves as an epistemic object connecting many different actors.

The next chapter, the first of the two studies of two major corporations, pro-vides support for the thesis that the gradual change from hierarchy to market, from bureaucracy to post-bureaucracy, is by no means unified and conclusive but is, instead, to be seen as a mixture of opposing tendencies and managerial activities. The bureaucratic organization, then, is not of necessity on its way out, but may emerge in a form that embodies the virtues and benefits of the bureau-cratic and post-bureaucratic organization forms.

4 The innovative bureaucracy, Part I

The entrepreneurial bureaucracy

Introduction

In the analysis of the literature on bureaucracy and various forms of post-bureaucratic organizations, it was argued that the conventional view of bureaucracy has gradually lost its status because it is incompatible with more recent and fluid images of society, the market and the world of business. However, as suggested by du Gay (2005), for instance, bureaucracy is not a once-and-for-all unified and enclosed organization form but, instead, appears in many forms and in many arrangements. Such a more fluid and permeable image of bureaucracy, which still remains affirmative of functional organization, is more representative of how bureaucracy emerges in real-life settings. In addition, such an image eliminates the dual separation between bureaucracy and non-bureaucracy and undermines the supplementary role of bureaucracy in management discourses. In this and the following chapter, a study of innovation work in two contemporary bureaucracies will be examined. Rather than assuming that bureaucracy is a poorly functioning organization form in terms of providing favourable conditions for innovation and creativity, it will be examined in terms of being an organizational arrangement actually supporting and reinforcing innovation while, at the same time, being able to respond to external changes. Thus, the research question is not whether bureaucracies *can* be sites for innovation or not, because in the two cases under consideration this is undoubtedly the case, but *under what conditions* innovations takes place in large, functionally organized organizations, hosting many different expert and specialist groups.

Are large firms bureaucracies?

The definition of bureaucracy adhered to in this book does not assume that it is a form of organization exclusively denoting public administration. Instead, bureaucracy refers to the principles formulated by Max Weber. As Shenhav (1999) points out, Weber did not distinguish between public administration and private firms. Here, we follow Bendix's (1956: xx) definition: " 'Bureaucracy' refers to the universal tendency of men [*sic*] who are employed in hierarchical organizations to obey directives and to identify their own interest and ideas with the organization and with all those persons in it who shares this identification." The two firms studied are both organized into functional departments with specific roles and employing certain expertise, are hierarchically structured with clear vertical chains of command and communication, and regard their employees as being specialists dealing with certain clearly defined and bounded activities and processes. Thus, when speaking of them as "bureaucracies" we do not mean they are demonstrating certain behaviours, operations or dysfunctions but that they are organized in accordance with certain *bureaucratic structures* and *principles*. The emphasis, then, is not primarily on *outcomes* but on the *morphology*, the form, of the organization. Speaking of structure, we follow Barley's (1986: 79) view of structure as being "[a]bstract, formal relations that constrain day-to-day action in social settings". Barley also points out that the notion of structure is by no means what is once and for all fixed in specific positions but what is under the influence of social actions. Barley writes:

> As Goffman (1983) was fond of observing, in everyday life actors are simultaneously the marks as well as the shills of social order. While it is difficult to see how social structure can arise except out of actions of people, people's actions are also surely shaped by forces beyond their control and outside of their immediate present. A full account of structural change therefore appears to require a synthetic view of structure as both a product and a constraint of human endeavor.
>
> (Barley, 1986: 79)

Human action, then, simultaneously reproduces social structures and draws on social structure. As a consequence, social structure is totally fixed but is gradually shifting when certain groups deviate from instituted behaviour. In terms of bureaucracy, the bureaucratic structure is that which is under the influence of the organization members' activities, yet those activities are rooted in the bureaucratic standard operating procedures and rules. In other words, bureaucracy is by no means once and for all put in place but, rather, is under the continuous influence of the joint agreement and actions of all employees in the organization; bureaucracy is *recursively reproduced*. Large firms and organizations in a variety of contexts are modelled on the Weberian bureaucracy model. Since private firms are competing under fierce market conditions, one may not even think of them as bureaucracies but as something else, for example, as just "large firms". The supplementary role of bureaucracy in the doxa of bureaucracy critique thus places bureaucracy in opposition to private firms. In this and the next chapter, this narrow and essentially misguided idea is challenged. Instead, the two large multinational firms are regarded as inextricably bound up with their hierarchical and functional organization. To put it another way, bureaucratic mechanisms and organizational principles are not opposing innovative activities and creative thinking but are, on the contrary, a *sine qua non* for being able to compete within two industries demonstrating hard competition and a great deal of complexity, namely the automotive and pharmaceutical industries.

Methodological considerations

The study lasted for two years but, prior to that, a number of different research projects had been conducted in the two firms. In Volvo Cars, research on product innovation and organization change management had been conducted over the period 1999 to 2005. In AstraZeneca, a series of studies of knowledge-management practices and creativity in new drug-development activities were undertaken over the same period. Needless to say, systematic research into domains such as new product development in the automotive industry and new drug development activities can only enable a partial and highly fragmented view of the complexity of the operations. In most cases, qualitative methodologies can enable some insights into the field of practices but such insights are nonetheless still only partial and can only account for a subset of the multiplicity of activities making up the entire work process. One of the good things about maintaining long-term relationships with specific companies, especially in a collaborative research setting (Adler *et al.*, 2004), is that one may build fruitful relationships with individuals in the collaborating firms, individuals that may be able to describe and explain in greater detail what is happening in organizations and provide insights into the "tricks of the trade" of the field. In this section, the methodology of the study is accounted for. Prior to issues of data collection and data analysis, the very notion of methodology is critically examined.

Habermas (1988) speaks of methodology as a form of cartography, a form of joint sense-making to clarify how to proceed:

> Regardless of whether methodology reflects on a research practice that is already in use, as in the case of physics, or whether, as in the case of sociology, its recommendations precede the research practice, methodology sets out a program to guide the advance of science. Thus it is not meaningless to discuss methodological requirements, even if they have not yet been fulfilled by research practice: they influence the way sciences articulate their self-understanding. In part, methodological viewpoints set standards for research, and in part they anticipate its general objectives. Taken together, these two functions establish the system of reference within which reality is systematically explored.
>
> (Habermas, 1988: 44)

For Habermas, methodology is not strictly a matter of data collection but, equally, addresses the epistemological and ideological facets of a scientific programme. Therefore, methodology can never be regarded solely as a matter of collecting and analysing data but must always include the addressing of the wider social implications for each scientific programme. The present study is located within a qualitative methodology tradition emphasizing what Max Weber (1949) calls *Verstehen*, understanding, at the expense of *Erklärung*, explanation (see also Dilthey, 1988). In the qualitative methodological orientation, there is less emphasis on causal relationships and the establishment of linear relations between entities or processes, but instead constructs such as meaning and understanding guide the research. For instance, Bakhtin emphasizes that human beings are speaking, self-reflective beings and must be examined as such:

> The human sciences are sciences about man and his specific nature, and not about a voiceless thing or natural phenomenon. Man in his specific human nature always expresses himself (speaks), that is, he creates a text (if only potential). When man is studied outside a text and independently of it, the science is no longer one of the human sciences (human anatomy, physiology, and so forth).
>
> (1986: 107)

Qualitative methodologies shed some light on the conditions wherein human beings collectively constitute meaning and understanding. In many cases, the use of qualitative methodology implies some kind of social constructivist framework wherein the human condition is essentially embedded in what is agreed upon in communities and groups of humans. But qualitative methodologies may also be based on other epistemological positions such as materialist thinking, for instance Marxist theory. In this view, human action and behaviour are, if not determined, at least strongly dependent upon the material conditions under which humans operate. For instance, the activities on the shop floor are strongly affected by the relationship between the employer and the employees and to what extent the employer demonstrates trust in the employee (see, for example, Fucini and Fucini, 1990; Graham, 1995). The notion of trust is here an operationalization of the material conditions producing subject positions such as the manager, the employee, the employer and so forth.

However, not all kinds of materialist thinking are of necessity Marxist or even oriented towards antagonist relationships. For instance, actor-network theory (Callon and Latour, 1981; Law, 1991; Czarniawska and Hernes, 2005) and the science and technology studies (STS) tradition (Bijker *et al.*, 1987; Bijker, 1995; Jasanoff *et al.*, 1995) are two examples of theoretical frameworks that emphasize the coalitions and networks constituted equally by humans and non-humans. Such networks of human and non-humans are prevalent in everyday life and in highly specialized laboratory settings. For instance, high-energy physics can no longer be fruitfully examined separately from the tools, computers and machinery mobilized in the research (Traweek, 1988; Knorr Cetina, 1995). Therefore, STS scholars use the notion of technoscience (see, for example, Lyotard, 1984; Latour, 1987) to capture the integrated frameworks of heterogeneous resources underpinning a variety of social processes. In this particular study, there is no clear allegiance declared to any specific and unified theoretical model, but instead some organizational processes are regarded as *predominantly* socially constructed while others are *predominantly* materially embedded. In other words, at times, say, a laboratory technician may speak of standard operation procedures in laboratory work as being imposed as a regulatory practice from the monitoring authorities and thus adheres to a constructivist view, while in other cases the same person may speak of his or her work as being inextricably entangled with the mastering of a series of laboratory practices including tools and machinery, thereby safeguarding the laboratory setting from constructivist influences. Since social work is always already an assemblage of social, cultural, embodied, technological and symbolic resources, there is little use in separating different entities and processes into compartmentalized domains (Schatzki, 2002). Both social and organizational life are based on heterogeneity and need to be examined as such.

Data collection

The principal data-collection methodology in this study was semi-structured interviews with relevant actors within the two organizations. Even though interviews remain one of the most widely used qualitative methodologies in the social sciences, they is largely based on the individual interviewer's skills and the interlocutor's will to contribute to the conversation. Such skills and agreements determine the outcome and, therefore, practical advice and systematic methods can only be of limited importance. In addition, the epistemological status of the interview is always a contested terrain. For some writers, the interview is little more than a structured reflection on how the interviewee perceives everyday work-life. For others, an interview is a form of symbolic violence (Bourdieu and Passeron, 1977) on the part of the interviewer, a way to project various beliefs and assumptions onto the interviewee. The Czech author, Milan Kundera, is notorious for his dislike of interviews:

> [T]he interview as it is generally practiced has nothing to do with dialogue: (1) the interviewer asks questions of interest to him, of no interest to you; (2) of your responses, he uses only those that suit him; (3) he translates them into his own vocabulary, his own manners of thought.
>
> (1988: 133)

Briggs (2003) is highly critical of how the interview is used in popular culture where it serves to instil legitimacy through mimicking scientific rigor and objectivity:

> Interviewing is . . . a "technology" that invents both notions of individual subjectivities and collective social and political patterns and then obscures the operation of this process beneath notions of objectivity and science – or, in the case of journalistic and television interviews, of insight and art.
>
> (Briggs, 2003: 245)

Such qualities are little more than chimeras for Briggs who disapproves of the tendency to reduce any answer to questions to clear-cut findings and opinions. Instead, Briggs argues, drawing on the work of Mikhail Bakhtin, that "responses are like crossroads at which multiple paths converge, with signs pointing in all directions" (Briggs, 2003: 248). Bakhtin (1986: 92) speaks of utterances as being "filled with dialogical overtones", that is, utterances reflecting other previous utterances:

> Utterances are not indifferent to one another, and are not self-sufficient; they are aware of and mutually reflect one another. These mutual reflections determine their character. Each utterance is filled with echoes and reverberations of other utterances to which it is related by the communality of the sphere of speech communication. Every utterance must be regarded primarily as a *response* to preceding utterances of the given sphere (we understand the word "response" here in the broadest sense). Each utterance refutes, affirms, supplements, and relies on the other, presupposes them to be known, and somehow takes them into account. After all, as regards a given question, in a given matter, and so forth, the utterance occupies a particular *definite* position in a given sphere of communication.
>
> (1986: 91)

Bakhtin continues:

> The topic of the speaker's speech, regardless of what this topic may be, does not become the object of speech for the first time in any given utterance; a given speaker is not the first to speak about it. The object, as it were, has already been articulated, disputed, elucidated, and evaluated in various ways. Various viewpoints, worldviews, and trends cross, converge, and diverge in it. The speaker is not the biblical Adam, dealing only with virgin and still unnamed objects, giving them names for the first time.
>
> (1986: 93)

No utterances, then, in the strictest sense are original; they merely reflect what is said – they reside in intertextuality. However, in what Denzin (2003) calls the "interview society", the interview is often abused in terms of being regarded as, unproblematically and with low costs, being able to gain insight into all sorts of problems and conditions. As a qualitatively oriented management researcher, one needs to recognize that speaking to people and observing people are the two major opportunities for gaining insights about certain practices. In a recent publication addressing the status of the interview, Gubrium and Holstein argue that today there is a need to be more sceptical about the role of the interview and what sorts of understanding it enables: "Interview roles are less clear than they once were. ... Standardized representation has given way to representational invention, where the dividing line between fact and fiction is blurred to encourage richer understanding" (2003: 3). MacIntyre shares this view of story-telling, believing that the construction of plots is what undermines the idea of truth: "There are not and there cannot be any true stories. Human life is composed of discrete actions which lead nowhere, which have no order; the story-teller imposes in human events retrospectively an order which they did not have while they were lived" (1981: 214).

Writing on the basis of interviews thus disturbs the positivist line of demarcation between fact and fiction (White, 1987). As a consequence, one need use concepts such as "certainty", "truth" and "objectivity" more carefully: "The possibility of certainty must be regarded skeptically, if not rejected outright," Gubrium and Holstein (2003: 4) argue. Notwithstanding such remarks, Gubrium and Holstein present an affirmative view of the interview. They want us to be aware of the frail epistemological grounds of the interview and to address all sorts of concerns regarding the qualities of an interview in public rather than sweeping the issue of epistemology under the carpet. In another paper in Gubrium and Holsten's edited volume (2003), Atkinson and Coffrey argue that "[w]e cannot take the interview as a proxy for action" (2003: 117). Again the interview is envisaged as a situation in which the interviewee is constructing an image of the self: "[I]nterviews are occasions in which are enacted particular kinds of narratives and in which 'informants' construct themselves and others as particular forms of moral agents" (Atkinson and Coffrey, 2003: 116). Atkinson and Coffrey suggest that there is a need to be aware that the interviewee may use an interview for strategic purposes. Moreover, the interview is an event wherein collective beliefs and enactments are articulated: "[I]nterviews become equally valid ways of capturing shared cultural understandings and enactments of the social world" (Atkinson and Coffrey, 2003: 119). In summary, the interview is never capable of enabling full understanding of an individual's view of the world but can nevertheless provide small glimpses and insights into the particular social fabric the individual is part of. The epistemological fragility of the interview per se implies that certain formulations become problematic, for instance the assurance that certain conditions exist and that some events unfolded in a particular manner. In all kind of narrative communication, the issue of truth and falsity can never be finally resolved but, instead, more or less credible and interesting accounts can be provided.

In terms of practical activities the study comprised two series of interviews. The first series, conducted in January and February 2005 included twenty-eight persons, twelve representing Volvo Cars and sixteen representing AstraZeneca. The second series, conducted over the period June–August 2005, included twenty interviews at AstraZeneca. The interviewees included managers and co-workers in the R&D organization, in design departments, in marketing and in support functions such as information technology systems support. All the interviewees had significant organizational tenure or a long-term engagement within the industry and related institutions such as the university system. All interviews were structured in accordance with an interview guide and were tape-recorded. The interviewers transcribed important passages in the interviews. The interview duration time was about one hour and fifteen minutes. The three participating researchers coded the interviews individually. Codes were derived from both the interviewees' own vocabulary (emic categories) but also from the conceptual framework developed in the bureaucracy literature (etic categories). In addition to the interviews, tentative findings were presented to the interviewees at a seminar and the interviewees were asked to reflect and comment upon the analysis. This iterative research design enabled new opportunities for joint reflection on the work conditions in large organizations.

I. Volvo Cars: the entrepreneurial bureaucracy

The automotive industry

The automotive industry is commonly characterized as being a mature industry with limited growth potentials (at least in the Western world), high overcapacity, commoditized product offerings, and with a fierce competition with high price pressures on the market and internal pressures for increased efficiency (Rådberg Kohn, 2005; Wickelgren, 2005). As a consequence, the reliance on scale economy in the operations is significant: it is claimed that about 30 per cent of sales volume is related to fixed costs, and therefore a 3 per cent loss in sales volume has been calculated to reduce operating profits by 24 per cent. Today, a number of major automotive companies make the lion's share of the profit from their financial services rather than from the manufacturing of cars. Furthermore, the high sensitivity for prices and sales volumes and the emphasis on shorter new product development cycles have led to significant consolidation of the industry to achieve the demanded economies of scale. For instance, in 1964 there were fifty-two independent automobile producers, while in 2004 only twelve remained (Rådberg Kohn, 2005). Some examples of mergers and acquisitions include the merger of Mercedes-Benz and Chrysler, General Motors' acquisition of SAAB, the Ford Motor Company's acquisition of Jaguar, Volvo Cars and, most recently, Land Rover, and the alliance between Renault and Nissan. Among the major automotive companies, Toyota stands out as the single most profitable and high-performing corporation. Liker offers some insight into Toyota's impressive track record:

- "Toyota's annual profit at the end of the fiscal year in March 2003, was $8.13 billion – larger than the combined earnings of GM, Chrysler, and Ford, and the biggest annual profit for any automaker in at least the decade. Its net profit margin is 8.3 times higher than the industry average" (2004: 4).
- "While stock prices of the Big 3 were falling in 2003, Toyota's shares had increased 24% over 2002" (2004: 4).
- "Toyota has the fastest product development process in the world. New cars and trucks take 12 months or less to design, while competitors typically require two to three years" (2004: 5).
- "Much of Toyota's success comes from its astonishing quality reputation. ... In 2003, Toyota recalled 79% fewer vehicles in the U.S. than Ford and 92% fewer than Chrysler" (2004: 5) .

Not only does Toyota offer a portfolio of profitable small and medium-sized cars, they have also managed to enter the premium brand segment with their

Lexus – at least in the USA, but to a lesser extent in Europe – which "[i]n 2002 outsold BMW, Cadillac, and Mercedes-Benz in the U.S. for the third year in a row" (Liker, 2004: 4). In addition, Toyota's Prius hybrid model has aroused substantial interest in terms of being the first mass-produced hybrid car.

In general, the premium segment has been more profitable than the middle and the discount segments. While the middle segment has been comparatively large and automotive companies such as Opel or Ford (in Europe) have been capable of making profits, today the situation is changing as the premium and discount segments grow, leaving the middle segment companies in a precarious market position (see Figure 4.1). Speaking in the terms used by Micheal E. Porter (1985), the middle segment companies are increasingly being "stuck in the middle", offering too little additional value to the customer to justify their higher prices, yet being incapable of moving up to the premium segment where customers have far higher expectations of the product.

In addition to the pressure on automotive companies to lower new product development cycles and the challenge to make new products stay as long as possible in the market before new products are introduced, the Western, Japanese and Korean automotive companies anticipate increased competition from Chinese and Indian producers, capable of exploiting lower production costs and highly skilled, yet less costly, engineering competencies. Even though the automotive industry may be portrayed as mature, this does not mean that the industry is saturated or not under pressure to change. On the contrary, the last fifteen years have witnessed a revolution for many automotive companies. For the time being, the "Big Three" major American corporations, General Motors, Ford Motor Company and Chrysler, are facing fierce competition in their own home market from Japanese competitors such as Toyota, Honda and Subaru, all

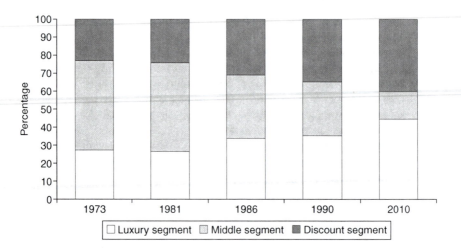

Figure 4.1 Market segment trends for consumer goods in Germany (adapted from Rådberg Kohn, 2005: 8).

having their own manufacturing plants, their "transplants", in USA (Fucini and Fucini, 1990; Florida and Kenney, 1992; Schroeder *et al.*, 1992; Cuther-Gershenfeld, *et al.*, 1994; Ebrahimpour and Cullen, 1994; Wilms *et al.*, 1994; Graham, 1995). Taken together, the automotive industry is an industry characterized by great complexities and continuous change.

The Volvo Car Corporation

The Volvo Car Corporation is an automotive company started in 1927 with its Head Office in Gothenburg, Sweden. In 1978, Volvo Cars formed a separate company within the Volvo Group, a conglomerate including Volvo Bus, Volvo Trucks and Volvo Penta. The company has been owned by the Ford Motor Company since 1999, employing about 28,000 people. Volvo has moved from the middle segment and has entrenched a position in the Premium Brand market segment of the automotive industry (Wickelgren, 2005). Volvo produces about 450,000 cars annually and approximately one-quarter of the production is sold in the USA. Volvo is generally renowned for pioneering safety in automobiles and has been the leader in this field since the 1950s. Volvo has developed several safety innovations that are now available in all car models, for instance the three-point safety belt. The emphasis on safety has positioned Volvo – at least according to some of the Volvo co-workers – as a not very adventurous brand, a brand of preference for families and persons concerned with safety. Over the last few years, Volvo has worked hard to get rid of this somewhat bland image and has, for instance, sponsored the Volvo Ocean Race sailing competition (formerly known as the Whitbread Race) to associate the brand with more daring endeavours. Besides the features of the product, Volvo became internationally recognized when they developed assembly-line production in the Kalmar and Uddevalla plants in the 1970s and 1980s, challenging the Japanese mass-production system (Cusumano, 1985; Berggren, 1990, 1994; Kenney and Florida, 1993). Over the years, Volvo has developed a strong engineering culture (see Kunda, 1992; Pelto-nen, 1999; Wallace, 1999) wherein employees are expected to play a central role in the company's performance (Jacob and Ebrahimpur, 2001). In common with many manufacturing companies, the culture can also be claimed to be *masculine* in terms of giving priorities to technical features, favouring quick decisions and actions over talk, and idolizing strong leaders and managers standing up for their projects, functions or areas of responsibility. One of the consequences of this masculine culture is that women do not always play a central role in development projects. For instance, Bragd (2002: 158), who studied the development of the successful XC90 SUV car model, reports: "[V]ery little can be reported about the women's influence in the process. In fact, they were quite invisible."

Why Volvo is an innovative company

Developing a new car model is a very complex matter, including a variety of resources and competencies. In the automotive industry it is customary to distinguish between *concept phases* where new ideas and concepts are conceived of and elaborated upon, and the actual *new product development process* wherein the new car model is being developed. In today's industry, different companies very often collaborate on one single platform, that is, a unifying framework specifying some of the characteristics of the model, but also some of the joint components and other technical features. Even though the automotive industry has been revolutionized in terms of reducing cost and compressing time to develop new car models – a process that have been championed by Japanese companies such as Toyota and Honda (Mair, 1999; Liker, 2004) – a new car project is still a very large undertaking in terms of budget and the amount of people involved. Since automotive companies remain functionally organized, project leaders often invest a significant amount of time and effort to coordinate activities between departments and specialist groups. In the new landscape where firms increasingly collaborate across firm boundaries, the demands on coordination and joint decision-making increase, rather than being reduced in importance. Jönsson (2004: 85) reports that a FIAT product-development manager claimed that about 7 per cent of the total budget went to travel costs. In alliances, joint ventures and other collaborative arrangements, it may be that this cost is substantially higher.

In practical terms, a new car product proceeds along a tight time-planning schedule and has to pass a number of go/no-go gates. Time, quality and cost are the three parameters determining the process and, at Volvo especially, the cost factor has been emphasized after Ford's acquisition. Being a skilful and successful project leader is one of the principal criteria for building credibility in the industry. Heavyweight project leaders gain respect and prestige through being able to lead and monitor complex projects. In Volvo Cars, the period from the end of the late 1980s to the beginning of the new millennium has included a strategic re-positioning – from being firmly located in the middle segment, represented by brands such as Opel, Toyota and Renault, to the premium segment, including competitors such as Mercedes, BMW, SAAB, Audi and Lexus. It is generally believed in the industry that it is more complicated to make money in the middle segment and that this is the principal domain for increased competition from Japanese and Korean competitors. In contrast to the middle segment, the premium segment offers opportunities for more technical features and better qualities of the cars. However, being able to compete with brands such as Mercedes and BMW demands that the cars are excellent in terms of technical features, design and quality. In the period of 2005–2006, Volvo regarded themselves as being part of the premium segment, albeit at its lower strata, being more of a competitor for Volkswagen than for Audi, BMW, Mercedes and Lexus. This shift in strategy and gradual movement from being, at least in Sweden, an "everyman's car" to a more exclusive position was achieved through the launching of a series of new car models to reposition Volvo as a premium brand. The *pièce de résistance* was perhaps the much-praised SUV car model, Volvo XC90, which became Volvo's smash hit after its launch in 2002. In addition to the renewal of the portfolio of car models, essentially modelled on BMW's strategy to operate in three different segments (represented by the

3 series, the 5 series and the 7 series) in the premium market, Volvo aimed at developing a new design idiom while maintaining its strong reputation as the leading automotive company in terms of safety.

Safety was, from the outset, one of the key prioritized areas for Volvo. The founders of Volvo, Assar Gabrielsson and Gustaf Larsson, were committed to the idea of producing cars that would suit the demands of the customers in Scandinavia and thought of safety issues as being of major importance. The second CEO, Assar Gabrielsson's successor, Gunnar Engelau (1956–1971) continued this tradition and established Volvo as the leading company in terms of safety. A great number of safety features derived from Volvo under Engelau's direction and still, today, Volvo takes great pride in its contribution to the domain of safety. Volvo is the Centre of Excellence in safety in the Ford conglomerate. However, this strong emphasis on safety may be appreciated by the customers when actually being involved in accidents and other unfortunate events, but it also gave Volvo the reputation of being the car of choice for the less adventurous and the family car buyer. Volvo thus had to deal with the somewhat dull image of the brand particularly in comparison to, for instance, Mercedes and BMW, the two foremost representatives of the premium segment; these two competitors sell cars on the basis of factors such as quality and elegant design (Mercedes) or engine specifications and extraordinary driving qualities (BMW). The Volvo executives believed the image and the design of the car had to change. Volvo had to "inscribe values" into their cars that customers, existing and potential, appreciated and desired (see, for example, Gartman, 2004). Since the late 1980s, Volvo has worked hard to get rid of the image of being a dull and "boxy" middle segment car and has aimed at moving up the hierarchy of brands. The change to a more contemporary design idiom in particular has been highlighted as a major quality of the new Volvo portfolio of car models. Figure 4.2 shows that Volvo Cars has compressed the new product development time and extended their product portfolio.

So what makes Volvo an innovative company? First, Volvo has, over the years, developed a flat and informal organization form fuelled by an entrepreneurial culture wherein the co-workers are expected and encouraged to take initiatives in order to contribute to the company. Volvo is still the leading company in terms of safety – generally separated into active safety (prevention of accidents) and passive safety (safety when accidents occur) – even though Volvo co-workers often claim that investments in safety today have diminishing returns vis-à-vis other features such as design and advanced information technology. Similarly to quality, safety is becoming part of the qualifying, rather than an order-winning, criteria in the automotive industry (Beckman, 2004). Over the last ten years, Volvo has developed and launched a number of car models that have been equally well-received among motor journalists and customers. While other companies in the middle segments (e.g. Opel, Ford, FIAT) demonstrate less-positive trajectories and suffer harder from the increased competition from Japanese and Korean competitors, Volvo can demonstrate a movement upwards in the market segments. A similar movement can be seen, for instance, in the

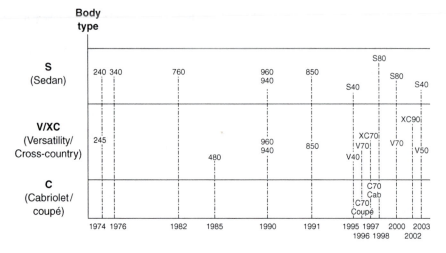

Figure 4.2 Illustration of Volvo Cars' new product launches, 1974–2003 (source: Volvo
Cars, Public Affairs, adapted from Rådberg Kohn, 2005: 9).

Audi brand. German competitors, however, do have a larger home market (about
eighty million people), while Sweden, with a population of nine million, has two
automotive companies, SAAB and Volvo. Consequently, Volvo exports the bulk
of its production. The strategic re-positioning, from being in the middle price
segment to moving to the lower strata of the premium segment, is very much an
accomplishment embedded in the Volvo co-workers' ability to contribute to the
firm.

All the car models that today (in 2005) make Volvo a highly profitable
company, accounting for a substantial part of the Ford Motor Company Group's
total profit, were developed prior to Ford's acquisition in 1999. Even though one
must not underrate external factors such as macroeconomic events and economic
policies, it is reasonable to argue that the lion's share of the accomplishments
can be found in the management of the resources internal to the firm. This
resource-based view of the firm (see, for example, Barney, 1991, 2001) suggests
that it is the ability of firms to develop, exploit and share resources and assets
that is the primary explanatory factor when understanding sustainable competitive advantage. In comparison to, for instance, SAAB, the other Swedish automotive company, today owned by General Motors and in a less-favourable
position because of its failure to make profits for the last fifteen years (with very
few exceptions), Volvo has been successful in slowly and gradually changing its
strategy and portfolio of products. Volvo co-workers thought of SAAB as being
a particularly sad case of mismanagement because SAAB was always the more
technically adventurous and experimentally oriented company of the two, but
also feared the consequences for the Swedish automotive industry if SAAB
would fail to live through the crisis the company experienced at the beginning of
the new millennium. For instance, the access to suppliers and qualified co-

workers and technical expertise is dependent on a reasonably large automotive sector. Altogether, one may argue that Volvo is an innovative and creative company in terms of being able to orchestrate and manage complex new product-development processes in an industry characterized by shortening cycle time, increased competition and the entrants of new competitors.

Staying innovative in mature markets

In this section, we will address the importance of creativity for the competitiveness of the company, the influence of new managerial practices, and the effects of managerial control and procedures.

The role of innovation and creativity

At Volvo Cars, all of the interviewees argued that the firm's capacity for innovation and creative thinking was of great importance. Since the end of the 1980s, Volvo has re-positioned itself as a premium brand alongside Audi, BMW and Mercedes. Although the Volvo workers were aware that Volvo belonged to the lower strata of this segment and, in fact, were competing with Volkswagen rather than with, say, BMW, the new position of the brand implied that the company was no longer competing on the basis of price but on technical features and design. This strategic position in the market further accentuated the need for being innovative and creative. Brands such as Toyota, Skoda and Renault were focusing on a mass market where it was generally believed that it was difficult to make any money because of the price competition and the entrance of new competitors, primarily from producers in Asia, such as the Korean automotive companies. In addition, the interlocutors thought of Volvo as being creative over time, especially in the field of safety, both active and passive, where the company had a strong reputation and was regarded as the industry leader. Since innovation and creativity are tricky concepts in terms of operationalization into, for instance, specific activities and actions – that is, innovations do not emerge as discrete and predictable events and occurrences but are, instead, distributed between a great amount of actors, processes, decisions and so forth – the interviewees did not conceive of their work as being innovative and creative all the time. Instead, innovative and creative ideas emerge every now and then and, in many cases, such ideas are never brought forward into the decision-making process. However, no matter how vague the notion of innovativeness and creativity are, they were still of central importance for the long-term and medium-term competitiveness of the company. One of the technical project leaders was asked if it was important for the company to be creative, and answered:

> Yes, that is a key success factor. ... It's all about being able to offer something good, something special, something better to the customer than others are capable of offering. We can never compete on price and then we need to develop a good climate for innovation. ... At the same time, we need this

"product innovation factory" to safeguard quality and to have this critical mass to be able to quickly develop new models.

(Project manager)

By "production innovation factory", the project manager means a standardized and well-functioning procedure to develop new car models. To date, new product-development activities at Volvo Cars have been, the interviewees argued, not exactly standardized, but the individual project leaders have maintained their jurisdiction. The project manager saw the benefits with a more structured process but was concerned that the new ways of working would negatively affect creativity:

> You move from a somewhat chaotic new product development process to a situation where you have a "new product development factory": "This day, the specifications arrive and then I need to do this and that and I have four weeks available, and that day I need to deliver it" ... There is less and less space for doing anything that is outside of the original specifications. You close the case much, much earlier to be able to safeguard the quality and then you shrink the space for all the creative solutions. There are both pros and cons with this tendency. ... The risk is that we standardize all product and kill all the good initiatives.
>
> (Project manager)

Many of the interviewees welcomed Ford's more standardized model as that which may make Volvo's new product-development process less susceptible to individual decisions and ambitions. Yet, several interviewees pointed to the need to provide "spaces of exploration" within an otherwise streamlined processes. The project manager continued:

> If you examine a couple of our real hits, then you notice they have been turned down a number of times in the process. But then people continued to work on them because they thought they were of great importance. One of these things ... won the Ford Technical Award, the highest prize you can get [in the company]. ... This group did not give in. ... Each and everyone have been very good at developing their gadgets cheaper, more efficiently, but also more streamlined. There is a risk that we lose our competitive edge and lose our source of attraction.
>
> (Project manager)

This "double nature" of the innovation-management activities, that of simultaneously standardizing and streamlining the NPD process *and* enabling for experimental thinking, was brought into the discussion by several interviewees. One of the technical experts specializing in fuels advocated the presence of areas wherein not everything was controlled in details: "I am absolutely convinced that in order to generate new ideas, then you need these islands within the company where you do not control everything in detail" (Technical expert). One of the engineers argued that creativity and innovation were of central importance but that processes enabling for innovation are complicated to manage. Therefore, innovation and creativity are what are produced in the actual work situation – "in the battlefield":

> I think that the really good things, they are conceived of in the battle field. … There needs to be time for building these prototypes, to make these investigations where you conceive of these new ideas. You cannot be so lean that everyone is busy delivering exactly what is asked for and nothing more.
>
> (Engineer)

However, innovation and creativity in the automotive industry are, she continued, not trivial matters because of the complexity of the product. Virtually all new ideas have immediate consequences for a number of other groups' work and therefore creative thinking is, from the outset, already restrained by practical matters:

> Developing a new car implies such a long chain of activities. It is not very easy to bring a good idea, because this good idea actually affects a multiplicity of things during a long period of time and implies an expensive process. It is not that simple.
>
> (Engineer)

She continued: "It's hard bringing new ideas. … It probably depends on the high investments and the cost of making a new car. … Such is the nature of the industry." One of the designers addressed the immense complexity of the car as what delimits creativity: "Before, you could do your thing and then that's it. … I did not ask nobody but today I need to discuss with our project leader about everything. Every single change affects a lot of things today" (Designer).

Under the new regime of Ford, new limitations for innovative thinking were also introduced. For instance, one of the principal ideas that came with Ford's ownership was that several models should be developed on the same platforms. In such "family of car models", the same components should be used, thereby reducing the costs of procurement and making the logistics and access to components less costly. One of the designers thought of this orientation as having implications for his work:

> There is this scenario that makes creativity go down: the ambition to find synergies between the Ford companies that they have bought to use "carry over" [The use of the same components in different car models and brands]. If you have a cycle plan where you organize the car manufacturing around this principle, then you need to engage much earlier in the process and to be able to tell what implications this has for the design. I believe that will

become a problem; it will reduce our creativity because we have already been locked up in "hard points" [specifications not possible to negotiate] . . . we are too focused on the synergies and that we should produce joint components in all these companies. There is always someone that has to pay.

(Designer)

In summary, innovation and creativity were treated as capacities of central and pivotal strategic importance for Volvo; without the ability to develop new technical features, clients would have few reasons for buying the car, the interviewees argued, and therefore Volvo had to be capable of managing innovative work. The interviewees did point to a number of conditions, changes and tendencies that, in different ways, contributed to a situation where innovation and creativity becomes more problematic and complicated. First, they highlighted the differences between a Scandinavian management culture, emphasizing consensus, joint decision-making, informal relations and mutual trust between managers and co-workers, and an Anglo-American management culture. Second, increased administrative and management control procedures implemented in the organization were a source of annoyance and regarded as time-consuming procedures pushing innovation and creativity from the agenda. However, several of the interviewees pointed to an increased standardization of the operations as one of the potential solutions to the continual loss of time dedicated to innovation.

New managerial values and practices

Volvo Cars were subject to an acquisition in 1999 when Ford Motor Company, one of the "big three" American automotive companies, bought the Volvo Car Corporation from the Volvo Group. The rationale for the Volvo Group, the former owner of Volvo Cars, to sell its automotive company was that, in an industry increasingly emphasizing economies of scale and shared R&D and new product development costs, a minor player like Volvo, producing about 450,000 cars annually, needs to collaborate with some major corporation. Ford, who already owned a series of companies and brands such as Jaguar, Land Rover, Mazda and Aston Martin, thought Volvo would fit into the portfolio. However, the differences between American management style and culture at Ford and their Scandinavian counterpart caused some concerns for the co-workers at Volvo. For instance, while Volvo encouraged an entrepreneurial attitude towards work, Ford were regarded as a centralized company. Jönsson (2004), in discussing a study of the new car-development process at Volvo, emphasizes the idiosyncratic Scandinavian leadership style, often misunderstood by newcomers as being permissive. Jönsson writes:

The Swedes have this urge to achieve consensus which makes them unclear in their decision-making. This is often misunderstood since the urge is really to reach agreement about what the problem is. Such agreement will automatically coordinate action, it is (implicitly) assumed, and on the basis of this, decision-making is widely delegated. Since people are assumed to behave responsibly, they will contact their boss if there is a problem. The Swedish managers, consequently, have an open-door policy. This is seen, by their Dutch and Japanese colleagues alike, as passive leadership. Managers should be out there looking for problems to solve, monitoring and following up. The Swedish trust their subordinates to be responsible people who want to contribute. Management is the art of persuading them to want to contribute. This is done by reasoning and agreeing about what the problem is (long meetings without proper decisions).

(Jönsson, 2004: 119–120)

This Scandinavian leadership tradition, resting on the mutual trust between manager and co-workers, was praised by most of the Volvo interlocutors. For instance, one of Volvo's technical specialists sketched a scenario wherein workers are no longer expected to be entrepreneurial and take action but merely to engage in predefined work assignments:

I believe we eventually will become a real American company where people await instructions and do as they are told. . . . In one of our gas projects, I had to figure out how to handle the cars when they got to the repair shop. Can you start to weld right away, or do you need to empty the fuel tank or should you add hydrogen gas, or how do you do it? I started to look for Ford's instructions [on the intranet]. On every single question . . . it stated: 'Ask your supervisor'. In that case, it all became very conspicuous.

(Technical specialist)

One of the designers addressed a similar theme:

We Swedes are used to taking responsibility and be given responsibility, that is why we have a flat organization structure. In the U.S. you never do more than the boss tells you to do. If you do that, you're fired, even if you do the right thing. You *never* by-pass a boss. You ask your boss who in turn asks his or her boss. You mustn't forget anyone. We do not have such a society. Here, any employee can, more or less, walk up to the CEO and complain about me or anyone else. It is a possibility, but not in the U.S. . . . It's a good thing because it makes all people committed.

(Designer)

For the Swedish co-workers, this emphasis on adherence to rules and strict job descriptions was thought of as a degradation to a mere rule-following. In addition, it was thought of as being an indication of the disappearance of the egalitarian culture praised by the Swedish co-workers. One of the managers at Volvo said of the new situation after Ford's acquisition: "You notice that each and everyone are not equal – which we tend to believe in Swedish company culture. You notice as soon as some top guy from Ford comes in and demands 'do it like this'" (Manager). A designer at Volvo provided an example of the cultural differences between Sweden and the USA:

> American culture and our culture – that's a bit of a culture shock! They want to control from the top what we do, and they think that if you can control something – that's perfect! We never think in those terms at Volvo. I mean, if I am going to Düsseldorf or Frankfurt or America, then I won't fly Business Class for fun: I always try to get an economy class ticket. ... But it seems like ... if you give an employee free hands [in the USA], well then *he will* fly first class. This demonstration of suspicion that you notice is not in line with our culture.
>
> (Designer)

Another manager thought of Ford's rules of conduct, the formal policy regarding a series of activities, as being an indication of this kind of suspicion:

> There are rules that are outright absurd. ... They formulate the rules in a manner ... that makes it impossible to follow them. Here, we are used to having *a bit* of rules, and those rules are formulated so that we may actually follow them. But the Ford rules [are like]: "We forbid it all."
>
> (Section manager)

Another perceived difference between Scandinavian and Anglo-American culture is the strong emphasis on financial performance, especially in the USA. Several interviewees at Volvo Cars argued that what they thought of as a one-sided focus on finance had detrimental effects on innovation and creativity. One of the Project managers at Volvo Cars stated:

> When you develop a new product, you balance qualities and money. Ford is wholly managed by the money – you get some money and then you get a certain degree of quality, period! Money talks. At Volvo, it used to be that we wanted to reach a certain level at an approximate cost. ... The money did not always weigh that much in the scale. The money is much more important [in Ford]; to keep the budget, to keep the price of the component, to keep the price of the tooling, and so forth. ... It's a very clear change there.
>
> (Project manager)

Another Volvo co-worker pointed at the need to follow the budget as one of the principal virtues in the American regime:

> We Swedes, we reach for the stars and then we make it halfway. For the Americans, if you reach for the stars, then you need to go all the way. You cannot say afterwards that "well, well, we gave it a shot". You cannot do that. That is a difference of culture.
>
> (Designer)

Perhaps the most recurrent theme causing anxieties in the interviews was the perceived difference between Anglo-American individualism and Scandinavian collectivism. Among the Volvo co-workers, collectivism was praised as a significant source of competitive advantage, manifested in the ability to work in cross-functional teams, to make joint decisions and some other activities, and individualism was more or less treated as a managerialist fad, supported by a variety of reward and incentive systems implemented by Ford. Those reward systems were also regarded as some kind of Trojan horse, brought into the firms notwithstanding the local conditions and traditions. One of the Section managers at Volvo argued:

> It's an enormous difference, especially when we work with our friends in England. The attitude is completely different; this fact that your personal goals are something that determines your behaviour when you're dealing with a problem or an issue. Very few here think in such terms and above all no one would frankly *say that is the case*, because that is not something you admit.
>
> (Section manager)

The section manager did not approve of this movement towards a more individualistic perception of work because it was regarded as something preventing collective innovation work.

Even though there were several concerns on the part of the Swedish co-workers regarding the Anglo-American culture, there were also numerous interviewees pointing at the positive outcomes from the encounter between "the two cultures". One of the managers remembered that it was actually not that easy for many Volvo co-workers to see the benefits from having a new owner: "It's been hard for some people to see that there are a number of advantages with the Ford corporation and that there are opportunities for win–win situations. They are not the world's third largest automotive company for no reason" (Manager). She continued:

> Both systems have their pros and cons. We are really bad on communicating clearly, on decision-making, and this eternal strife for a consensus makes the system inert. Foreign colleagues coming here to work just blow their top because of that. Those are our weaknesses.

One of the senior managers argued that it was his role to communicate that Ford and Volvo were, in fact, part of the same corporation:

> Ford is blamed for everything that is wrong. They [Volvo co-workers] say that Ford managers are nothing but PowerPoint presentations and a lot of talk and little action. People say that they demand a lot and that they change jobs all the time. Unless you change job in Detroit every 18th to 24th month you're a loser. People don't see that the Americans are under just as much

pressure as we are. A key to my job is to communicate what I understand of Detroit to our employees.

(Senior manager)

One of the designers also pointed at the ability of the Ford managers to appreciate and demonstrate an understanding of what they were expected to perceive as an alien culture:

> That is always on the agenda when we do a presentation and we discuss what we need to change. They say: "You mustn't lose you identity, what is Volvo specific, because you need to be able to develop your brand, and you cannot do that if you become Ford." I don't think it is a deliberate strategy that "let's turn them into Ford – 'Fordify' them", but it is more about this colossus having all these [management] *systems*: MPR systems and leader goals and bureaucratic systems for control of travel expenses and costs. This issue of how these systems affect the Volvo culture is never discussed, I suppose, but they just roll out the same administrative procedures as elsewhere ... if we are to become a unified company, then it is quite natural that we try to develop the same structure, and then it is a side-effect that the structure influences the culture.

(Designer)

He continued:

> I believe there is still a "Volvo spirit" ... you don't break it that easily. If you continue to pump in Americans, of course it will change ... if Ford wants to take over and make this an American world, then they need so many Americans that we [Swedish co-workers] become a minority ... the American culture is just here during work time. When you leave, then you enter the Swedish society, which is based on the belief in caring for one another. The Volvo spirit is a bit like that: We take care of one another; we are concerned and proud about our product.

(Designer)

In summary, the merger and the acquisition were not without pains, with an alien culture started to influence what was previously a rather homogeneous and clearly confined cultural universe. One of the strategies to cope with all the worries, anxieties and concerns was to formulate critical or affirmative views of the new cultural changes. Even though the interviewees approved of the American and British culture per se – the interviewees did not demonstrate a provincial attitude towards new influences as such – they were concerned that the new practices and activities derived from new managerial regimes would have detrimental effects on the company culture.

New forms of management control and administrative procedures

The co-workers portrayed their Volvo as an informal workplace, rooted in a mechanical engineering culture and a concern for the well-being of the customers, yet being capable of responding to external changes and of being a professional and highly competitive company navigating in an industry characterized by intense competition. In addition to rather harsh market conditions, the American owners imposed certain modes of thinking regarded as alien to the Volvo culture. During the time of the research, Volvo reported a significant positive financial performance and achieved an all-time-high in terms of sold cars in 2004. These successes, however, did not lead to any feeling of complacency among the Volvo co-workers. Quite the contrary. The intense cost-cutting in the industry and the awareness of the financial hardship of many automotive producers – for instance, in the Swedish automotive company SAAB, owned by Ford's competitor, General Motors, and located in Trollhättan, some 70 kilometres away from the Volvo Head Office in Gothenburg – allowed only a modest optimism about the future. The need to consolidate resources and, in many cases, to implement more systematic management control routines and mechanisms imposed new work assignments on the Volvo managers. One of the section managers, responsible for the powertrain software in the cars, argued:

> In general, there is a harder climate today. Everybody feels they need to clarify who's to blame and that yourself is not responsible. . . . We have less resources to do the job and at the same time personal performance and personal goal achievement are emphasized. We used to work as a collective.
>
> (Section manager)

Another consequence of the cost-cutting programme was that slack that previously enabled explorative work and activities off the beaten track was now more or less eliminated. One of the engineers argued: "If there is no slack whatsoever anywhere, then it is not that easy to allow for creativity, because that has to cost something." Another engineer said: "A few years ago, you could point at the necessity of a skunk work. Back then, you could start something and try something out. Now, it's quite hard." A senior manager thought that the strong focus on short-term financial performance on *all levels* of the firm was potentially a threat to the long-term competitiveness of the company:

> I wish we were able to convince the investors to show a bit of patience so that we did not have to be profitable in every single R&D department every third month. It kind of takes its time to show any results and we need a bit of extra margins we can make use of. I can feel a certain impatience and a fixation on short sight even in the innovative domains.
>
> (Senior manager)

When being asked about their evaluation of the increased influence of bureaucratic procedures, most co-workers claimed they though of a strengthening of the management control and administrative routines. At least, the procedures and systems had changed over time. One of the technical experts was disgruntled over inflexible and time-consuming reporting activities and offered some examples of how she had to involve managers at Ford in operations she had previously been handling herself. Moreover, when Ford managers were involved, there were certain rules and regulations that could stop the entire activity because they could not be by-passed, even in cases when there were solutions available that were not acknowledged by the system. Procurement activities were one such recently reorganized activity. She said:

> There were a bit of bureaucracy before, but you could handle it. Today we attain a lot of information about things you're supposed to do through the mail system, and in many cases the language [in the instructions] is really unintelligible. ... A variety of special words on how to proceed is introduced.

One of the section managers argued that it was complicated to remain creative when being exposed to a number of administrative systems aimed at standardizing the work routines:

> I don't think that we in the management team of the Powertrain department are really creative. It feels like as soon as you enter this administrative machinery you lose much of the ability to think in new terms: the systems are just chewing things over and over: "We have these problems and how do we solve them?"
>
> (Section manager)

In other cases it was not easy to determine if increased work pressure in terms of administrative workload was an actual problem for the managers or just a general complaint about the new situations. An engineer argued:

> I've heard people say that for managers, there are much more papers and stuff. I think there is a truth in the claim that the bureaucracy has expanded. In some cases the bureaucracy may have just changed, you use a new spreadsheet and you do it a bit differently. ... Maybe, it is not always bad that you standardize quite hard, like they did at Ford.

A majority of the interviewees claimed that they thought of the new Ford systems of management control and reporting as being complicated to use. Still, some of the interviewees argued that standardization of routines would have a long-term positive effect on the capacity to innovate:

> You may think that standardization is in opposition to new thinking, but I don't think so. A certain degree of law and order may in fact enable new thinking since the rest of it just goes on. It would make many people happy

if we had fewer problems and would be able to anticipate problems and solve them.

(Manager)

A project leader argued in similar terms:

> I think Ford are much more stringent regarding responsibility, the delega-
> tion of tasks, how they are dealing with specifications, and on how to deal
> with a number of issues. I regard that that they "steer up this situation" in
> positive terms. Previously, it's been too much of "doing it your own way"
> for no reason; things that had little to do with the very creative development
> process and the quality assurance process.

(Project leader)

Another perceived direct implication from the increased emphasis on financial performance, cost-cutting and leaner new product development activities was that some processes were made reversible in that decisions that had already been made could be brought into discussion anew. The designers pointed out that when they designed, say, a new seat for a new car model, they presented, for instance, three different alternatives representing the cost levels, such as "cheap", "medium" and "costly". When the project leader makes a decision for, say, the medium-priced seat, this choice led to certain design alternatives being abandoned while others are implied. For instance, more expensive materials such as leather may be discarded while other technical features may be agreed upon. Then the car is on the verge of being introduced, the "rationalization engi-neers" working with "ratio" – a nickname for the "rationalization" of the activ-ities in Volvo (in fact "cost-cutting") – may come back to the designer to ask them to cut additional costs besides those already being agreed upon when choosing one particular seat. One of the designers expressed his critical view of this change of decision *ex post facto*:

> You can see it coming: every time we have done a change in the design,
> then somebody wants to change a detail, because then we save five crowns.
> (approximately €0.45) ... Then I have to make the decision: "is it worth
> it?" ... This is so prioritized within Ford and Volvo: to cut costs to save a
> crown. In that field [cost control] there are no limits for the investments and
> then we get additional work. ... In many cases, we refuse to do it [change
> the product] because we regard it as being of value for the customer. Here,
> there are immense conflicts of interests. They only do their job, but it
> implies a significant additional workload for us.

(Designer)

Therefore, what was originally an irreversible decision – a "go/no-go" type of decision – then proved to be what is again open to negotiation. For instance, the "ratio engineers" may ask if it was possible to make different choices of materials and fabrics in order to cut costs while, for the designers, such decisions are a matter of reducing the entire design to a set of components that could be individually separated and replaced. Instead, they thought of such *ex post facto* decisions as being in conflict with their design work, essentially conceiving of the car as a coherent and unified entity rather than an assemblage or patchwork of individual components. The designers thus thought of such interventions into their domain of expertise as mindless and degrading.

Taken together, many of the Volvo co-workers were concerned about the influence of a management control ideology which they thought of as being of Anglo-American origin and as being in some kind of opposition with the engineer culture's emphasis on experimentation, labouring and tinkering. While several of the interviewees argued that one must not complain about all sorts of practical concerns and present preoccupations that one does not appreciate, there was a general concern in the company for the short-term thinking and the Ford management system emphasizing control. The entrepreneurial engineering culture of the company was in many cases emphasized as being incompatible with such managerialist thinking and its one-sided emphasis on financial performance.

Summary and conclusion

The automotive industry is characterized by fierce competition and lower margins, and, consequently, there are numerous alliances and collaborations between firms. Today, few automotive companies stand without partners. Volvo Cars is a minor player in the industry, and therefore Ford Motor Company's ownership of Volvo helps in sharing R&D resources. Interviews with managers, development engineers, designers and a number of other Volvo co-workers suggest that, while Volvo remains functionally and hierarchically organized, employing a number of expert groups specializing in different domains of new car development, the company is still capable of managing complex and advanced forms of innovation work. The capacity to remain innovative and creative is perceived as one of the most central drivers for sustainable competitive advantage, and therefore factors potentially threatening such capacities were regarded with scepticism.

The interviewees at Volvo Cars addressed two major challenges for the future. First, the influences from British and American management culture were two-sided. On the one hand, there were great opportunities for learning things when sharing resources with one of the world's largest automotive conglomerates. Planning, project management and decision-making were domains where some of the Volvo interviewees thought they could learn a great deal from Ford. On the other hand, the British and American cultures were envisaged as being hierarchical, formal, anti-egalitarian and inflexible. Therefore, the new management culture posed a threat to the predominant entrepreneurial culture wherein all co-workers engage in the activities for the sake of Volvo. The Volvo interviewees tended to lament the tendency to further emphasize formal management systems over what may be called "thoughtful improvisation". The existing innovation system is, of course, highly regulated and organized by a number of formal decision-points, milestones, toll-gates, deliverables and so forth. But the Volvo co-workers argued that one must not mistake the map for the territory and therefore one must be capable of responding to unanticipated changes in the innovation process. In the present Volvo regime, engineers and project managers are capable of dealing with such events, but they were concerned this would not be regarded a legitimate management practice in the Anglo-American management system. As a consequence, many of the interviewees pointed to a tighter management-control system as an indication of the lack of trust on the part of top management in Ford. Rather than leaving the day-to-day work decision to the co-workers, the new systems of management control provided an increasingly tighter network of detailed control.

Even though the co-workers at Volvo were concerned about the effects of the emerging American management regime on the predominant *modus operandi* anchored in a Scandinavian managerial tradition, they were positive regarding the opportunities for undertaking innovative and creative new product development work. They also claimed that just as much they had to adapt to Ford's way of working, Ford may learn from Volvo. Several of the managers argued that the Ford executives were emphasizing that Volvo should preserve its Scandinavian traditions, culture and operating procedures. Speaking in terms of bureaucracy critique, it is noteworthy that neither of the new management practices derived from inside the organization but, on the contrary, they are imported into the firm from the outside. In the case of Volvo Cars, there is no evidence of any "iron law of bureaucratization" wherein large companies of necessity petrify and fall prey to their own internally developed mechanisms. Much of the bureaucracy critique literature tends to treat bureaucracies as intrinsically determined to become inefficient and engaged in responding to its self-imposed mechanisms and routines. In contrast to this image of the bureaucracy as gradually becoming less and less concerned with matters of the outside world, the Volvo co-workers actually defended their reasonably structured and controlled ways of working against more formally enacted procedures. In Volvo, all co-workers are expected to act a bit entrepreneurial in order to be able to provide new products to the market with limited resources. Emphasizing management control and other forms of mechanisms regulating the internal procedures add further costs and, therefore, the Volvo co-workers did not endorse a more formal management system. Taken together, the case of Volvo Cars does not support the bureaucracy critique claiming that large, functionally organized and hierarchical firms are more or less incapable of innovating. Quite the contrary, Volvo Cars is a good case to illustrate how a limited amount of resources can be used wisely to provide highly competitive products even in markets characterized by hyper-competition. Volvo Cars is therefore both organized in a bureaucratic manner *and* a highly innovative and creative company.

5 The innovative bureaucracy, Part II

The science-based bureaucracy

Introduction

In this second empirical chapter of the book, the case of the British–Swedish pharmaceutical company, AstraZeneca, is examined as an example of a bureaucratic organization capable of undertaking advanced science-based innovation work. While Volvo Cars are operating in an industry characterized by lower margins, hyper-competition and an emphasis on cost-cutting, the pharmaceutical industry (although sharing some of these characteristics) also have the issue of new drug development, which consumes an increasing amount of financial resources in society. As opposed to the automotive industry, wherein most companies have adopted Japanese concurrent engineering management procedures and thereby have substantially shortened the new product development process, the new drug development process in the pharmaceutical industry is, in fact, consuming more time and money now than ever. The most widely recognized explanation for this predicament is the increase in close regulation of the industry by the authorities. Innovation work in the pharmaceutical industry is controlled and regulated from outside of the firm. This, however, does not suggest that there are no opportunities for creative and innovative work in the pharmaceutical industry; the last ten years has brought a veritable explosion of new scientific practices and know-how within what can be called the "new biology", that is, in domains such as genetics, genomics and proteomics, providing new means for developing drugs targeting human diseases. Although, the automotive and the pharmaceutical industries share some characteristics, there are areas where they differ substantially. What this chapter intends to show here, notwithstanding these intersections and divergences, is that large, functionally organized and hierarchical organizations are fully capable of orchestrating innovative work.

The pharmaceutical industry: an overview

New drug development is inextricably entangled with the laboratory sciences. The laboratory is, of necessity, a fabricated milieu: "It would seem," Knorr Cetina (1981: 4) writes, "that nature is not to be found in the laboratory, unless it is defined from the beginning as being the product of scientific work." Therefore the new molecules must always be related to external environments such as biological organisms and, later on, large groups of patients in the clinical trails. The ability to add value to molecules through their association with, and connections to, biological organisms is the key capability of pharmaceutical companies. Hara, drawing on a sociological perspective of science and technology, characterizes such a process as being a production of "facts" that are not inherently "objectively true" themselves:

> A drug discovery is here defined as a discovery of the "fact" that a natural or synthesized chemical has a particle of biological activity which can be applied to the treatment of diseases. However, from the viewpoint of the social shaping of science and technology, I do not intend to suggest that the "fact" is an objective matter, which exists independently of social processes.
>
> (Hara, 2003: 7)

Barry describes the drugs provided by pharmaceutical companies as being "informed materials":

> Pharmaceutical companies do not produce bare molecules – structures of carbon, hydrogen, oxygen and other elements – isolated from their environment. Rather, they produce a multitude of informed molecules, including multiple informational and material forms of the same molecule. Pharmaceutical companies do not just sell information, nor do they sell material objects (drug molecules). The molecules produced by pharmaceutical companies are more or less purified, but they are also enriched by pharmaceutical companies through laboratory practice. The molecules produced by a pharmaceutical company are already part of a rich informational material environment, even before they are consumed. This environment includes, for example, data about potency, metabolism and toxicity and information regarding the intellectual property rights associated with different molecules.
>
> (Barry, 2005: 58)

The process of producing "informed material" is carried out in the stages of discovery activities in the laboratory, the development of the molecule qua candidate drug, and finally the testing of the molecule in large-scale clinical studies. Therefore, being able to manage the entire chain, from the laboratory to final drug application and the launching and marketing of a new drug, are key capabilities of pharmaceutical companies. This process is heterogeneous and includes a variety of expertise. For instance, Knorr Cetina (1983: 123) points to the complexities the novice encounters when studying a technoscientific activity:

> If ethnographers of science had hoped to come up with a set of parameters which neatly specify this process they were quickly disappointed. A day in

the laboratory will usually suffice to impress upon the observer a sense of the disorder within which scientists operate, and a month in the lab will confirm that most laboratory work is concerned with counteracting and remedying this disorder.

Similarly, Latour and Woolgar point to the complexity of laboratory practice: "A body of practices widely regarded by outsiders as well-organized, logical, and coherent, in fact consists of a disordered array of observations with which scientists struggle to produce order" (1979: 139). Thus, the analyst of new drug development is very much exposed to claims and arguments of the practising scientists. However, this predicament is not unique to the pharmaceutical industry, but is innate to most professions and organized activities. The work of, say, construction workers may be less complex than laboratory work but, for the outsider, there are still significant events and processes that are not immediately open for inspection and analysis.

Beside the complexities "inside" the laboratory and the various new drug development activities, pharmaceutical companies are continually influenced by external changes. Casper and Matraves (2003) found that the governance structures in Germany and the UK affected pharmaceutical firms' innovation capabilities. While German firms were successful in developing new chemical entities (NCEs), the active molecules of a new drug, the UK firms were significantly better in delivering blockbuster drugs. The corporate governance structure in the UK, Caspar and Matraves (2003) argue, enabled UK firms to quickly adapt to changes, while the German firms had a more long-term perspective on their research and development. Besides the governance structure, industry standards for clinical practice strongly affect the cost and development times of new drugs. Abraham and Reed (2002), when considering the influence of regulatory demands, show that there is an iterative process between authorities and pharmaceutical companies in terms of negotiating regulatory practice. They write: "[T]he complex relationship between regulation and innovation may not be unidirectional: scientific and technological innovations can influence regulatory developments" (2002: 338).

Abraham and Reed (2002) studied how the International Conference on Harmonisation of Technical Requirements for Registration of Pharmaceuticals for Human Use (generally shortened to ICH), arranged during the 1990s, sought to establish new regulatory standards that would promote innovation and new thinking in the industry. They suggest that, in fact, the ICH standards did not, contrary to the official declarations, rest solely on scientific evidence, but the demands for toxicity testing were lowered to enable new innovative projects. Abraham and Reed (2002: 360) conclude: "The foregoing analysis demonstrates that the ICH's standards for drug judgments are not 'technical' in the sense of being divorced from political judgments and social interests." Such a conclusion is also made by Busfield (2006), who argues that pharmaceutical companies are more concerned with their financial performance than with engaging in healthcare concerns, as suggested by the formal rhetoric. For instance, the blockbuster drugs in 2003 were two cholesterol-lowering statins, an anti-psychotic and a drug to reduce blood pressure, arguably all drugs aimed at treating the health problems faced by the richer countries rather than diseases of the developing world. This portfolio of blockbuster drugs is representative of what Clarke *et al.* (2003) refers to as "biomedicalization", the increased emphasis on individual health as a variable dependent on the use of technoscientific resources such as drugs, but also on the individual's "ongoing moral self-transformation" in terms of a systematic "care of the self". In a biomedicalized society, health is not just a matter of luck or coincidence but is actively produced through human action. While Abraham and Reed (2002) point at the negotiable nature of the *scientific* standards in the industry, Busfield (2006) addresses the social and sociological consequences of the systematic production of pharmaceuticals. She concludes:

> Pharmaceutical producers use their ideological, economic and political power to play on the anxieties and discontents of life in late modern society creating a market for products that extends well beyond obvious health needs. Health services, which are supposedly based on considerations of welfare and professionalism and a commitment to patients' interest, become the means of generating large profits for a highly commercial industry that uses scientific fact making as a tool to serve its own interests as much, if not more, than the interests of health service users.
>
> (Busfield, 2006: 310)

The comparatively strong position of the pharmaceutical industry calls for some reflection, especially in terms of patient security. Clarke *et al.* (2003: 169) report that a study showed that industry-sponsored research is 3.6 times more likely to produce results favourable to the sponsoring company than publicly sponsored research. Technoscience, then, is not self-enclosed but remains open to external influences.

In addition to political and social interests, advances in the life sciences and biomedicine disciplines continuously affect the pharmaceutical industry. Over the last fifteen years, a number of new techniques and scientific programmes, such as pharmacogenetics, high-throughput screening and systems biology, have been developed and adapted by pharmaceutical companies. Zucker and Darby (1997) show that incumbent pharmaceutical firms have to invest substantial time and energy to implemented new biotechnology practices in their discovery work. Biotechnology here

> [m]eans the revolutionary breakthroughs in life sciences over the last two decades including especially, the use of recombinant DNA to create living organisms and their cellular, subcellular, and molecular components as a basis for producing both therapeutics and targets of testing and developing therapeutics. Recent developments focus on structural biology, combinatorial chemistry, and gene therapy.
>
> (Respondent, cited by Zucker and Darby, 1997: 432)

Zucker and Darby continue: "[B]iotech is a dominant technology for at least some areas of production of biological agents, for creation of targets for screening and evaluating potential pharmaceutical products, and as a methodological base for creating pharmaceutical products" (1997: 432). Even though the "biotechnological revolution" offers new opportunities for identifying new targets and therapies, there are still significant challenges facing pharmaceutical companies when aligning "old" and "new" methods and techniques. Hedgecoe and Martin (2003) examine the emergence of pharmacogenetics as one specific biomedical approach to new drug development that raises a series of problems and concerns, but also opportunities for the industry. Hedgecoe and Martin here provide some background to the new scientific practices:

> Coming into the 1990s, a number of new technologies such as polymerase chain reaction and high-throughout screening gave scientists greater understanding of genetic variation and increased the interest in pharmacogenetic studies. In addition to these technical developments, there were also ideological changes which, in the wake of the Human Genome Project, started to restructure medicine in terms of genetics (Bell, 1998). Perhaps most importantly, pharmcogenetics finally aroused the interest of the new genetic technologies with a focus on drug discovery and development. Around this time a new term began to be used to describe the discipline: Pharmacogenomics.
>
> (2003: 333)

When conducting large-scale clinical studies of a particular medicine, all patients were more or less treated as a homogeneous group. With the help of pharmcogenomics, one may be able to sort out individuals who respond differently to the substance on the basis of genetic analysis and to identify explanations – in terms of genetics, that is – for the unfavourable response. The drug may then be modified to suit the individual's "genetic markers". In Hedgecoe and Martin's formulation: "The 'disease dependent' vision of pharmacogenetics aims to identify associations between genetic markers for drug response and those genes directly involved in the development of different forms of pathology" (2003: 337). They point to the clinical value of such an analysis:

> If a strong correlation between a genetic marker and drug response of disease prognosis can be demonstrated, then this will have immediate clinical value, even if the biology of this link remains a mystery. This opens up the prospect of the rapid introduction of routine clinical genetic testing based on nothing more than a statistical association between a marker and the response to a particular drug.
>
> (Hedgecoe and Martin, 2003: 340)

Pharmacogenetics remains one single technical effect from what can be called the "new biology", yet it produces a series of ethical, juridical, managerial and scientific concerns that must be addressed prior to the implementation of such new genetic methods. The point is that new drug development is a social practice continually being reformulated and reshaped on the basis of scientific and technological advances. For pharmaceutical companies and their co-workers, there is a demand for being able to continuously adapt to new conditions. Therefore, taken together, new drug development must be conceived of as a most complex social practice, embedded in a variety of social, scientific, technological and managerial processes and undertakings, in many cases crossing one another and thereby producing an intricate texture of activities. These different levels of resources and assets cannot be reduced to one another but must be examined as an assemblage comprising a number of different connections and interactions. Hara (2003: 19) uses the concept of *discovery*, not in terms of the identification of the compound per se, but in terms of the "causal relationship between chemical and the biological activities". Thinking of drug development in such *relational terms* (Cooper, 2005) is one promising approach to the analysis of new drug development.

The case of AstraZeneca: the science-based bureaucracy

Why AstraZeneca is an innovative company

AstraZeneca is a major international healthcare company engaged in the research, development, manufacture and marketing of prescription pharmaceuticals and the supply of healthcare services. It is one of the world's leading pharmaceutical companies, with healthcare sales of over $24 billion in 2005 (AstraZeneca, *Annual Report* 2005). The company operates within seven therapeutics areas: neuroscience (CNS and pain control), cardiovascular, gastrointestinal, cancer, respiratory and inflammation. AstraZeneca is ranked number five in the industry for R&D expenditure (2003): they spent $3.4 billion on R&D in 2005, employing more than 12,000 researchers. The Head Office is located in London and the company has seven sites in Sweden, UK and the USA. The AstraZeneca product portfolio includes ten medicines generating annual sales of more than $1 billion each. The blockbuster drugs include the gastrointestinal medicine, Nexium, accounting for $4.6 billion in annual sales, and the cardiovascular medicine, Seloquel, accounting for $1.7 billion annual sales. In addition, the number of nominated candidate drugs has increased over the last three years from fifteen in 2003, to eighteen in 2004 and twenty-five in 2005.

In order to account for a pharmaceutical company's capacity for innovation and creative thinking, one needs to examine the product portfolio of the focal firm. AstraZeneca has had an extraordinarily successful track record. Zeneca[5] had previously been successful in the 1930s up to the 1950s; a success covering a relatively wide product range including antiseptics, antibiotics and cardiovascular therapeutic areas. In the late 1960s, the company's most significant domains of research were cardiovascular and, later on, cancer treatment (Pettigrew, 1985). Important breakthroughs were made in the cardiovascular area (propranolol, Inderal™) in the early 1960s, which also resulted in a significant expansion of the R&D organization. For Astra, an important breakthrough in the late 1960s was the launch of Aptin™, for high blood pressure. That was a starting point for Astra's further expansion (Östholm, 1995). More breakthroughs followed, including the first-in-class drug (omeprazole, Losec™) that eventually became the best-selling medicine in the world for a period of time (Sundling, 2003).

Today, despite an increasing emphasis on shareholder value and stock market performance – combined with a stronger regulatory environment (Sundgren, 2004) and increasing cost (twelve years, on average, with an estimated cost of $900 million) to develop a drug (DiMasi *et al.*, 2003) – AstraZeneca can be categorized as an innovative company. In 2004, eighteen candidate drugs[6] (CD) were selected (fifteen in 2003 and eleven in 2002) and, by the end of 2004, the company had thirty-one projects in the pre-clinical phase and seventeen projects in clinical phase one, seventeen projects in clinical phase two and twenty-five projects in clinical phase three.[7] In addition, the company has recently been successful in developing and launching competitive medicines such as Nexium™ (proton pump inhibitor and successor of Losec™), Crestor™ (treatment of dyslipidaemia) and Seroquel™ (treatment for CNS disorders) which all have a large potential to establish strong positions in their therapeutic areas.[8]

In terms of intellectual-property issues, AstraZeneca file, on average per year, 300 to 350 new patent applications. The company has a patent portfolio consisting of more than 16,000 patents worldwide, and 14,400 pending applications. AstraZeneca sales in 2004 totalled $21.4 billion with an operating profit of $4.8 billion.[9] The R&D organization has expanded over the last three years and today consists of 11,900 people at eleven R&D centres in seven countries: Sweden, the UK, the USA, Canada, France, India and Japan.[10] In summary, AstraZeneca is a company that has proven to be able to demonstrate what Dougherty and Hardy (1996) call "sustainable product innovation" and have been reporting significant financial performances for a number of years.

The new drug development process in the discovery organization

New drug development is a complex undertaking including the alignment and combination of a number of scientific skills and practices into a technoscientific procedure (for a detailed discussion of new drug development, see Chiesa, 1996: 640; Styhre and Sundgren, 2005: 51ff). The whole process is presented in Figure 5.1.

Drug discovery and development is a lengthy and costly process, taking an average of fifteen years (Yu and Adedoyin, 2003). On average, it costs a company more than US$800 million to get one new medicine from the laboratory to the pharmacist's shelf (DiMasi *et al.*, 2003). This amount includes expenses related to the interrupted development of molecules that failed to meet specific characteristics required for commercialization. It also includes the cost of capital investments. Unpredictability in the research process is also an

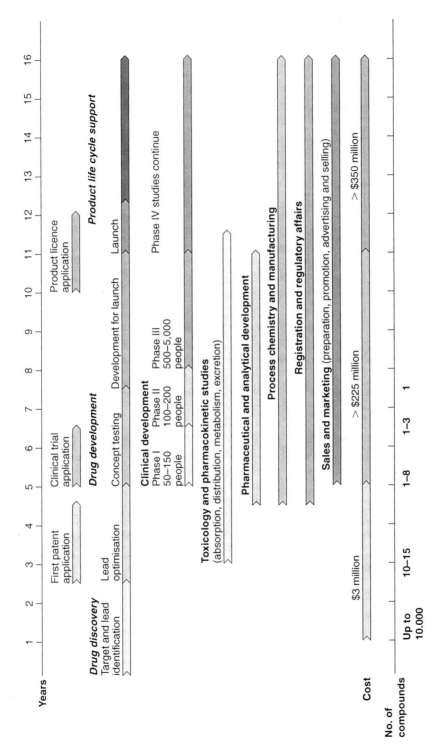

Figure 5.1 Overview of the research process (adapted from AstraZeneca, *Annual Report*, 2001).

important issue. Most pharmaceutical companies have experienced high project attrition: only 1 per cent of early discovery projects end up as products (DiMasi, 2001). Blau *et al.* (2004: 228) write:

> [A]lmost half of the resources that U.S. industry devotes to NPD are spent on products that fail or are cancelled. In the pharmaceutical industry this problem particularly is challenging because of long development times, low success rates, high capital requirements for building a manufacturing facility, and broad uncertainty in sales estimates.

Abraham and Reed (2002: 341) have pointed out the increased new drug development times: "The cost to bring a new chemical entity to market can be as high as US\$350 million, and it is estimated that the time from first synthesis of a new drug to its marketing quadrupled from 1960 to 1989."

Development of a pharmaceutical product can be generalized by dividing pharmaceutical R&D into three major processes: (1) discovery, (2) development and (3) product support and life-cycle management (Hara, 2003). For the pharmaceutical industry, the discovery of a new drug presents an enormous scientific challenge, and consists essentially in the identification of new molecules or compounds. Ideally, the latter will become drugs that act in new ways upon biological targets[11] specific to the diseases requiring new therapeutic approaches. Hara (2003) points to the heterogeneity of the drug development process:

> [T]he process of drug discovery and development can be regarded as involving heterogeneous elements including:
>
> 1   human actors such as chemists, pharmacologists, toxicologists, different functions in the company, corporate managers, academics, doctors, patients, government officers, politicians, activists and the general public
> 2   non-human entities such as drugs, materials, instruments and facilities; and
> 3   institutional and structural factors such as strategies, organizational linkages, human networks, organizational capabilities, funds, markets, regulations, sciences and clinical trails.
>
> (Hara, 2003: 32)

The drug discovery (pre-clinical) process can be divided into five stages (Sams-Dodd, 2005) separated by milestones to indicate significant progress, demonstrated in Figure 5.2. Moving from one phase to the next depends on meeting different criteria. It normally takes three-to-five years to produce a CD (Jones, 2001).

Figure 5.2 The drug discovery research process.

Target identification and validation

The identification of therapeutic targets requires knowledge of a disease's etiology[12] and the biological systems[13] associated with it. The duration of this phase may range from several months to several years. Target identification attempts to identify new targets, normally proteins, whose modulation might inhibit or reverse disease progression (Zuccato *et al.*, 2005). The role of target validation is to demonstrate the functional role and biological relevance of the potential target in the disease phenotype.[14] Target validation facilitates the identification and timely progression of lead molecules to provide effective improvement of diseases and, at the same time, it helps in reducing the risks of failures from incorrect biological hypothesis. In many instances, however, drug targets are newly discovered and thus their full biological role is not known. This necessitates constant updates of the connectivity of a target throughout the lifecycle of a drug discovery project (Apic *et al.*, 2005).

Hit and lead identification

Once the therapeutic target has been identified, scientists must then find one or more leads (e.g. chemical compounds or molecules) that interact with the therapeutic target so as to induce the desired therapeutic effect. In order to discover the compounds whose pharmacological properties are likely to have the required therapeutic effects, researchers must test a large variety of them on one or more targets. The term "hit" refers to when a compound has sufficient activity to warrant it being a candidate for clinical studies, providing it meets toxicity and other peripheral requirements (Walker *et al.*, 2004). Many pharmaceutical companies have large libraries of synthetic or natural compounds, ready to be tested. To test the chosen compounds in large numbers, scientists use an entirely automated process known as high throughput screening (HTS). In general, of the thousands of compounds tested, barely 1 per cent will qualify for further and more probing analysis (Potoski, 2005). An important task is to ensure that the chosen compounds have the desired therapeutic effect on the target and to check relative toxicity bioavailability *in vivo* on animals.

Lead optimization

Lead optimization is defined as those activities required to optimize a screening hit to a pre-clinical candidate (Baxter and Lockey, 2001). The purpose of this stage is to optimize the molecules or compounds that demonstrate the potential to be transformed into drugs, retaining only a small number of them for the next stages. To optimize these molecules, scientists use advanced techniques. For example, data allow the medical chemists to modify the structure of the selected molecules or compounds, if necessary, by screening, thereby creating structural analogues. The creation of hundreds, possibly thousands, of analogues is aimed at, for example, improving the effectiveness, diminishing the toxicity or increasing the organism's absorption of the drug. This phase requires close collaboration between the biologists and chemists, who form a feedback loop. In this phase, biologists test the biological properties of compounds on biological systems while the chemists optimize the chemical structure of these compounds in the light of information obtained by the biologists. This optimization stage aims at developing new substances that are more effective than known compounds. The latter are then subjected to a specific evaluation involving broader biological tests such as preliminary toxicology, computer-aided drug design, *in vitro* and *in vivo* studies planned for testing in humans (Clark and Newton, 2004).

Candidate drug nomination

The development potential of a candidate molecule depends essentially on its capacity to be administered to humans and show therapeutic effectiveness with an acceptable level of side-effects (Hara, 2003). Before testing candidate molecules on humans in clinical trials (the development phase), scientists must show that the candidate drug (CD) does not present an unacceptable level of risk, given the expected therapeutic benefit. Regulatory authorities require pharmaceutical companies to demonstrate the safety of the drug for humans and to prove that the therapeutic advantages of the compound greatly outweigh any associated undesirable side-effects (e.g. migraine or high blood pressure in the case of cancer treatment). These studies are conducted in conformity with the rules of the regulatory bodies. During this stage scientists (e.g. biochemists, pharmacologists and toxicologists) continue to evaluate the pharmaco-kinetic, pharmaco-dynamic (i.e. how the drug affects the body and how the drug is affected by the body, respectively) and toxicological properties of the compound *in vitro* and *in vivo* (on animals).

Development and clinical trials

If the CD is found to be safe, an application (investigation of a new drug, IND) is filed with drug-regulatory authorities and ethical committees to obtain approval for testing on humans. After authorities approve the IND, clinical studies can begin. The required three-part clinical trials process,[15] which judges the efficacy and safety of potential treatment, is a major undertaking. After completion of phase 3 studies, the final documentation can be compiled and submitted to the appropriate national regulatory agencies (e.g. the American Food and

Drug Administration) for review (new drug application, NDA) (Hullman, 2000). After approval, the product can be marketed. Adverse effects are followed meticulously through all clinical phases and after approval of the drug for launch. In the entire new drug development procedure, the discovery process is the most complex and unpredictable and involves many factors that could influence the success of the outcome (Zivin, 2000).

To conclude, the Discovery organization is accountable for the drug developing projects in the first five stages, after which accountability transfers to the Development organization. However, the involvement of the Discovery organization does not end at CD nomination, but must partner the Development organization into the sixth stage, the Proof of Principle Testing phase (containing pre-clinical development and initial clinical testing) aiming for the successful delivery of each drug project.

Functions in the new drug discovery process

The respondents represent the four major functional departments within Discovery AstraZeneca R&D in Mölndal, Sweden, that are all working on the design and synthesis of new compounds within AstraZeneca cardiovascular (CV) and gastrointestinal (GI) drug discovery. The Discovery organization includes different areas, including Gastrointestinal Biology, Cardiology, Metabolism and Vascular Biology, Toxicology and Laboratory Animal Resources.

Medicinal chemistry

Medicinal chemistry is a chemistry-based discipline concerned with the invention, discovery, design, identification and preparation of biologically active compounds, the interpretation of their mode of action at the molecular level and the construction of structure–activity relationships. The medicinal chemistry department comprises of about 190 employees. The department has core competencies in organic chemistry and medicinal chemistry, together with parallel synthesis and computational chemistry, analytical chemistry, separation sciences as well as extensive support functions.

Integrative pharmacology

Pharmacology is a biological-based discipline, which studies the pharmacological changes in whole systems (i.e. animals) by chemical substances, especially the actions of drugs, substances used to treat disease. Integrative pharmacology focuses on to increasing the functional understanding of compounds and target mechanisms of action in animal disease models. Although other methods (*in vitro*, molecular biological, and *in silico*) have provided critical details about the mechanisms of action from compounds in various disease states, studies in the whole animal are a cornerstone of drug discovery. The department consists of about 140 employees.

Molecular pharmacology

The role of molecular pharmacology, in contrast to integrative pharmacology, is focused on *in vitro* approaches (e.g. from molecules to cells, tissue to organs) to study effects of drugs on their respective molecular targets. The department comprises of about 200 staff working on a broad range of interrelated sciences such as genomics, biochemistry, cell biology, target validation, cellular physiology, immunology and bioinformatics. One important goal of the department is to explore and invent new concepts and experimental models in order to identify and validate new targets within different disease areas.

Drug-metabolism, pharmacokinetics and bioanalytical-chemistry (DMPK&BAC)

This department supports discovery project phases by investigating biologically active compounds and studying their metabolism (i.e. absorption, distribution, metabolism, excretion properties). The goal is to provide support to pharmacology and medicinal chemistry functions in target-and-hit evaluation and to minimize attrition during the Development phases. Another goal is to support bioscience disciplines in obtaining plasma concentrations of compounds of interest. The department is also responsible for documenting CDs and providing biological sample analysis to support pre-clinical studies and on through all clinical phases of drug development. The department consists of about 100 staff and includes core competencies in analytical chemistry and pharmacokinetics, together with physical and computational chemistry.

Staying innovative in regulatory regimes

In this section, we will – just like in the previous chapter – address the importance of creativity for the competitiveness of the company, the influence of new managerial practices, and the effects of managerial control and procedures.

The role of innovation and creativity

The new biology and challenges for the pharmaceutical industry

Similar to all pharmaceutical companies, AstraZeneca has experienced a long period of increased regulatory demands on their research activities. In the 1960s, the first integrated and systematic demands for regulatory control were raised and, over the years, a tight network of regulatory control has gradually been established. Among the AstraZeneca co-workers there was a great degree of understanding and acceptance for this need for monitoring the industry. Everyone wanted to avoid any large-scale disasters as a consequence of some neglected by-effect, both because of ethical considerations but also because of liability issues. The regulatory frameworks imposed a certain framework of operations on the industry and the discussions regarding the possibilities for innovation and creativity evolved around the possibilities provided within the regulatory framework. Nevertheless, all interviewees thought of their employer and the pharmaceutical industry as being innovative and essentially grounded in the co-workers' ability to conceive of new solutions to perceived problems. However, it is important to acknowledge that all innovation is embedded in scientific procedures and practices and that creative co-workers are, of necessity, also capable of mastering a specialized scientific field. Many studies testify to the scepticism towards new laboratory technologies among practising scientists in cases where they regard the technology as displacing their professional scientific skills. One such new technology predicted to wield great influence in the pharmaceutical industry was the mapping of the human genome, successfully completed in the beginning of the new millennium. Contrary to what was assumed among some of its spokespeople, such new techniques and technologies have not eliminated traditional scientific modes of thinking. One of the senior managers argued:

> A couple of years ago, the tendency was clearly that one should only do *in vitro* research, that one would be able to deal with all kinds of problems in cell research, but that did not work. . . . Three–four years ago, one believed that as soon as one knew the genome it would be possible to just ship out new medicines, but it has actually been quite the opposite. I believe this sort of solid integrative knowledge about how things interact in complex models is still as important today as twenty years ago. I do not side with those who believe that we will be able to scan the human body into a computer and then be able to predict everything. . . . We're a long way from such a situation.
>
> (Senior line manager)

Technological optimism has faltered and, instead, a more tempered view of the influence of new technology prevails at present. In addition to the human genome technology, the senior line manager also pointed at the use of High-Throughput Screening (HTS), a common name for a number of methods and techniques employed in laboratory studies examining how a biological entity reacts to exposure to various chemical compounds, as another disappointing technological development. Instead, a more systematic organization of information was regarded of greater importance:

> Our output of candidate drugs has increased significantly the last two–three years. When all these genome technologies, HTS and all that were introduced, you thought that it would revolutionize it all, that you would be able to virtually throw out loads of new drugs, but that proved to be wrong. But now we have undertaken a variety of activities, better libraries, and one should be able to predict how it [a new candidate drug] should look.
>
> (Senior line manager)

Needless to say, some of the interviewees were more sceptical and thought of laboratory research as losing status and becoming more and more organized in accordance with pre-defined goals and objectives. One of the synthesis chemists talked about such research activities as "template research", that is, standardized and "uncreative" research activities:

> We are doing a lot of "template research" here. We have these spread sheets … and there we tick the boxes, "now we have done this", "now we have done that", "now we have done that". But that isn't proper research. Research is by definition when you really do not know what is supposed to happen. Otherwise it is, for me, a development of a process or a product where you can predict outcomes. Research implies that you are taking some risks; you don't know the outcome but you have your scientific intuition and try to build a scientific test of proof.
>
> (Synthesis chemist)

One of the Disease Areas Scientific Leaders (DASL)[16] defended the rationale for the templates:

> We had quite a bit of discussions regarding the templatization and the process orientation. On the one hand, I can see a need for this in an organization this large; you cannot have a "Wild West" so it is probably a good thing to standardize practices at the sites and so forth. … Then, on the other hand, I think there are too many templates and guidelines. I know that when we started to discuss this … there were a lot of loud protests but I thought that we are wise enough to use these templates in a rational manner. Today, I need to admit that we have very much abandoned such beliefs.
>
> (DASL: integrative pharmacology)

One of the pharmacologists pointed to the importance of promoting ideas to top management and the various committees evaluating the suggested projects, and spoke of much of his work as "PowerPoint research" wherein the most "marketable" findings were reported. In a similar vein, one of the synthesis chemists addressed the loss of risk-taking in large organizations as a major impediment for the progress of the industry: "Large corporations take proportionally lower risks than small companies. … You should use smaller units because that is the only thing that works" (Synthesis chemist). He also pointed to the small companies in his field of interest as being role models:

> There are less and less innovations in large corporations and more and more outside of the large companies. … It differs a bit between disciplines. … In my discipline there are a number of companies working on nanoparticles. If you examine how many patents they file and how many the pharmacology unit at Astra files, you notice that a company employing about 50 people files substantially more. You need to be careful when

counting and so on, but it is still an indication of their activity in these innovative parts.

(Synthesis chemist)

He continued:

> I fear that . . . we won't be able to deliver another Seloken Soc or Losec – or omeprazol as the substance is called – because in this template mode of thinking it would get too many "red ticks in the boxes" or whatever you may call it. . . . You cannot exclusively run such risk projects . . . but a large company needs to be able to take larger risks than a small company. That is not the case, all over the world. We should be able to run a number of somewhat odd [high-risk] projects
>
> (Synthesis chemist)

One of the most important explanations for the lack of radical breakthroughs derived from what the laboratory scientists called the "new biology" was the absence of time for reflection and analysis. One of the molecular pharmacologists argued that there was, in fact, a great deal of scepticism towards the use of new biological technologies:

> I think there is a great fatigue. We have so much muscle, so much technology, access to so much information. This dream they discussed when they segmented the human genome came true: the massive access to information. The thing is, there is always a shortage of resources . . . sooner or later, you reach a point where somebody needs to take a look, conduct an analysis, and make a decision. AstraZeneca here in Mölndal has no tradition in this field. The managers are not trained in this spirit. . . . This new "era" in the biology – I am thinking of genomics and genetics where you can obtain much information, and the technique I work with myself where you can evaluate the genetic code of a cell – creates incredible amounts of information. In addition, there is information provided by the research community, available in databases on the Internet. . . . I don't think we are used to and prepared to receive all this information, and I think that people celebrate when they realize that this new deal also implies disappointments like any other previous technology. I think people are relieved when they hear that HTS has not generated any new significant drugs on the market. I think people are relieved when they hear that genetics has not produced any new forms of therapy.
>
> (Molecular pharmacologist)

Another pharmacologist working in the field of gastrointestinal medicine addressed the same topic:

> In one way or another, there is a firm belief in technology. For instance, we are now building a big *Imaging Centre*: new technology should solve

everything. .... If you are crass, what you see is that biology is a rather complex matter. This will solve nothing of it. You might get a clearer or more detailed picture of what is happening but that is not the way forward; that is not the main concern. We will not be able to characterize everything in detail. .... It is [the ability to exploit] the unexpected that will bring new blockbusters.

(Molecular pharmacologist)

Another line manager in the pharmacology department emphasized the central importance of access to qualified experts and researchers:

In general, we have doubled few functions in Discovery. Even though we have a modern research site it is quite common that just one single person knows one field. If he or she is absent it will actually affect the activities. It is amazing this is still the case in 2005. All this automatization and the explosion in all other areas cannot eliminate the fact that skilful persons cannot be substituted. We become aware of that now: when a person cannot join a meeting, all of a sudden that input is missing.

(Line manager, integrative pharmacology)

In other words, the specialization within the research implies that it becomes increasingly complicated to get a full picture. Some parts are often missing. In general, the pharmaceutical industry has to be capable of accommodating a series of new scientific innovations and techniques captured by the new term of "new biology". In many cases, new methods and approaches clashed with the more traditional *in vivo*-based new drug development regime. The intensification of research activities was something that most interviewees deplored, especially in terms of the overloading of data that demands proper scientific analysis. The lack of time thus becomes a major concern for the researchers.

The lack of time for analysis and reflection

The absence of time for systematic reflection and analysis was addressed as a most significant factor for the effectiveness of the discovery work. The principal target for the critique was the increased number of projects each researcher was expected to participate in. The tendency was that resources were spread too thin over a larger number of activities. One pharmacologist argued:

One person is doing too many things, I agree, because with this matrix [a management control system] thing ... the whole idea is that your fingers should be in several pies at the same time, and everybody should have several things to do. And accountability becomes difficult. I think we got fantastic people, but I think that we have the natural instinct in human being to do the least if we can. ... A lot of resources are lost there and that is the whole issue; we should rethink it like this: should people really work with three or four things at the same time? Can they actually be efficient when they work on three different targets at the same time?

(Molecular pharmacologist)

One of the managers in the DMPK department pointed to the impact on motivation for the individual:

All my co-workers will be working in two to three projects. . . . If they had one project they were engaging in, they would have been able to create very good relationships with the project co-workers. . . . Now everyone have to be fully committed to two additional projects because the number of projects have been increased while the personnel remain the same. This implies a conflict situation.

(Manager, DMPK)

The emphasis on running a larger number of projects meant that the researchers had, again, little time to engage in greater detail with the scientific and methodological challenges they were facing in the project. Besides dampening motivation, the multi-project organization further broke up the working day into pieces, thereby preventing the researcher from committing to one single task at a time.

One of the DASLs was critical of the lack of time for reflection:

The co-workers are overloaded with work assignments and they do not have the time to reflect; in many cases, they do not have the time to sit down and see what the results stand for . . . to see a pattern in a series of experiments. You rarely have the time to put these pieces together.

Similarly, one of the senior managers deplored the present situation: "We have always tried to dedicate 10 per cent of the time to your own ideas. Today we are not able to fulfil that objective. We do then not have enough time for 'curiosity research'. The increased emphasis on delivery makes this objective problematic." A synthesis chemists argued in a similar vein:

Back then, about 15 per cent of the total pharmacy resources were invested in what one may call "explorative knowledge creation". Then, after the merger, they found out that we had the largest pharmaceutical organization in the world. . . . Then the boss – who is still the boss – said that from now on we should invest only about 5 per cent in explorative work. . . . And then some of the managers are surprised that the amount of patent applications has lowered. . . . I would like to claim that they are half of what they used to be the last couple of years.

(Synthesis chemist)

Another critique was the concern for what was regarded as an excessive use of meetings in the organization. Native Swedes and co-workers with other backgrounds both thought of this as being a "Swedish problem" specific to the Swedish sites of the company. Several interviewees criticized the reliance on meetings as the principal arena for information and knowledge sharing. One of the molecular pharmacologists lamented: "This organization is plagued with meetings." One of the integrative pharmacologists argued: "The number of meetings have accelerated and is of course related to the size. It is mostly about informing different parts because we are farther and farther away from one another. There is an inflation [in meetings]." One of the project leaders in the DMPK department testified to her own ambivalence towards formal meetings:

> I have this strong sense of aversion against our way of working: this meeting hysteria is remarkable. Still I sit here and contribute myself with quite a bit of meetings and then I need to be able to reflect on how to deal with this situation. There must be other ways of handling it. . . . There is this firm belief, I would say, that we should handle everything at meetings. Meetings do not really put much demand on us and you can spend a great deal of time talking at meetings.
>
> (Project leader, DMPK)

Most of the interviewees regarded meetings as a necessary evil, but they also thought there could be fewer and better-run meetings. Some of the senior scientific experts could almost fill their entire working week with meetings, although many were only of marginal interest for them. Another concern was the lack of informal meetings and discussions. One of the project leaders in the Integrative Pharmacology department pointed at the small but nevertheless significant example of the lack of a shared coffee room as an indication of how complicated informal meetings have become:

> We used to have one coffee room and there were always loud discussions. People came there to drink coffee and talk about whatever. We used to have so much fun there. We discussed football and hockey, but also scientific matters. Now, we no longer have a coffee room but there is a shared one for the whole of the department and we are like 150 persons. It is located in another building and it is located a few storeys down. This means that the most of us, say 98 per cent of us, very rarely go there to drink coffee. Instead we sit like this [in the offices]. That is a damn simple thing, but also an important thing as I see it.

When complexity increases, new means of communication evolve. At the Mölndal site, meetings appeared to be the preferred arena for communication.

Another concern for the Discovery researchers was the emphasis on the accumulation of large amounts of data. Because the entire new drug development process was based on the ability to screen large number of substances and to sort out the most promising candidates, there was a continuous production of data that were, in most cases, stored in databases. One of the molecular pharmacologists regarded this ones-sided emphasis on storage at the expense of analysis and reflection as being outright "ridiculous" since, in general, there was no defined use of the data generated:

> We emphasize the logistics, to document data and make it available for everyone. I think it's ridiculous! It is of course a good thing to be able to share data and make it visible in the company, but it is much more important that there is an end-user receiving it. You do something for a reason and the person who submitted the question needs to be the end-user, because only that person is capable of seeing the full value of the analysis. If there is no such person, you mustn't think that AstraZeneca co-workers are "browsing around" in some computer database someplace saying "well, here's someone who did an interesting thing six years ago" and bring that research forward. That's silly! I think we focus on the wrong things: investing such amounts of time to categorize and make data available when there is no proper end-user.
>
> (Molecular pharmacologist)

One of the senior scientists in the DMPK department pointed to the downside of the massive production and storage of data:

> At times, I believe that there is too much information. There is always that risk. In the development projects, you synthesize like 3,000 substances . . . a real good substance may easily disappear then. . . . I think we've seen that tendency, that you miss something. It would have been great if we could reduce output and think more.
>
> (Senior scientist, DMPK)

Taken together, this strategy to cover vast domains in the discovery process gave rise to new problems (data storage, logistics of information) were created along with competition over already scarce resources. One such significant resource was the access to the researcher's time.

Nostalgia

Some interviewees formulated a positive view of the possibilities for innovation and creativity. One interviewee, engaging in clinical research – the testing of new candidate drugs on populations of patients – argued: "Even though there is the regulatory control, I think there are some opportunities for investigating, to test new ideas." A senior scientist, being critical of the lack of risk-taking in the industry, also acknowledged the possibilities for running "skunk works" parallel to the regular formal assignments in the organization:

> It is rather easy to do skunk work; if you have a hypothesis, like "If you do like this or like that, then it may come out well", then you can find a

specialist. Through this network, you rather easily – it sounds a bit strange, right? – get help, at least the first help ... to check whether this hypothesis works. ... I believe that is a successful way of conducting R&D work.

(Senior scientist)

"Oldtimers" at the site said this used to be a rather common way of running projects and, at times, their narratives bordered on nostalgia. Thus a concern for some of the newcomers in the organization took the form of nostalgia from the older co-workers. The 1980s was a periods of substantial scientific breakthroughs (e.g. the registration of the blockbuster ulcer medicine, Losec, developed at the Mölndal site) at the same time as the size of the firm was still comparatively small. It was commonplace among some of the co-workers to refer to this period as some kind of "golden age" for both the company and the pharmaceutical industry. One of the pharmacologists argued that one must take all these nostalgic reveries with a pinch of salt:

There are many encouraging stories told, like the Losec story. ... In this research setting, people are prone to tell stories about people who "despite" management accomplished things. Those are exciting stories but you never hear about those who staunchly maintain their work but fail to deliver something. We never speak about them. Quite frankly, they are outnumbering the success stories I would say.

(Pharmacologist)

One of the department managers was critical of the bleak and dystopic outlook formulated by some of the old-timers, claiming that the sense of sharing an integrated company culture and a feeling of embarking on an exciting experience is very much lost as the company grows larger and the industry is more and more tightly integrated and monitored, and oriented towards the financial markets with their emphasis on shareholder value. Instead, such reveries were dismissed as backward nostalgia that did not take into account the extensive changes in industry and in the broader society:

It wasn't better before. Of course, there was less control. The demands for delivery were completely different. If you delivered a candidate drug, that was fine, but if you did not, it did not really matter. At that time, when the turnover increased by about 30 per cent annually ... when Losec was at its height, 1999, its turnover was five billion US dollars, and when everything grows by 20–30 per cent per year, then life is easy. ... That "it used to be better" idea, I don't buy that. Of course it used to be better if there were no demands and there was plenty of time for everything.

(Senior line manager)

One of the younger co-workers, a chemist working in the molecular pharmacology department, argued that the culture at AstraZeneca is rather "academic". She claimed that some of her co-workers had a hard time coping with the new situation wherein more substances had to be explored at a faster pace: "Some of the people working in the *discovery phase* are very academic persons. They are not used to work very focused. That is not their best quality. They are very concerned with details. . . . I think these persons need some management." Rather than deploring the loss of the *ancien régime*, the chemist recognized the need for moving forward.

Taken together, the bureaucratization of activities and the demand for significant performance essentially derived from the outside in terms of increased competition and higher regulatory demands from the authorities, not from within the organization in accordance with some self-perpetuating "bureaucratic logic". Just as in the case of Volvo Cars, the interlocutors addressed two concomitant processes. First, the integration and blending of a Scandinavian and Anglo-American management culture implies some conflicts and misunderstandings that needed to be fruitfully dealt with. Second, the increased emphasis on managerial practices and an orientation towards financial markets implied a number of challenges for the scientific ideologies and mindset dominating the day-to-day activities of the site.

New managerial values and practices

Scandinavian organizations are often characterized in the literature as demonstrating flat organization structures, consensus, joint decision-making and anti-authoritarian leadership. "Low degree of power distance" and "feminine values" are Hofstede's (1980) two distinguishing features of the countries of Sweden, Norway, Denmark, and the non-Scandinavian country, the Netherlands. Among the Swedish AstraZeneca co-workers there was a general concern regarding their ability to make their voice heard in an organization now populated with American and British co-workers speaking their native language and therefore enjoying significant advantages vis-à-vis their Scandinavian peers. Beside the obvious concern for the use of English in the operations, more deeply ingrained differences between the UK, USA and Sweden were pinpointed. The most persistent theme concerned the more hierarchical organization and management styles in the USA and UK: "It [the company] is more managed from the top, one may say. You must expect that – Sweden is the flattest you can think of," one of the synthesis chemists said, clarifying that he was not surprised of the outcomes from the merger. "American companies are much more managed from the top," one of the senior line managers argued, siding with his colleague. One of the senior scientists, who had worked for a number of years in the UK, recalled her first encounter with British management culture:

> It was like traveling back to the stone age in comparison to Sweden. The *rigidity* and the *hierarchy* of the organization were incredible! You wouldn't believe it. And the view of the co-workers! We left that twenty-five years ago: how to treat co-workers, how to make use of

co-workers, and how to speak to them. That was different to what I was familiar with.

(Disease area scientific leader)

One of the managers in the Molecular Pharmacology Department indicated what he thought was the principal shortcoming with the English management tradition: the inability to exploit co-workers' creativity:

If they have a problem, it is the creativity: they have a much larger challenge than we do. They are incredibly locked up in their hierarchies. ... They are more controlled by the process. They like boxes and flow-charts and such things. You see that coming here as well.

(Manager, molecular pharmacology)

On the other hand, another senior scientist emphasized the effectiveness of an organization that remains focused on a few central and agreed-upon activities:

They [the English] are much better at process thinking. ... It depends on that they do not expect their co-workers to be creative and think on their own. ... This means that out in the laboratories you have "hands" but no "brains"; you don't ask for people's ideas – you don't ask them whether they think this is a good way of managing the activities. That is decided upon by top management.

(Disease area scientific leader)

One of the management practices that caused much concern was that each of the co-workers were not given the right to speak directly to his or her colleagues in similar positions in the USA or UK sites, but always had to ask for permission from the manager. For the Swedish co-workers, this procedure was unnecessarily complicated and caused much more work for all persons involved. One of the clinical researchers shared such experiences with others:

We have different traditions ... we speak differently. We are very to the point and informal in Sweden. ... I, in my role on the shop floor – if you put it that way – if I know I have to speak to this person in my position elsewhere, say, in England, then I cannot speak to that person directly but I have to inform that person's boss. It is supposed to be like that. ... That creates a great deal of inertia.

Another cultural difference was how to perceive one's career. One of the managers in the DMPK department emphasized the differences between Swedish and British co-workers. The whole of AstraZeneca had implemented what was called "broadbanding" after the merger. Broadbanding was a form of career system in which one could either choose the "scientific ladder" or the "line management ladder". All co-workers were located in a specific segment (a "band") that implied certain qualifications, assignments, demands for further career advancement and a span for the salary. The manager argued that Swedish co-workers did not care very much about the broadbanding system and cared little about advancing in the hierarchy, while the English co-workers thought of the system as being of central importance:

> So far, we never use this [system], neither to manage interests, nor for developing people. Nobody tells me that "I'm in band C and I would like to move to band B" when I talk to them. They just don't think in those terms. But when I talk to the Englishmen at the site: these bands are the only thing on their minds. For them, it is very important to advance a step further.
>
> (Manager, DMPK)

The British co-workers were more concerned with individual careers, while the Swedes emphasized the project work, the DMPK manager argued. Again, two different national cultures were claimed to demonstrate specific traits.

Since all the clinical research work is organized into project teams, thus imposing demands for quick and easily managed communication between different co-workers, in many cases representing different functional specialist roles, the structuring of communication around the line managers became a great concern, especially for the clinical researchers. But not all problems were caused by cultural differences. In some cases, the Swedish co-workers thought they were too anxious to involve American co-workers in particular in every single project, thereby at times making things more complicated than they needed to be. However, the integration of the Scandinavian and Anglo-American management cultures was not a trivial operation. Still, most of the employees thought of the merger as being successful in terms of making the different sites collaborate more closely with one another, and in terms of sharing resources and competencies within the firm. Still, the Scandinavians had some worries that their local organization culture would not survive the colonialization of the Anglo-American management cultures. As a variety of management practices and routines penetrated the everyday work-life, some of these beliefs were proved to be worthy of consideration.

Management control and administrative procedures

The use of output performance measures

One of the consequences of the merger with British Zeneca was that the activities in the different therapeutic areas were consolidated and integrated in order to meet future challenges. Over a number of years, the pharmaceutical industry had demonstrated a diminishing return on investment in R&D; that is, fewer blockbuster drugs generating annual income in excess of one billion USD were launched. In addition, pharmaceutical companies became more and more dependent on financial markets and oriented towards the "quarter economy"

predominating the contemporary capitalist regime. As a consequence, managerial work in pharmaceutical companies became more and more influenced not
only by scientific interests but also by management practices and the political
skills of entrepreneurs. One of the synthesis chemists described the new situation like this: "What you see now is that there are loads of these 'task forces'
that 'deal with issues' that the line managers . . . really have to try to stay away
from. You are easily captured by such activities". New managerial activities
were continuously brought into discussion and slowly started to affect the
modus operandi of the day-to-day activities. One of the managers in medicinal
chemistry pointed to the effects of the process model being implemented in the
company:

> The process orientation is much more clearly implemented. All the *three-
> pagers, five-pagers* [reports to various evaluation committees], and so forth.
> . . . Much more "tick-boxes" . . . I think it is very exhausting. I want more
> discussions and dialogue regarding each specific case. These "tick-boxes"
> are quite easy to use . . . but they are simplifying. . . . There are other things
> that are not covered.
>
> (Line manager, medicinal chemistry)

Even though a transparent and widely understood process helped to guide the
drug discovery process, all the spreadsheets and standardized reports could not,
the manager argued, substitute for proper scientific thinking.

The implementation of the key performance indicator (KPI) "number of synthesis per time unit" among the synthesis chemists had caused much debate in
the organization. One of the synthesis chemists expressed his concern for the
emphasis on performance measurement: "How many formulations you do per
time unit, and bla bla, bla. Everything is to be measured now." The chemists
thought the KPI was a one-dimensional construct that was only weakly related
to actual performance, that is, the performance measure was not taking into
account the *quality* of the substances. Quality is here primarily seen as the possibility of turning an actual substance into a new candidate drug. One of the synthesis chemists argued:

> But what does this number tell you? I can set up twenty reactions every day
> and write that eighteen reactions did not work. But management cannot read
> all the procedure, they just see the numbers. I am afraid it is going in this
> direction, that everyone [now thinks] that they judge me by the number of
> reactions that I do, so why not set up this one as well . . . then I have one
> reaction more.
>
> (Synthesis chemist)

In addition, the chemist pointed to the importance of being a qualified project
leader and how this was not indicated in the new performance measures implemented:

It is not the number of compounds, the number of reactions [that matters] ... [but] also the contribution to the discussion: how do you help your colleagues? How do you push your project forward? ... But it is difficult to measure. How do you measure this?

(Synthesis chemist)

When the KPI was implemented, it had immediate consequences for how the co-workers acted. For instance, substances could be reported before they were thoroughly evaluated and developed because individual quotas had to be filled over a period of time. One of the chemists at the DMPK department reported:

You'd rather deliver in December 2004 than in February 2005 because then you can report it "the right year" ... but it might be that it would have been better to wait for two months and do a few tests and maybe be able to say that "no, this one does not qualify".

(Researcher, DMPK)

In other words, the KPI had latent and manifest functions.

Even though the interviewees did not resist the standardization of activities per se, but rather thought of the standard operating procedures (SOPs) governing the day-to-day work as a meaningful way to organize activities and make them transparent, the all-too-close adherence to the SOPs was a standing concern. Since such scripts were written as a general instruction, it was complicated to determine exactly in how much detail the SOPs should be followed. Some of the interviewees spoke of the "SOP fundamentalists" (Swedish, *Bokstavstrogna*) who did not allow for any deviation from the SOPs. For instance, one of the senior scientists argued that the ambition to satisfy authorities' demands was slightly exaggerated:

It is the ambition of the company to be better than what the authorities demands. Then you block yourself: it is as if the activities are there for its own sake, not to respond and help us move forward. It is like they are here to perform better than what the authorities demands. ... If the authorities says 'jump!', then we jump three times as high.

The risk-aversion and the fear of failing to meet expectations and regulatory demands were substantial in the company. However, for most of the interviewees, the managerial control of the operations was regarded as being justifiable given the significant risks in new drug development. One of the researchers argued: "There are such enormous amounts of money in this type of industry so one needs to keep an eye on it, check what is done, and what is the basis for results and the arguments ... of course there are legitimate reasons for it" (Researcher). The pharmaceutical industry was generally regarded as operating under specific conditions that demanded close monitoring of activities. A senior line manager reflected on the nature of the industry: "In this industry, you can

easily spend six billion crowns, and then when approaching the large-scale clinical studies, one realizes that 'we did not think about this or that' and then you
drop the drug."

In addition to the SOPs, a significant amount of the interviewees voiced
concern for the MITP system (Management of Individual and Team Performance), an internal tool designed to help individuals agree, record, plan, carry out
and review personal objectives. These objectives are linked to the functional
targets, together with identified training and development, guiding everyday
work through the formulation of a series of goals and objectives for the individual. Within the MITP model, each co-worker specifies some goals that
should be accomplished during the year; the ability to meet these goals served
as the basis for salaries and bonuses. For the Swedish interviewees there were
at least two major flaws with this model. First, the MITP promoted a sub-opti-
mization of the activities in terms of each individual being enticed to formulate
easily accomplished goals rather than goals that were less easy to fulfil and,
therefore, more useful for the organization. Expressed differently, the intrinsic
motivation of central importance for the scientific mindset and the scientific
ideology was substituted with a model based on extrinsic motivation factors
such as monetary rewards and bonuses. Second, the MITP model explicitly
addressed individuals rather than teams, project groups, departments or any
other social group around which the operations were structured. One female co-
worker, a chemist working in the DMPK department, was critical of the whole
idea of MITP. She thought that the whole of the company promoted a "male
mode of thinking" [Swedish, *Ett manligt tänkande*] and that MITP was a
typical male innovation: "There is much more male dominance now. They prioritize and promote male behaviour much more than before . . . the emphasis on
performance, the leadership is much more inflexible. . . . It is a tougher
situation" (Chemist, DMPK). She continued:

> MITP is a typically male invention. A woman would not conceive of such a
> system. A woman would not approve such a reward system. It is very
> inflexible . . . and everything should be quantified. If you work in a team
> like we do, there is quite a bit that cannot be measured and that is actually
> important for the activities. Those things are never formally rewarded.
>
> (Chemist, DMPK)

MITP may, similarly to the key performance indicators, be at odds with local
cultures and work practices. One of the synthesis chemists even thought of
MITP as being what is essentially alien to Swedish culture: "Quite un-Swedish
[Swedish, *osvenskt*]. . . . Like getting the grades once a year" (Synthesis
chemist). Since it is individual goals and objectives that are formulated, the
alignment of the individual and the collective becomes one of the central issues
with the MITP model. Therefore, individualized and subject-centred management control models pose a threat to both a Scandinavian collectivistic culture
but also to the scientific ideologies serving as the bedrock for the entire organi-

zation. At AstraZeneca, all interviewees except one expressed their scepticism towards the implemented system. One senior principal scientist argued:

> There is no appreciation of the strategic efforts, the incentive systems are designed so that it is a prerequisite that what is aimed at is possible to express in quantitative terms, which leads to that the only things that are aimed for are those that are *possible* to quantify. Stuff that work like lubricants, such as good advice to others, helpfulness, own initiatives, do not count at all. The individual ensures his own context and you are supposed to underline your own efforts. Many Swedish co-workers consider this difficult while American co-workers are excellent on expressing their own qualities.
> (Senior principal scientist)

Another co-worker at AstraZeneca argued in similar terms: "We take a tactical perspective, not a strategic one. Before, you were rewarded when taking personal risks aiming at discovery, today we are rewarded on whether we follow working procedures or not" (Senior Manager).

Several of the interviewees cited the influence of managerial thinking and managerial careerism as a recent phenomenon in the firm that would eventually represent significant challenges for the predominant scientific culture. One of the synthesis chemists argued that the status of laboratory work had deteriorated during the years and it needed to be re-appraised in order to safeguard the future performance of the firm: "After all, it is the experimental work that is of the greatest importance; that is the core and should be given much more status. It is a problem when everyone wants to become something different [than laboratory scientists]." He continued: "Rather few people are in the laboratory. ... You must avoid dirtying your hands." The line manager career appeared to be more appealing than staying in the laboratory. In AstraZeneca, top management candidates were recruited from among the skilful scientists with degrees in the laboratory sciences and not among the salespeople or any other significant groups. By tradition, scientific skills and qualifications had a high status and were praised among the co-workers. Many of the co-workers even expressed their own feelings of insufficiency in terms of failing to follow the progress in relevant scientific fields. The new emphasis on managerial practices and managerial objectives, in some cases regarded as being inextricably entangled with the Anglo-American culture, was therefore regarded with significant scepticism. The "new world order" implied new management practices and, for most of the interviewees, such isomorphisms with other industries and the American and British business worlds emerged as an unavoidable and self-regulating force which could not be resisted.

The influence of leadership

One central activity in complex and highly integrated innovation processes, especially in science-based innovation work, is the creation of a vision and the formulation of objectives and the coordination of activities, that is, *leadership*. It may appear paradoxical that highly qualified and specialized scientists are expecting clear leadership guidance, but the ambiguities regarding the market situation and the position of competitors in the pharmaceutical industry requires a continuous rewriting of the map. New drug development is therefore not solely a scientific undertaking but is equally a matter of strategy and decision-making. In the new regime, where a larger number of concomitant projects are running, there is also a great need for help in prioritizing between different assignments. However, in an increasingly complex system, there is continuously a lack of time to see leaders. One of the line managers in the medicinal chemistry department stated:

> Our managers are not really visible. For instance, our head of the department: I think I've talked to him twice since I started here. . . . He does not have the time. We are 250 persons or something and how should he be capable of talking to each and everyone and develop a relationship with them? It is really hard.
>
> (Line manager, medicinal chemistry)

Absent managers primarily caused two kinds of problem for the co-workers: a lack of clear and transparent decision-making and unclear priorities. One of the molecular pharmacologists pointed to the need for formulating priorities for the co-workers:

> When we have a most inefficient pharma company today, I think that the most important thing they [top management] have to do is to give us a clear direction on what kind of target we should be looking at, how much risk we should take on this target, and how much validation we should be doing with this. That kind of thing would be nice rather than just telling me "that you're inefficient". They should be able to have an overview to see "where are we inefficient?"; tell me where are we inefficient? Are we equally inefficient? Are we inefficient in some aspect? Can we change that?
>
> (Molecular pharmacology)

At the time of the study, the Mölndal site had been compared to some of the UK sites and it was the top management that claimed that the Swedish site lagged behind in terms of number of synthesized substances. Rather than providing an analysis of what needed to be accomplished to deal with this concern, top management, some of the interviewees argued, were finger-pointing and repeating that Mölndal "had to do better". This lack of leadership and authority was annoying for the Discovery researchers because they had a firm belief in their own skills and capabilities, and thought that the evaluation was one-dimensional and thus incapable of representing underlying actual scientific expertise. Furthermore, the interviewees argued that it was complicated to understand how decision-making was conducted in the company. Too many managers shared too many decision-making responsibilities. One of the Disease area scientific leaders argued:

> There is a weak line of command concerning decision-making. There are ambiguities . . . regarding who have the responsibility and mandate to make decisions. Everybody really wants to run back to their bosses and ask if they should do this or not, and that makes time pass. Then you feel that the only thing you do is repeating what's been said for the last half a year in presentations at different meetings. You need to get all the managers into the same boat so they dare to make the decision.
>
> (Disease area scientific leader, integrative pharmacology)

A synthesis chemist working in the DMPK department emphasized that many decisions were delegated without proper information and instructions being provided:

> I miss clear decision-making. They declare something and then it's on our desks but we get no further instructions; then we are supposed to manage the whole thing without knowing what the objectives are. Even if we appreciate working on our own, you need to know in greater detail what to achieve and how to achieve that objective.
>
> (Chemist, DMPK department)

In general, many of the co-workers agreed that, while the whole new drug development process had become much more complex and integrated, and that the number of concomitant projects had increased in number, leadership had not developed at the same pace. Co-workers, therefore, were at times left mostly on their own, exposed to a series of ambiguities, yet subject to performance measurement and monitoring. A manager in the DMPK department said that top management had failed to foresee the consequences of the new regime:

> Regarding the leadership . . . I am not fully impressed, I must say. I don't think they are seeing the consequences of the complexity of drug development. . . . They try to eliminate some of the steps in the chain to make things easier for us. I think that is the right way to go. There have been too many decision-makers and too little mandate in the projects.
>
> (Line manager, DMPK).

For instance, while the activities have became more complex, decision-making has remained largely centralized and distributed over a number of scientific committees serving as advisory boards in the company. In the new organization, the DMPK line manager hoped to see a stronger project organization where more mandates were given to the project leaders. In addition, many of the interviewees pointed to the lack of risk-taking as a structural problem for the industry. One of the managers in the molecular pharmacology department pointed to the higher stakes in the industry and how this implied a preference for a risk-averse leadership practice.

> There is so much money involved that one does not dare being first on the market because the authorities are sceptical towards new ways of thinking, a new "class" of pharmaceuticals. You have to fight fiercely to get something approved. If you join the next wave then the market is prepared a bit for these new medicines. It's hard work being first. . . . Then you rather play the safe cards first.

Moreover, one of the synthesis chemists pointed to the fact that most new drugs were aimed at dealing with "more biologically complex diseases", suggesting that there were greater scientific challenges facing pharmaceutical companies. The authorities' lack of acceptance for side-effects was also brought up as a key factor that strongly affected pharmaceutical companies. "The pharmaceutical industry is facing a tough period, I'd say," one of the interviewees said. Taken together, all these different factors contributed to a situation wherein leadership was of central importance. Particularly in these times of uncertainly and increased demands, several of the leading scientists and managers called for more charismatic leaders who could provide a source of enthusiasm and self-confidence. One of the molecular pharmacologists remarked:

> Our managers are so boring it's getting a kind of occupational health problem. If we at least could reflect society as a whole and have at least a few charismatic persons. I am not asking for everything; you can be scientifically competent and ambitious, or you can be a charismatic person – a strong person making people enthusiastic, or intimidating them, or whatever, but there is no such thing now.
>
> (Researcher, molecular pharmacology)

Some of the interviewees spoke of a former manager who demonstrated a particular ability to formulate a vision for the coming period and to emphasize the creative and innovative work in the organization. Today, there were few such charismatic individuals taking the lead.

Summary and conclusion

The interviewees at AstraZeneca argued that they had great opportunities for creative and innovative work: they had access to state-of-the-art technology and world-class laboratory facilities and were working in a company hosting a great variety of expertise in targeted therapeutic areas. However, the interviewees were also concerned about the new demands for "delivery" in terms of the number of new chemical substances provided and the number of new candidate drugs "in the pipeline" (the favoured metaphor for the new drug development process in the pharmaceutical industry). These more clearly articulated goals and objectives derived, the interviewees argued, from two sources. First, more detailed demands on new drugs enacted by the American Food and Drug Administration and other national authorities imposed a need for scanning and identifying more substances that may hold water throughout the entire new drug development process. The authorities are, in short, a much tougher negotiator these days. Several interviewees told stories wherein today's most well-known drugs (e.g. aspirin) would not have been accepted by the authorities because of known or potential side-effects. Second, the emphasis on the financial markets, some of the interviewees argued, led to a predominantly risk-averse attitude in pharmaceutical companies. Large firms took relatively lower risks than small firms, according to some of the interviewees. The orientation towards the financial markets also put pressure on the company to present a promising and well-balanced portfolio wherein new drugs were being launched on the market on a regular basis. To be able to pool the risks, this portfolio corporate governance model implied that top management presented a goal-breakdown structure wherein all parts of the organization could formulate rather detailed output goals. Even though most of the employees thought of the top management strategy as being legitimate and justifiable given such predicaments, they also thought of this one-sided emphasis on output as being detrimental for long-term innovativeness. For instance, one of the line managers said that, during his last meeting with the head of the R&D organization of the firm, the major concern was how to make financial investors understand the quality of the R&D activities in the firm and not how to manage the R&D work internal to the firm. The focus of top management may then change to conditions external to the firm. This may imply a loss in momentum in the R&D activities.

The bureaucracy literature, suggesting that innovation and bureaucracy are mutually excluding categories, says that all factors negatively affecting the capacity to undertake creative and innovative work derive from inside of the firm, from the very fabric of the bureaucratic organization form. The bureaucracy critique literature does not suggest that bureaucracies are incapable of innovating because of *external* conditions. On the contrary, bureaucracy is presented as a self-enclosed and non-adapting form of organization only marginally capable of responding to the changes in the environment. The case of AstraZeneca shows that large, functionally organized and hierarchical firms are, in fact, eminent domains for highly innovative work. The AstraZeneca Mölndal site is one of the world's most outstanding innovative sites in terms of blockbuster drugs and, in the more tightly regulated regime of today's pharmaceutical industry, the site continues to deliver substantial amounts of new candidate drugs. The factors negatively affecting the innovativeness of the firm, such as market expectations and more detailed regulatory demands, derives from pressures external to the firm. The case of AstraZeneca is thus, if nothing else, an example of how bureaucratic organizations are, in fact, capable of adapting to its environment and to institute mechanisms and practices safeguarding the long-term survival of the firm. Similar to the case of Volvo Cars, AstraZeneca is an advanced, science-based bureaucracy with substantial adaptive capabilities, continuously altering its practices to respond to external changes. Bureaucracies must therefore be examined as the outcome of a recursive adaptation process rather than being self-enclosed structures. If the latter was the case, firms would not be large, functionally organized and hierarchical structures. There is ample evidence to suggest that such is the case. Therefore, the longstanding critique of the innovative capacities of bureaucracies must be critically examined.

6   Bureaucracy in an age of fluidity

A vitalist view

Introduction

This final chapter is an attempt at examining the empirical material accounted for in Chapters 4 and 5 and at developing an alternative image (in the various senses of the term) of bureaucracy than that prevailing in the present bureaucracy literature. The two cases did not suggest that hierarchically and functionally organized companies relying on rule-governed action and various specialist and expert competencies are not, of necessity, incapable of innovating, nor are they failing to offer highly stimulating and interesting work assignments and career opportunities. Both Volvo Cars and AstraZeneca have proven to be sites where numerous innovative solutions have been developed and creative thinking is deeply rooted.

Still, these two firms adhere to a number of central bureaucratic principles and regimes of organization. These two cases are not anecdotal examples of how large companies organize their innovation work. A substantial number of industries and companies are organized in accordance with the Weberian principles of bureaucracy. The idea that large bureaucratic firms are incapable of innovating is one of the persistent themes in contemporary management thinking as well as in common-sense thinking, but little empirical evidence supports such claims. Of course, at times, small firms prove to be highly innovative and there are examples of how large firms fail to make the correct strategic decisions, thereby failing to respond to external changes and new challenges, but for every small firm being successful there are numerous cases of firms that disappear, become subject to mergers and acquisitions, and in other ways fail to maintain their individual status. Similarly, for every large firm that has been modestly successful in responding to various external changes, there are numerous examples of large firms being highly innovative and pioneering different technologies, services and products. If that was not the case, the ecology of the business world would simply not demonstrate the presence of large conglomerates, companies and corporations. To a certain extent, Karl Marx was right: capitalism would enable capital accumulation in a few places. Contemporary capitalism is, no matter what the enthusiasts for the entrepreneurial and enterprising personality type think, an economic regime highly dependent on large corporations (see, for example, Perrow, 2002). Still, there are opportunities for small and medium-sized companies to play an important role as sites where new alternatives and new thinking evolve and become established, for instance in the biotechnological firms that were started in the 1970s and 1980s (Rabinow, 1996, 1999). However, thinking that large firms are incapable of orchestrating similar explorative endeavours is simply not true; instead, major corporations such as Microsoft, Siemens, Toyota, Philips and Mitsubishi are extraordinarily creative organizations notwithstanding their size, functional organization and hierarchical structure. In many cases, it is not the size and functional organization and other bureaucratic features of such organizations that are brought into the analysis as central factors determining their "above-normal" performance, but more abstract and ambiguous concepts such as "culture" or "charismatic leadership" are favoured. Since the bureaucratic organization form is taken for granted in times of good performance and immediately made the single most important explanation in less-productive times, the bureaucratic organization's role as supplementary to other managerial and organizational resources is reinforced. This longstanding treatment of bureaucracy will be examined in greater detail in the rest of this chapter.

Innovation in large, bureaucratic organizations

The two dominant axial assumptions of the bureaucracy critique have been the inability of bureaucracy, that is large rule-governed and specialized organizations, first, to adapt to external changes and new demands, and, second, to provide interesting and stimulating jobs. In both the two cases accounted for here, these two strands of critique can be, if not falsified, at least put into question. First, large organizations do not poorly adapt to emergent conditions and new demands imposed by either new forms of competition or regulatory authorities. Quite the opposite. Large organizations have established a series of mechanisms identifying such external changes and orchestrating responses to them (Lawrence and Lorsch, 1967; Thompson, 1967). In the case of Volvo Cars, the competition in the mature automotive market created the need to merge with some major player in the industry to achieve economies of scale in R&D activities. In AstraZeneca, a similar demand for consolidating research activities in a variety of therapeutic areas, such as gastrointestinal and cardiovascular medicine, and broaden the portfolio led to the decision to merge with Zeneca. In both these cases, there were no intrinsic, supposedly "bureaucratic logic" that prevented action from being taken. Instead the two companies demonstrated accurate responses to the need to take action to deal with the new challenges. In addition, the interviewees did not express any dissatisfaction with their work situation in terms of the interdependencies with the size of the organization. Instead, most interviewees argued that the actual size of their employing organization enabled certain opportunities that would not have been available in smaller or medium-sized firms. The worries and concerns expressed by the interviewees essentially derived from the complexity of their respective operations and the increased demands for a continuous and ongoing exchange of information and communication. Above all, the interviewees did not think a smaller company would be able to undertake such large-scale development activities but would have been destined to manage only a subset of the activities. In both the firms studied, interviewees expressed their pride over the fact that they more or less fabricated the whole product "in house". At Volvo, some interviewees regretted that some part of the development work would be located at Ford and saw this as an indication of the loss of a sovereign position in the market and exposure to decision-making outside of the company. In AstraZeneca, substances in new candidate drugs that were in-sourced from smaller biomedical companies were treated with some scepticism because they were thought of as an indication of the shortcomings of the company to be unable to develop its own compounds. Therefore, size provided opportunities.

Just because large bureaucratic organizations are capable of responding to changing conditions and providing meaningful jobs, it does not mean there are no controversies and debates regarding day-to-day operations. In the two firms, interviewees listed a number of changing conditions they thought would pose a real challenge for the firms. For instance, in both companies the professionalization of the managerial function and managerial work were regarded as in opposition, or at least not in full harmony, with the entrepreneurial culture at Volvo Cars and the scientific culture at AstraZeneca. The increased influence of what may be named a "management culture" (or what critics may call "managerialism") implied a stronger focus on individual performance rather than team or work-group performance, a demand for clear, objective and measurable goals that could serve as the basis for career advancement and individual salaries and bonuses.

In organizations where innovation and creativity are praised – be it in terms of engineering, scientific work or artistic work – as central to the long-term competitiveness of the firm and for the quality or work-life, there are a number of implications for the movement towards a rationalist and instrumental management culture. First, there is a need for some slack and some excessive resources; resources that can be used to develop what is not always already specified and determined. In a performance-oriented management model preoccupied with objective measurement, business opportunities and new ideas may never be developed because of their inability to prove themselves profitable in the first instance (see, for example, Sundgren and Styhre, 2003). Second, reliance on objective measurement of virtually everything implies a "flight from ambiguity" that does not recognize puzzling and confusing phenomena as worthy of investigating but, instead, as what needs to be excluded from the investigation. In other words, multiplicities are reduced to singularities, multidimensional constructs become one-dimensional; innovative and creative thinking, then, is little more than adherence to predefined operating procedures. Third, in innovative and creative firms, innovation is rarely, if ever, the outcome of one single individual's thinking and work but, instead, emerges in what Leonard-Barton (1995) calls the "creative abrasion", the discussions, joint interpretations and debates within a community of individuals. Therefore, the individualistic, subject-centred management control model highly criticized in, for instance, AstraZeneca may impose another barrier towards innovation and creativity. However, no managerial model is solely good or bad per se, but has certain merits and shortcomings. What the interviewees in Volvo Cars and AstraZeneca are criticizing, then, is not the ambition to professionalize the management function or the implementation of systematic management practices but, rather, the differences between the favoured Anglo-American "tight control" models and the Scandinavian culture. What may appear as largely taken for granted in a British or North American company may not, of necessity, be what is embraced elsewhere.

In summary, the bureaucratic model as such is not what is preventing innovative and creative work. As opposed to a variety of texts dismissing bureaucracy as imposing self-perpetuating processes of bureaucratization imposing barriers to change and adaptation, major firms can demonstrate a capability to not only respond to changes, but also to anticipate them. Somewhat paradoxically, it may be that large organizations are at times *too* eager to adapt to external changes (Dahlsten, 2003). For instance, instituted management practices, in many cases of North American origin, are today distributed globally through the mechanisms of isomorphism and mimetic adaptation (DiMaggio and Powell, 1991). In some cases, the adaptation of new managerial practices would have been slower and more piecemeal if internal bureaucratic mechanisms imposed inertia in the system. For instance, the shift from traditional shop-floor organization to scientific management practices was slow and gradual in Sweden, but today, when the management culture is global and constitutes an industry in its own right (Thrift, 1998; Jackson, 2001), there is less room for resistance towards new managerial practices. No matter if most new management fads are sooner or later proven to struggle to live up to the promises of its spokespeople, management ideas are still seductive for managers. Therefore, bureaucratic virtues may in the future become re-evaluated in terms of resisting the "management fad of the month" culture.

Beyond the efficiency and humanist critiques

In the last two chapters, Volvo Cars and AstraZeneca were labelled as two forms of bureaucracy: the entrepreneurial bureaucracy and the science-based bureaucracy. In Volvo Cars, a strong entrepreneurial tradition, based on state-of-the art mechanical engineering skills, has prevailed over the seventy-five years, and more, of the company's history. The co-workers praise the capacity of the firm to mobilize employees in both formally decided upon development projects and a variety of skunk-work activities and other initiatives running adjacent to the standard operations.

In Volvo, interviewees said, you can make things happen if you know how to navigate the system and pull the right strings. As a consequence of the entrepreneurial culture, many co-workers spend most of their working lives in the company because they believe they can move on to new positions and assignments when they want to change their career. In AstraZeneca, scientific ideologies and concerns have always been privileged. Like most science-based companies, AstraZeneca employs highly skilled individuals with PhDs and Masters degrees in the biosciences and, therefore, the organization is strongly determined by what may be called university values and norms. Similarly to Volvo, coworkers at AstraZeneca conceive of themselves as active agents who control the means for taking action and influencing the firm's activities. The difference between Volvo and AstraZeneca is that the pharmaceutical company, to a larger extent, relies on scientific procedures and is subject to detailed regulatory practices. The engineering activities at Volvo are, of course, also dependent on specialized scientific skills and know-how, but since the day-to-day work does not directly intervene into biological organisms such as laboratory animals, human volunteers or patients, the demands from authorities are less explicitly formulated. Nevertheless, the two firms are comparable through their ability to mobilize and exploit the intellectual capital and know-how within the firms. Being entrepreneurial and maintaining the status of a state-of-the-art researcher means a company must stay on the move, in a state of continuous change and adaptation to new conditions. In Volvo and AstraZeneca, one therefore observes a restless adaptation to continuously changing conditions such as emerging technologies. In addition, new regulatory demands and the production of scientific facts that must be taken into account produce a situation wherein adaptation is seamless and ongoing. As a corollary to the demand for change, the work situation for the individual co-worker is not conceived of as problematic in terms of *too little* change but rather of *too much* change. Therefore, Crozier's (1964) talk about alienation as endemic to bureaucratic organizations cannot be supported by the research findings. In Robert Blauner's classic, *Alienation and Freedom* (1964), it was the workers who attended machinery and worked in assembly-work settings that experienced the greatest amount of alienation – defined as powerlessness, meaninglessness, isolation and self-estrangement – because they could not control their own work situation and saw little variation in their work (see also Graham, 1995 and Fucini and Fucini, 1990; see also Cavendish, 1982, on assembly-line work). The lion's share of the jobs in the two studied companies are, instead, qualified, complex and demand high levels of experience and formal training to carry out. However, it may not be a wholly fair treatment of Crozier's (1964) work to discuss the notion of alienation as the single most important construct. Instead, more recent psychosomatic illnesses such as "burnout" and stress may be of greater relevance to further research (e.g. Styhre *et al.*, 2002). Alienation has always been examined as if it is exclusively a matter for labouring people on the shop floor in production facilities. The work in knowledge-intensive organizations may be fraught with other concerns.

One of the consequences from these findings is that one needs to reformulate the two major thematic critiques on bureaucracy – that of the efficiency and that of the humanist implications regarding work opportunities – in new ways. Bureaucracies are not, of necessity, inefficient and incapable of responding to external changes, nor are they failing to provide meaningful work opportunities.

This does not make a large-scale organization a utopian place, combining all sorts of organizational benefits into one single structure; instead, bureaucracies represent one form of social arrangement that, under specific conditions, are capable at the lowest possible cost of delivering goods and services. Everyday work-life in contemporary bureaucracies is characterized by a stronger reliance on continuous communication, the continuous exposure to new managerial prac- tices, an emphasis on the latest quarter performance report and a loss of the slack resources that once enabled new thinking. It may be that the root metaphor of bureaucracy, and that of the entire modern episteme – that of the mechanical clockwork – is no longer an adequate model of how contemporary bureaucracies work and operate.

Bureaucracy and the metaphor of the biological organism: biophilosophical images of organization

> [A] century-old devotion to "conservative systems" (physical systems that, for all practical purposes, are isolated from their surroundings) is giving way to the realization that most systems in nature are subjects to flows of matter and energy that continuously move through them.
>
> (Manuel De Landa, 1992: 129)

> Life can be consciously comprehended only as an ongoing event, and not as Being *qua* a given.
>
> (Mikhail Bakhtin, 1993: 56)

> [A] lyric theme runs through Bergson's work: a veritable hymn in praise of the new, the unforeseeable, of invention, of liberty".
>
> (Gilles Deleuze 2004b: 30–31)

The literature on the use of metaphors in management writing is massive and therefore only a few samples from it are provided here (see, for example, Manning, 1979; Lackoff and Johnson, 1980; Morgan, 1980, 1986; Gergen 1992; Oswick *et al.*, 2002). Metaphor is a trope that "transports" – the etymological meaning of the Greek word – from its original meaning to something different. It thus draws on comparison or resemblance (Todorov, 1983: 71). Weick (1979: 49) writes: "A metaphor can often capture some of these distinctive, powerful, private realities that are tough to describe to someone else." For Czarniawska (1998: 7), "metaphor is a mode of substitution". Human cognition is, in many respects, strongly affected by the use of metaphors aimed at capturing what is ambiguous or multifaceted. It is complicated to think of a language completely devoid of metaphor.

The metaphor of the machinery is most widely used to capture the functioning of a bureaucracy. From an epistemological perspective, the machine is an unhappy choice of metaphor for denoting complex organizations because machinery is defined precisely in terms of its *inability* to change. Georges Canguilhem (1992) defines a machine as a man-made, artificial construction functioning by virtue of mechanical operations. The machine is also composed of parts and moveable mechanisms and, therefore, obeys strict, rational and economical rules: "The whole is rigorously the sum of the parts. The final effect depends on the ordering of causes" (Canguilhem, 1992: 56). Since machinery is, of necessity, determined by its components and, above all, by the relationships between them and their causes; there is no room for deviant cases, for "monstrosities". What is deemed teratological belongs to life because life does not adhere to the same principles as machinery (see Hacking, 1998). Canguilhem writes:

> Life is experience, meaning improvisation, acting as circumstances permit; life is tentative in every respect. Hence the overwhelming but often misunderstood fact that life permits monstrosities. There are no monstrous machines. ... Whereas monsters are still living things, there is no way to distinguish the normal and the pathological in physics and mechanics. Only among living beings is there a distinction between the normal and the pathological.
>
> (Canguilhem, 1992: 58)

Seen from this perspective, there is a disjunction between the narratives of the "dysfunctions" and "pathologies" of bureaucracy and the popular use of the machine metaphor in the same discourse. Either bureaucracy adheres to rational, economical rules or it is conceived of in biological or organic terms. In the following, the latter alternative will be examined.

One of the most widely used metaphors to capture social formations and social organization is the *organism*. In the dialogue *Republic,* Plato conceived of society as an organism susceptible to radical changes and, in conservative political thinking, this image has been embraced throughout the centuries. In this context, the metaphor of organism is not employed to side with such political conservatism. Rather than assuming that organisms are unable to respond to external changes, it is argued, quite on the contrary, that exactly such an ability to respond to changes is one of the distinguishing marks of a viable organism. Cummings and Thanem (2002) present a comprehensive critique of the organism metaphor in organization theory, claiming it represents a continuation of the mechanistic episteme dominating classic organization theory. Although Cummings and Thanem (2002) point to the connections between mechanistic models of organizations and biological models, they do not address process-based biological models. For instance, the vitalist biophilosophy of Henri Bergson has little to do with the functionalist images of organisms that Cummings and Thanem (2002) critically examine. In the following, the notion of the organism will be examined on the basis of the writing of Henri Bergson on becoming and change in organisms. Bergson's stance is fundamentally anti-Platonist because he does not make biological organisms a model for what is stable and predictable but, on the contrary, for what is continuously moving, changing and in a state of becoming (see also Schrödinger, 1946).

Bergson's philosophy of life

Bergson's thinking is often portrayed as once-fashionable but then it fell from grace and today is little attended to (Kolakowski, 1985; Riley, 2002). However, a number of books and papers testify to an awakened interest in Bergson's thinking (Mullarkey, 1999; Ansell Pearson, 2002; Lawlor, 2003; Linstead and Mullarkey, 2003). While this new concern for Bergson has initiated a variety of intellectual projects, in this setting we are primarily interested in Bergson's view of biological organisms as being capable of changing, yet maintaining its form. This philosophical position is called *vitalism*. "Vitalism seems to be," Chiari (1992: 245) writes, "above all, a reaction to eighteenth-century Cartesian dualism and materialism, from which the soul or psyche had been practically excluded." Vitalism is a philosophical tradition of thinking that seeks to apprehend what life is and how life can emerge in material matter (Teilhard de Chardin, 1959; Schwartz, 1992; Greco, 2005; Lash, 2006). Such questions were addressed in Bergson's work in new and creative ways. Around the turn of the twentieth century, biologists started to study "diachronic life processes" in emerging sub-disciplines such as embryology, genetics and evolutionary biology (De Issekutz Wolsky and Wolsky, 1992). The main impetus for the interest in vitalism was, of course, Charles Darwin's evolutionary biology formulated in his *Origin of Species* (first published in 1859). Darwin not only influenced biologists but also a range of other scientific disciplines. A physicist like Ludwig Boltzmann (1844–1906) (1974) was a great admirer of Darwin, and Erwin Schrödinger (1887–1961), a physicist of the generation succeeding Boltzmann's, addressed Darwinist implications for his work (Schrödinger, 1958). These scientific breakthroughs served as an impetus for Bergson's philosophy. Bergson called for a "vitalist biology" seeking the "the inward, invisible force of which the sensible forms [of living beings] are manifestations" (Bergson, 1975: 99). In *Creative Evolution*, perhaps Bergson's most well-known work and the book that started the wave of "Bergsonism" in the pre-First World War period that T.S. Elliot described as an "epidemic" (Burwick and Douglass, 1992: 3), the notion of *becoming*, for Bergson a principal ontological concept, is discussed on the basis of biological models and illustrations.

It is noteworthy that Bergson does not speak of biological organisms as metaphors but as the very foundation for the ontological and epistemological model he is advocating. A "theory of life," Bergson (1999: xiii) writes, and a "theory of knowledge seem inseparable." But Bergson's writing is also of relevance for "super-individual" organisms – "organizations" in Bergson's vocabulary[17] – such as human societies: "Whether human or animal, a society is an organization; it implies a co-ordination and generally also a subordination of elements; it therefore exhibits, whether merely embodied in life, or, in addition, specifically formulated, a collection or rules and laws" (Bergson, 1977: 27). When examining biological organisms, Bergson wanted to move beyond what Kant called the *Zweckmässigkeit* in organisms, its "goal-orientation" (Ansell Pearson, 2002: 122).[18] Instead, Bergson wanted to first develop a theory of organisms that is not based on teleology, finalism, and Aristotelian entelechism and hylemorphism, and, second, he aims to discuss life beyond its mere appearances. In a mechanical system, "all is *given*" Bergson (1998: 39) says. Bergson points at the continuous change of the human body or any other organism: "The truth is that we change without ceasing, and that the state itself is nothing but change" (Bergson, 1998: 2). In the book *Mind-Energy*, a collection of essays and lectures, Bergson says that *movement* is what defines life:

> Strictly speaking, there is no living being which appears completely incapable of spontaneous movement. Even in the vegetable world, where the organism is generally fixed to the soil, the faculty of movement is dormant rather than absent; it awakens when it can be of use.
>
> (Bergson, 1975: 14)

These "changes without ceasing" and "spontaneous movements" are not apprehended by mathematical calculation, Bergson (1998: 20) argues: "Organic *creation*, on the contrary, the evolutionary phenomenon which properly constitutes life, we cannot in any way subject to mathematical treatment." This is part of Bergson's "theory of knowledge": intellectual thinking is incapable of understanding change, and since life and biological organisms *are* change, intellect is incapable of understanding processes of becoming, that is, *life*. Life is, for Bergson, the coming together of consciousness and matter:

> Consciousness and matter appear to us … as radically different forms of existence, even as antagonistic forms, which have to find a *modus vivendi*. Matter is necessity, consciousness is freedom; but though diametrically opposed to another, life has found the way of reconciling them. This is precisely what life is – freedom inserting itself within necessity, turning it to its profit. Life would be an impossibility were the determination of matter so absolute as to admit no relaxation.
>
> (Bergson, 1975: 17–18)

Life, resting in duration and based on what Bergson calls *élan vital*, a "force of life" or "vitalist force", is continuous, creative and fluid. Erwin Schrödinger, who emphasized the association between evolution and consciousness, expresses a similar idea:

> In brief, consciousness is a phenomenon in the zone of evolution. This word lights up to itself only where or only inasmuch as it develops, procreates new forms. Places of stagnancy slip from consciousness; they may only appear in their interplay with places of evolution.
>
> (Schrödinger, 1958: 12)

Chiari speaks of *élan vital* as "the dynamic energy" of the living:

The *élan vital* is creative freedom, in the image of God, not confined to the biosphere which is itself connected, like everything else in our world, with the immanent duration of the universe. It is the dynamic energy which guides the evolution of the living; it is a concept born from a reflection based upon science and fused with a philosophical intuition which blends philosophy and science and thus matter and spirit. Bergson respects science and even goes as far as looking upon life as a kind of mechanism, but the question, for him, is to know whether the natural system which we call living beings could be equated with the artificial systems which science composes with matter, or whether it ought not to be assimilated to the natural system which is universe.

(Chiari, 1992: 253)

Bergson equates life with becoming:

[L]*ife is like a current passing from germ through the medium of a developed organism.* ... The essential things is the continuous progress indefinitely pursued, an inevitable progress, on which each visible organism rides through the short interval of time given it to live.

(1998: 27, emphasis in the original)

In addition, Bergson is sceptical of the concept of *individuality*; for him, the *élan vital* precedes any individuality. Ingold (1986: 107) argues:

Bergson, for his part, rejected the idea of absolute individuality in the organic world. "The living being," he argued, "is above all a thoroughfare", along which all the impulsion of life is transmitted. And as each individual, like a relay runner, takes up this impulsion and passes it on, as each generation must lean over and touch the next, so how can we tell exactly where one individual begins and another ends?

In this sense, Ingold (1986) argues, the individual *is* the past, an embodiment of the continuous unfolding or directed flow of creative time. It is, then, no longer possible to ascribe absolute boundaries between individuals qua biological organisms, i.e. "the bearers of life" (Ingold, 1986: 107; see also Ansell Pearson, 1997: 125, 142). The feminist philosopher, Rosi Braidotti (2006: 217), advocating a non-unitary nomadic subjectivity, expresses sympathy for such post-humanist ideas: "This is just one life, not *my* life. The life in 'me' does not answer my name: 'I' is just transient." The essence of life is not to be found in individual particles but in the totality of the *élan vital*. Contrary to the individuality so central to Darwinism and the theory of variation under natural selection, Bergson's philosophy envisages the world as "an undivided flux" – "more like a continuous elastic membrane than a vast collection of particles" (Ingold, 1986: 133). Chiari points to the coming together of material and conscious life in Bergson's organism:

Life for him is not simply biological life, but also psychic and psychological life conceived as becoming and creativeness. Duration is the consciousness of this becoming or, rather, the invasion by becoming of the subject's consciousness; duration is, in fact, pure, direct introspection of this becoming. It is an unmediated intuition of being as becoming, and this becoming naturally has a causality which entails its finality. This finality is not fixed by any external force; it pertains to life itself which evolves, not according to an already fixed pattern or plan, but according to the laws of the elements which compose it and which have, from the smallest particles to macrocells, their respective causalities, connecting one with the other so as to achieve the complexity of organisms. The end of life is to be life, and life itself is not concerned with knowing its own end, but only with being and becoming, without any possible end. If man is, for Bergson, the finality of the universe, this finality is inscribed in evolution itself, but it is neither imposed from the outside nor predetermined: it is part of creation itself, whose finality seems to be its spiritualization.

(Chiari, 1992: 253)

Recent insight into the genotype[19] the of biological organisms (that Bergson of course knew little of) suggest that, while the genome – the possible combinations of genes – is a stable entity, proteins, the molecules made from a long sequence of smaller subunits called amino acids (Jones, 2004: 107), playing a central role for the biological organism, are constantly changing through the biochemical interaction with the genome and the environment. As a consequence, a comprehensive analysis of proteins and their functioning – what is called *proteomics* – is a very complicated scientific challenge because of the continuous change of the proteins.[20] Therefore, Bergson's thinking is still valuable when understanding how biological and biochemical models are constructed (De Issekutz Wolsky and Wolsky, 1992); he presents a model of the organism that radically puts into question a number of assumptions regarding forms of knowledge and doctrines of teleology and finalism. While it is rarely Bergson's theory of the organism per se that is emphasized outside of what Ansell Pearson (1999) calls "biophilosophy", in this case this model of biological organisms captures the qualities we are interested in when defending the bureaucratic organization form. However, there are other schools of thinking that have demonstrated an interest in Bergson's work on evolution.

Bergson's followers

Bergson's contemporary, Alfred North Whitehead, is the other great process philosopher of the twentieth century in addition to Bergson. For Whitehead (1978), influenced by Bergson (Kolakowski, 1985: 45), the world needs to be examined as being in a state of becoming and what we refer to as entities, e.g. elementary particles, such as electrons in physics research, are therefore to be conceived of as *events*: "An event is a nexus of actual occasions inter-related in some determinate fashion in some extensive quantum: it is either a nexus in its formal completeness, or it is an objectified nexus. . . . For example, a molecule is a historic route of actual occasions; and such a route is an 'event'" (Whitehead, 1978: 80). Pedraja (2002: 83–84) explains the idea thus:

> [R]eality is a fluid interplay of relations between concrete actualities and infinite possibilities. As a result of its dynamic and interrelated nature, reality cannot be limited to any given or static or fixed concept without reducing its fluid nature to a rigid abstraction.

While Whitehead continued Bergson's work on process metaphysics, an ontology of becoming, other theoretical discourses have shown interest in Bergson's work on biology. Feminist philosophers such as Elizabeth Grosz (2001, 2004) have demonstrated a detailed interest in Bergson's thinking. Since Bergson conceives of biological organisms in terms of becoming, the notion of difference so central to post-structuralist feminist thinking and especially in the writings of Luce Irigaray, is examined through Bergson's philosophy. Grosz (2004) examines texts of Darwin, Nietzsche and Bergson to identify alternative ontologies and epistemologies that can support a feminist mode of thinking affirmative to difference. Grosz (2004: 3) writes:

> [W]e need to understand the body, not as an organism or entity in itself, but as a system, or a series of open-ended systems, functioning within other huge systems it cannot control, through which it can access and acquire its abilities and capacities.

The human body, or any biological organism, is, for Grosz, not self-enclosed and unified once and for all; instead, bodies are open systems or a "series of open-ended systems". In addition, such bodies are never wholly stable but are always operating under the influence of what Bergson calls "duration", being within a temporal horizon. Grosz argues:

> States, especially psychical states and processes, cannot be understood as distinct, more as fugitive emanations, as processes, than as atoms or units. States merge one into the other, with no clear-cut separation between one and the other; their translation is indiscernible. If we artificially arrest this indiscernible transition, we can understand states as separate entities, linked by succession, but we lose whatever it is that flows in change, we lose duration itself.
>
> (Grosz, 2004: 195)

Grosz thus emphasizes the Bergsonian theme of becoming by rejecting the simple location of states as discrete and separated bodies. Instead, what we refer to as states are always processes of continuous change and movement, in many cases complicated to detect and identify, and only eventually observable. For

Grosz (2004), Bergsons's thinking of the biological organism as inherently becoming without submitting to any finalist or teleological doctrine is important because it assumes that difference (difference between sexes, races, etc.) cannot be pre-determined and predicted. Becoming, then, is always open-ended and therefore undermines any essentialist assumptions. Grosz (2004: 261) writes:

> The most radical and deeply directed projects of feminist, queer, antiracist, and postcolonial struggles involve a welcoming of the unsettling of previous categories, identities, and strategies, challenging the limits of present divisions and conjunctions, and reveling in the uncontainability and unpredictability of the future.

Bergson's thinking is therefore a radical theory of difference, of *differentiation*. Judith Butler (1993) advocates another feminist material theory of the biological organism and, more specifically, the human body. Although Butler (1993) does not rely on Bergson – he is only referenced in one single footnote – she is speaking of the human body in material and fluid terms: "[a] process of materialization that stabilizes over time to produce the effects of boundary, fixity, and surface we call matter" (Butler, 1993: 9, original emphasis removed). From this perspective, bodies are never fixed but are made up of material resources and the symbolism humans inscribe into such materiality. Feminist thinking, then, has paid attention to process philosophies such as that of Bergson and Deleuze, as in the case of Elizabeth Grosz, and Foucault, in Judith Butler's writing.

Bergson's thinking has been recognized in various disciplines. De Landa (2002) cites the Physics Nobel Prize winner, Ilya Prigogine, to support a process-based view similar to that of Grosz (2004):

> [A]s Henri Bergson and others emphasized, everything is given in classical physics: change is nothing but the denial of becoming and time is only a parameter unaffected by the transformation that it describes. The image of a stable world, a world that escapes the process of becoming, has remained until now the very ideal of theoretical physics. ... Today, we know that Newtonian dynamics describes only part of our physical experience.
> (Nicolis and Prigogine, 1989: 52, cited in De Landa, 2002: 83)

Physical and biological bodies are then no longer exactly cut off from movements and changes but, rather, are to be examined within such an ontological and epistemological model affirmative of becoming and fluidity. William James, the great American pragmatist philosopher, and one of Bergson's earliest followers, says that "what really *exists* is not things but things in the making" (James, 1996: 263). What is of particular interest here is the notion of the biological organism so central to Bergson's *Creative Evolution*. Gilles Deleuze, perhaps Bergson most outstanding follower in contemporary philosophy, speaks of Bergson's biological models in terms of *actualization* and *virtuality*. Here, the life of biological organisms denotes the continuous movement and actualization of the organisms; organisms differentiate, evolve and become in an ongoing series of transformations and changes. Deleuze writes:

> Life as *movement* alienates itself in the material *form* that it creates; by actualizing itself, by differentiating itself, it loses "contact with the rest of itself". Every species is thus an arrest of movement; it could be said that the living being turns on itself and *closes itself.*
>
> (1988: 104)

For Bergson, a biological organism is without doubt to be examined as a form of *organization*, a systemic entity dominated and regulated by specific rules and mechanisms. In addition, such an organization is never operating under Aristotelian laws of entelechism and hylemorphism (Aristotle, 1998a, b) wherein any biological organism carries within its own potentiality, its own specific possible trajectories and potential modes of development. On the contrary, Bergson strongly resists any form of finalism and insists on seeing biological organisms as following fundamentally open-ended and indeterminate paths. Therefore, biological organisms are by no means predetermined to become what it is intrinsically programmed at the becoming but are, instead, the effects of both internal dispositions and external conditions.

The problem of individuation: the concept of transduction

A final example of biophilosophical thinking is the philosophy of Gilbert Simondon (1924–1989), a French philosopher and a student of Georges Canguilhem and Maurice Merleau-Ponty. Although Simondon's work, published in the 1950s and 1960s, has been recognized as seminal contributions to Continental philosophy and served as an important influence in, for instance, Deleuze and Guattari's discussion of what they refer to as *machinic phylums* in *A Thousand Plateaus* (1988),[21] very little of his work has unfortunately been translated into English. Therefore the overview is restricted to one single text and a comprehensive introduction by Adrian Mackenzie (2002). Simondon formulates a critique of Aristotelian hylemorphism that shares a number of similarities with Bergson's biophilosophy (see also Stiegler, 1997: 67ff; Lecourt, 1998; Deleuze, 2004a). Simondon examines the notion of *individuation* as the process wherein the individual is constituted qua "individual". Rather than subscribing to a "hylemorphic scheme" (Simondon, 1992: 316), using the static notion of *form*, Simondon seeks to outline a more dynamic process of individuation taking into account the becoming of the individual. For Simondon, a living system is a "system of individuation" but also a "system that individuates itself" (Simondon, 1992: 305); there is a dynamic relationship between the constituted entity (i.e. individual) and the constituting process. Simondon explains:

> The living entity is both the agent and the theater of individuation: its becoming represents a permanent individuation or rather *a series of*

approaches to individuation progressing from one state of metastability to another. The individual is thus no longer either a substance or a simple part of the collectivity. The collective unit provides the resolution of the individual problematic, which means that the basis of the collective reality already forms a part of the individual in the form of the preindividual reality, which remains associated with the individual reality.

(1992: 307)

When a system individuates itself, it becomes "metastable". Metastability is different from "stable equilibrium and rest" because it takes into account the potential energy of the system, the notion of order and the increase in entropy. Simondon (1992) is here speaking of *ontogenesis* (i.e. how something is *coming to be*) rather than *ontology* (i.e. how something *is*) and is thus interested in what is the very process of constitution. Simondon uses the term *transduction* to denote the entire process of individuation into a metastable unity. Transduction thus means any process, "physical, biological, mental or social" (Simondon, 1992: 313), in which metastability emerges (see also Mackenzie, 2002: 15–16). The concept of transduction is used in a range of scientific disciplines to denote various processes of change in form or matter. For instance, in molecular biology, transduction denotes a specific event in which a virus carries new genetic material over into the DNA of bacteria (Mackenzie, 2002: 17). In biophysics, transduction denotes the process where one form of energy (e.g. electric energy) of the so-called *donor* is transformed into another class of energy (e.g. chemical energy) in the *receptor*. Transduction thus captures the transformation of one form into another. Transduction is therefore a concept emphasizing the radical openness and emergence of any entity. Simondon writes that individuation must be understood as a *recursive* process between the individuated (the agent) and what individuates (the structure):

A being does not possess a unity in its identity, which is that of the stable state within which no transformation is possible; rather, a being has a *transductive unity*, that is, it can pass out of phase with itself, it can – in any area – break its own bounds in relation to its center. What one assumes to be a *relation* or a *duality of principles* is in fact the unfolding of the being, which is more than a unity and more than an identity; becoming is a dimension of the being, not something that happens to it following a succession of events that affects a being already and originally given and substantial. . . . *Instead of grasping individuation using the individuated being as a starting point, we must grasp the individuated being from the viewpoint of individuation, and individuation from the viewpoint of preindividual being*, each operating at many different orders of magnitude.

(Simondon, 1992: 311, emphasis in the original)

He continues:

Transduction corresponds to the presence of those relations created when the preindividual being becomes individuated. It expresses individuation and allows us to understand its workings, showing that it is at once a metaphysical and also a logical notion. *While it may be applied to ontogenesis, it is also ontogenesis itself.*

(Simondon, 1992: 314, emphasis in the original)

Simondon similarly speaks of the "unfolding of the being" (1992: 311) as the process in which the entity or individual is "individuating":

The transductive process is thus an individuation in progress. Physically, it might be said to occur at its simplest in the forms of progressive iteration. ... Transduction occurs when there is activity, both structural and functional, which begins at a center of the being and extends itself in various directions from this center, as if multiple dimensions of being were expanding around the central point.

(Simondon, 1992: 313)

For instance, to use a trivial example, an individual is not simply inscribed with qualities, potentialities and shortcomings but actively makes use of resources, be they material, emotional, social or cultural, to influence or alter the view of the individual. For instance, a person may develop interests and habits to actively promote one's own social life or to "make oneself more interesting". The *transductive unity* (Simondon, 1992: 311) accomplished, however, is only metastable since the ontogenesis of the individual is always a matter of ceaseless becoming. For instance, when humans are ageing they tend to take on different identities and subscribe to different beliefs than, say, children or teenagers – they gradually change in the process of individuating. Another example is provided by Sherry Turkle's (1996) analysis of how Internet users create new personas and identities when collaborating with the new information and communication technology. In Turkle's study, the metastable transductive unity produced is an assemblage comprising humans and technologies; single humans may use multiple identities that, in themselves are transient and contextualized.

Simondon's notion of transduction is equally applicable to biological organisms and social organizations. Mackenzie (2002: 17) argues:

Life is transductive too, but involves temporal and topological complications. The living encounters information understood strictly as the unpredictability of forms and signals, as a problem. It resolves the problem through constant temporal and spatial restructuring of itself and its milieus. It develops and adapts, it remembers and anticipates.

The concept of transduction thus offers a concept that grasps how living and non-living processes differentiate and develop without presuming underlying substances or identity. Moreover, transductive unity is achieved through the combination of "physical, technical and affective realities" (Mackenzie, 2002: 35). Transduction is potentially useful in organization analysis because it focuses on the folding of different forces and elements together in the individuating of individuals, collectives and entities.

Similar to Bergson's thinking, Simondon (1992) and Mackenzie (2002) say that a living organism is capable of changing its innate structure to respond to external changes. There are never any fixed positions but equilibria are always transient and temporal; metastability is achieved in transductive processes where organism and environment are mutually adapting and interchanging. Mackenzie concludes:

> A transductive approach promises a more nuanced grasp of how living and non-living processes differentiate and develop. It understands the emergence of a mode of unity without presuming underlying substances or identity. Every transduction is an individuation in process. It is a way something comes to be, an ontogenesis.
>
> (2002: 18)

Mackenzie's development of Gilbert Simondon's thinking is a contemporary example of a critique of the Aristotelian tradition of entelechism and hylemorphisms, locating the possible trajectories of the living inside the organism. Such a self-enclosed view is subject to critical analysis and is displaced by more open-ended and vitalist views of the organism. Needless to say, the Aristotelian notion of potentiality in his entelechist thinking is today a viable tradition of thought in times where the human genome mapping programme has been successfully completed and various forms of genetics are regarded as the backbone for a variety of social, technological and scientific practices (see, for example, Rabinow, 1999). The human genome mapping project is based on the idea – to paraphrase Galileo's *Il Saggiatore* – that the book of nature is written in the genetic code. Simondon's (1992) contribution is therefore not uncontroversial in terms of locating the living in a network of interactions and resources rather than conceiving of qualities and potentialities as an innate matter of the organism.

Altogether, Bergson's model of the biological organism is dynamic because it points at the systematic organization without making such a system of mechanisms and processes deterministic. When using Bergson's writing on biological systems, one moves beyond the narrow Platonist image of the biological organism as essentially incapable of dealing with change. Instead, the Bergsonian image of the biological organism points to the two-fold nature of the organism as both residing in its own specific form, yet being capable of anticipating, recognizing and responding to external changes. Studies of biology qua laboratory or experimental practice (e.g. Lynch, 1985; Fujimura, 1995; Keller, 2002) support the idea that what constitutes life is by no means uncontested and once and for all agreed upon. Instead, a great deal of controversy and debate regarding the ultimate matter of life prevails. Therefore, Bergson's thinking is not only of interest in terms of his "theory of knowledge" but also in terms of the view of the organism.

Biological metaphors and models of recursivity in organization theory

Examples of how the biological organism serves as a metaphor for social organizations include Burns and Stalker's (1961) classic study of innovation in British industrial firms, introducing the very important distinction between *organic* and *mechanic* structures of firms, a dichotomy that Émile Durkheim (1933) used in his foundational sociological work on the division of labour in society. Another example is Karin Knorr Cetina's (1995) work on the community or field of High-Energy Physicists (HEP) as what she calls "a superorganism": "[H]EP collaborations can be considered as *movable, semi-detached corporations* located somewhere between the social movement and an organization in the vocabulary of social categories, but identical with neither" (Knorr Cetina, 1995: 123). HEP do not make up a complete society, neither do they constitute a social movement. They are instead operating under conditions similar to, Knorr Cetina argues, those of termites or ants; they contribute to the maintenance of a community and a field without being able to oversee the whole field. Instead, a number of generic practices and choices are guiding physicists throughout the world in working on a variety of legitimate physicist research questions. Another example of how the metaphor of organisms is invoked in social sciences, and especially in organization theory, is Nelson and Winter's (1982) evolutionary theory of economics (see also Aldrich, 1999). In Nelson and Winter's model, routines play a role in organizations similar to that of genes in a biological organism. Nelson and Winter (1982: 14) explain:

> In our evolutionary theory, these routines play the role that genes play in biological evolutionary theory. They are a persistent feature of the organism and determine its possible behavior (though *actual* behavior is determined also by the environment); they are heritable in the sense that tomorrow's organisms generated from today's (for example, building a new plant) have many of the same characteristics, and they are selectable in the sense that organisms with certain routines may do better than others, and, if so, their relative importance in the population (industry) is augmented over time.

Hannan and Freeman (1989) advocate a *population ecology* view of how organizations emerge, develop and eventually disappear or merge with other organizations or maintain their form. Population ecology represents – contrary to, for instance, Nelson and Winter's (1982) evolutionary theory – a holistic view and examines organizations on an aggregated level as industries, clusters or industrial regions. Hannan and Freeman (1989: 331) say that the population ecology of organizations is (1) "shifting the focus to the population level", (2) "moving from a static to a dynamic approach", (3) "recognizing the strong limits on the speed with which existing organizations can adapt to rapidly changing environments" and, finally, (4) "examining change in diverse but internally homogeneous organization populations over their full histories".

Another influential use of biological organisms in social theory can be seen in the biologists Huberto Maturana and Francisco Varela's (1980) notion of autopoetic systems, a central and indispensable influence in Niklas Luhmann's sociology. For Maturana and Varela, learning and self-consciousness are two central features of a viable biological organism: "Learning as a process consists in the transformation through experience of the behavior of an organism in a manner that is directly or indirectly subservient to the maintenance of its basic circularity" (1980: 35). They continue: "Man is a deterministic and relativistic self-referring autonomous system where life acquires its peculiar dimension through self-consciousness" (1980: 57). Luhmann's autopoetic model of social systems has attained some interest in organization theory recently (Seidl, 2003; Nassehi, 2005). Hernes and Bakken (2003) speak of Luhmann's theory of social systems as a recursivity-based theory wherein social systems are emergent and reproduce themselves through a continual interaction between the environment and the system. Here, the system is both constituted and constituting, that is, it is the social system that affects, say, human action, while simultaneously the social system is the outcome from such human actions. There is then no proper "beginning" of the social system or human action but they are, instead, reproducing and reconstituting themselves recursively (see also Barley and Tolbert, 1997). Schatzki (2002: 209) explains his version of recursivity:

> [I]t makes sense to say that an agent is both an arrangement and an effect thereof. An actor is its compositional network because anything is that which it is composed. An agent is also an effect of its compositional arrangements because its capacity to act as a single entity depends on the co-operation of its components.

Orlikowski (2000) provides a fine illustration of the idea in her analysis of technology. Technology, for Orlikowski (2000), is never a "matter-of-fact", a unified and finished exogenously given entity that humans uncomplicatedly relate to. Instead, humans in the very use of the technology continuously shape technology. Still, it is the technology that initially enables action; technology, then, is simultaneously constituted by and constituting human actions. Orlikowski writes:

> Structures of technology use of constituted recursively as human regularly interact with certain properties of a technology and thus shape the set of rules and resources that serve to shape their interactions. Seen through a practice lens, technology structures are emergent, not embodied.
>
> (2000: 407)

She continues:

> Technologies are ... never fully stabilized or "complete", even though we
> may choose to treat them as fixed, black boxes for a period of time. By tem-
> porarily bracketing the dynamic nature of technology, we assign a "stabi-
> lized for now" status ... to our technological artefacts.
> (Orlikowski, 2000: 411; see also Barley, 1986, 1990; Law, 2002: 2–3)

As a consequence, technology is never once and for all fixed but, instead, is
"temporally and contextually provisional" and implies that there are always
possibilities for contingent uses of technology. In Barley's (1986: 81) formulation: "[S]ince technologies exist as objects in the realm of action, one cannot
hope to understand a technology's implications for structuring without investigating how the technology is incorporated into the everyday life of an organization's members." In Orlikowski's (2000) account, technology is a socially
embedded and contingent resource that takes a more fluid and flexible shape
than the regular view of technology as something more or less fixed. For Hernes
and Bakken (2003), all organization evolves as recursive systems where action
and structure are closely entangled, yet separated.

Another concept that draws on a biological metaphor and a model of recursivity is what Drazin and Sandelands (1992) call "autogenesis", a self-organizing model similar to that of the recursive organization model. Drazin and
Sandelands (1992: 230) distinguished between *exogenesis*, a set of factors
derived from the environment that affects the organization structure, and *endogenesis,* change that derives from within the organization. Drazin and Sandelands suggest that the notion of *autogenesis* bridges the two complementary
perspectives and say that, "within an autogenesis perspective, organization
occurs through the self-organizing capacities of individuals interacting in a
social field" (1992: 231). Drazin and Sandelands (1992) list a number of theoretical developments that, they claim, are aligned with the autogenesis model of
organization; for instance, Ilya Prigogine's theory of *dissipative structures*. Furthermore, rules play a central role in bridging the exogenesis and endogenesis
perspectives. They therefore share with Luhmannian organization analysts such
as Hernes and Bakken (2003) the view that organization is essentially a self-
organizing process embedded in the interaction between structure and agent;
organizations are recursively constituted and therefore the long-standing
emphasis on separating outside and inside of organization becomes of less
central importance. It is simply a dichotomy that is losing its analytical value in
a recursivity-based perspective on organization.

In summary, the notions of the biological organism and vitalism are of central
importance for Henri Bergson's thinking because they are primary examples of
a process-based developmental model. As opposed to many conservative images
of organisms as being incapable of changing and, therefore, in need of protection – for instance, patriarchal thinking conceiving of women as more frail
beings than men and therefore in need of protection and exclusion from everyday society – an organism is here regarded as (1) a particular form of organization structured in accordance with specific mechanisms and rules, (2) yet

capable of responding to external and intrinsic changes and modifications. In terms of metaphor, this model of organization is capable of providing meaning and is also useful because it is rooted in immediately observable processes such as bodily growth and maturation. As all parents learn to know from observing their children, life is a continual movement at various speeds; at times quick and momentary, at other occasions slow and gradual. Nevertheless, all forms of organism demonstrate different degrees of adaptability and adjustment. Those are the qualities that, in the next section, bureaucracies are claimed to be capable of following.

Bureaucracies as adapting systems

The benefit of the biological metaphor is that life is, at least in the Bergsonian tradition of thinking, what is intrinsically capable of changing – that is, being in a state of becoming, yet obeying to a functionalist structure similar to that of a social formation such as an organization. Biological organisms are always already in a state of changing, both in terms of separate individuals and as a population, or even a population in relation to other individuals. It is little wonder, then, that a variety of philosophers and political thinkers have compared society with an organism. In many cases this metaphor has been invoked to point at the fragile nature of society, its naked dependence on external conditions for living and the access to a number of physical needs, such as food or water. In the use of the metaphor of the biological organism here, it is not such weaknesses that are emphasized but, on the contrary, the strength and viability of biological organisms, their ability to evolve and mutate under different conditions and to withstand extraordinary conditions, are emphasized. Seen in this perspective, essentially a Bergsonian one, life is capable of surviving the most strenuous of conditions and harshest treatments. In addition, there is no teleology or finalism in the biological model; life goes on and in such movements changes are always implied. Living is time and time per se is creation and change, a movement from virtuality to actuality, from *what will be* to *what is*. Speaking of organizations in terms of being organisms is, then, by no means a conservative and conserving metaphor in the tradition of Edmund Burke and other conservative political thinkers but is, on the contrary, praise for organizations' capabilities to differentiate in the course of action.

In terms of bureaucracy studies, one of the oldest themes in organization theory, the biological metaphor of the organism implies that there is no clear-cut and determinate line of demarcation between bureaucracy and post-bureaucracy qua practical arrangement. The post-bureaucratic form is what departs from bureaucracy, that takes some bits and pieces and introduces some new practices and operations. On the contrary, the bureaucratic form is never wholly "bureaucratic", as in the lexical definition, but is, instead, always demonstrating some of the skills and capacities of the post-bureaucratic organization. In the two companies studied in Chapters 4 and 5, there was little evidence of a loss of horizontal and informal communication and other virtues of the post-bureaucratic form.

Instead, the bureaucratic framework contained many organic organization arrangements that made the functional orientation run smoother.

Routines and adaptation

One of the key mechanisms in all bureaucratic organizations is the formulation and adherence to rule-governed routines. In analogy with the biological organism metaphor informed by Bergson's vitalist philosophy, routines have been examined as semi-fixed scripts that are continuously adapted to external conditions. In a series of papers, Martha Feldman and her collaborators (Feldman, 2000; Feldman and Rafaeli, 2002; Feldman and Pentland, 2003, 2005) have explored the dynamics inherent to routines. Rather than being inflexible standard operation procedures, routines are here the "grammars of action" (Pentland and Rueter, 1994) from which the skilful and knowledgeable co-worker can form individual practices. Feldman and Pentland write:

> We define organizational routines as repetitive, recognizable patterns of interdependent actions, carried out by multiple actors. We claim that organizational routines combine an ostensive aspect, the ideal or schematic form of a routine and a performative aspect, specific actions by specific people in specific places and times. Any particular routine within an organization can be analysed in terms of these parts and the interactions between them.
>
> (2005: 96)

Routines are always double-sided; they are anchored in ostensive definitions (Wittgenstein, 1953) showing how to perform a particular activity or operation and they are manifested as actual performances. Practice therefore emerges as that which circles around formal descriptions, yet is never fully accomplished qua ideal-typical activities. Elsewhere, Feldman and Rafaeli (2002) define routines in terms of being "recurring patterns of behaviour of multiple organizational members involved in informing organizational tasks" (2002: 311, original in italics). Here routines are again portrayed as based on repetition of patterns of actions. "As routines exist as multiple levels ... they are both stable and adaptable at the same time" (Feldman and Rafaeli, 2002: 325). In Feldman *et al.*'s view of routines, organizations are constituted not by fixed and immutable activities, but, instead, are dependent on the ability of the organizational members to understand, perform and adapt routine-based activities to changing conditions. Routines are always possible to negotiate in the face of uncertainty or newly emerging conditions; they are the grammars of action that make organizations flexible and adaptable (see Young, 1999). The strict and insensitive adherence to routines and rules, and the inability to understand routines in their context, are standard critiques of bureaucratic practice. Feldman *et al.*'s work shows that routines are not inherently in opposition to flexibility and the ability to adapt. Quite the contrary, routines are the scripts providing immense opportunities for skilful performances (Callon, 2002). Studies of routine work, for instance Leidner's (1993) study of fast food restaurant work or Paules' (1991) study of waitresses' work in a New Jersey diner, suggest that routines do not pose a threat to mindful work but, in fact, provide an agreed-upon and shared ground on which standard operation procedures can be carried out.

Speaking in terms of the metaphor of the biological organism maintaining its forms, yet continuously changing and adapting to external conditions, routines are by no means the smallest components in a mechanical system. Instead, it may be fruitful to conceive of routines as formal or informal scripts that enable a variety of individual performances. In the actual work situation, standard operations can be modified through sensitive adaptation to external changes and what Weick and Roberts (1996) call *heedful interaction* between individuals. For instance, a restaurant cook has to be trained in, and capable of responding to, the customers' preferences, as reported by the waiter or waitress (Fine, 1996). Scripts and action are therefore closely entangled, but they never fully intersect; the map and the territory remain separated. Seeing organizations in such terms, as simultaneously changing and maintaining their form, helps students of organizations to move beyond the mechanical metaphors that have been intimately associated with bureaucracy. Being affirmative to the increased fluidity of contemporary social life in terms of flows and exchanges of information and resources, while being capable of appreciating bureaucratic virtues such as specialization and standardized operations, makes us see bureaucracies in new perspectives. Rather than continuing the longstanding tradition of what Du Gay (2005) calls "anti-bureaucratic thinking", one may seek new ways of examining bureaucracy. Similarly to Feldman *et al.*'s re-conceptualization of routines, alternative and more positive accounts of bureaucracy may be helpful in the re-evaluation of the most widely criticized organization form.

Theoretical implications and research questions

Bureaucracy and supplementarity

The overarching theoretical perspective of this book has been that bureaucracy serves as a supplement to other forms of organization in much management writing. Speaking in terms of bureaucracy, this specific organization form is, in Derrida's analysis, playing a role similar to that of writing vis-à-vis speech. Bureaucracy is never introduced as a full and legitimate counterpart to other organization forms but is, instead, only a negative image with which the good features of the new organization form may be compared: network organization/ bureaucracy, virtual organization/bureaucracy, project organization/bureaucracy, and so forth; in all these cases, bureaucracy is brought into discussion as an example of an organization form that fails to demonstrate a variety of qualities and characteristics that these new images of organizations are claimed to embody. In terms of theoretical contribution, this study has pointed to the importance of critically reflecting upon the underlying assumptions guiding and structuring a field of research, that is, the *doxa* of a particular field. For instance, in Ferguson's (1984) substantial feminist critique of bureaucracy, it is bureaucracy per se, its structure and modes of functioning, that is portrayed as oppressing the workforce: Bureaucracy has, we recall, "a tremendous capacity to hurt people, to manipulate, twist and damage human possibility" (Ferguson, 1984: xii). Ferguson's critique is in parity with the darkest and most depressive texts of, say, Theodor Adorno, and sides with Michel Crozier's (1964) massively pessimistic account of the potentials of bureaucracy. Needless to say, Ferguson's text effectively undermines the image of bureaucracy as being capable of providing any social benefits. However, Ferguson does say very little about the supplementary role of the bureaucracy, that it is generally located in the same position as women, additional to and less valued than other organization forms, that it is always already judged and rejected beforehand, that it never gets a fair and just evaluation. In fact, somewhat paradoxically, Ferguson joins hands with a number of market enthusiasts (see Frank, 2000) in persistently claiming that hierarchies are, of necessity, less efficient than hierarchies. Ferguson's feminist thinking, then, reinforces the supplementary role of bureaucracy and fails to point to some of its obvious merits, concealed by its taken-for-granted qualities.

Bureaucracy needs to be examined on the level of *doxa*, on the level of ideology. As Althusser (1984: 49) points out, "Ideology never says: 'I am ideological'." Ideology is, by definition, inaccessible for common sense thinking; a "sublime object" (Žižek, 1989) outside of representation, belonging to, Žižek says, what Jacques Lacan calls the Real, that which is not capable of being represented by language or symbols (Roberts, 2005: 621). "[I]deology is the system of the ideas and representations which dominate the mind of a man or a social group" (Althusser, 1984: 32). *Doxa* is the ideology of a particular field. Being able to step outside what is taken for granted is a good starting point for bureaucracy studies in the new millennium. Conceiving of bureaucracy as a supplement suggests an ability to move outside of the present world order. The seminal bureaucracy studies of the 1950s and 1960s, the "direct studies" of Gouldner (1954) and Blau (1963) and the "indirect studies" of bureaucracy of Whyte (1956) and Mills (1951), did not assume offhand that bureaucracy was either this or that; they were fundamentally empirical in their orientation. According to Hans-Georg Gadamer (1975), history is irreversible in terms of "the principle of the history of effects" (*Wirkungsgeschichte*); all (literary) works are examined in the course of history, and later readers are more or less exposed to such initial treatments of the work that imposes certain preconceived ideas about it. Therefore, when reading Gouldner (1954), Blau (1963), Whyte (1956) and Mills (1951) today, one is aware of how their works have been examined and regarded through the decades since their publication. One can thus never give bureaucracy studies a "new fresh start" but must always operate within a field of intertextuality emerging from Max Weber's original writings. Nevertheless, research on bureaucracy may attempt at overcoming the *doxa* of bureaucracy supplementarity and examine the various positive and negative effects of a bureaucratic organization form.

Valuing bureaucracy on basis of performance

Those few who actually take the time to defend bureaucracy against its detractors (e.g. Sennett, 1998; Du Gay, 2000b) raise a number of issues and concerns regarding the work-life in contemporary society. However, somewhat paradoxically, they say rather little about bureaucracy per se. Just like writers criticizing bureaucracy because its is claimed to fail to perform certain activities that other organization forms are supposedly capable of, the defenders of bureaucracy are equally convinced that bureaucracy is the answer to a set of problems and challenges. Janning (2005) describes Sennett (1998) as a "utopist" who hopes for a world that will never come and that has never been. Critical theorists, such as Weber and Marx and their followers, have always emphasized work-life as being at least partially based on struggles between groups. In a Marxist understanding, it is the access to and control over capital that are the determining factors for social organization. For Weber, it is other factors, such as religious orientation or professional training, that underpin antagonist relations. More contemporary social scientists such as Pierre Bourdieu, at times regarded as a follower of Durkheim (1938) in terms of conceiving of social conditions as "social facts", point to the struggle over meaning and influence in a variety of fields (see, for example, Bourdieu, 1977, 1990). In all of these theoretical perspectives, there is no social life devoid of struggle and controversy. Therefore, portraying bureaucracy as some kind of safe haven, a place to retreat from the turmoil and clamour of the contemporary capitalist economic system, only helps to reinforce the supplementary role of bureaucracy.

Speaking in terms of bureaucracy, one should not succumb to utopian thinking and assume that the movement back to a society populated by "organization men", in the vein of Mills' (1951) and Whyte's (1956) studies, would make contemporary society a better place. Instead, one needs to examine and evaluate all social benefits and costs of the bureaucratic organization forms. Therefore, even though the emphasis on the social and human costs of an increasingly deregulated and market-based business world in, for instance, Richard Sennett's analysis, highlight some important issues regarding what Félix Guattari (2000) calls the "Integrated World Capitalism" (see also Hardt and Negri, 2000), it does little to support the bureaucratic organization form as such. In future engagements with bureaucracy studies, one needs to maintain a business perspective to make bureaucracy legitimate.

Who's afraid of bureaucracy? Implications for management practice

One of the first consequences of the study is that one should not be overtly concerned about the presence of bureaucratic structures in a firm. At times, unnecessarily "bureaucratic work" may inhibit the progress of innovation but, in most cases, structure and standards are promoting innovation and creativity rather than preventing it. At the same time, practising managers must keep an eye on

procedures and operations so that too much time is not dedicated to what strategic management theorists call "non-value adding activities", activities that do
not provide additional "user-value" to products or services. Second, practising
managers need to be aware of the supplementary role of bureaucracy in
contemporary business culture and that words such as "bureaucratic" and
"bureaucrat" are, as von Mises (1944) argues, invectives – labels used to debunk
practices and roles. This unhappy use of such terms is an indication of how
deeply imbued the everyday management language has become saturated with
disregard to bureaucracy. In organizations, there is a scepticism towards much
"management speak", but these uses of the terms derived from bureaucracy are
older than more recent management language games. Thus, one must not
mistake everyday complaints about "bureaucratic procedures" and so forth with
the actual consequences of bureaucracy; that is, to confuse the content and the
form. In the empirical studies there were little complaints about the bureaucratic
organization form as such, while the various managerial control procedures and
systems were regarded as taking time away from more pressing concerns.

In the two firms studied, the notion of bureaucracy is not synonymous with the
strictly functional and hierarchical organization but is, instead, more in line with
the biological organisms metaphor discussed in this chapter. That is, even though
the *formal* structure is functionally organized and hierarchical, the *informal* and
practical work in day-to-day operations are much more organic, fluid and changing. Scandinavian companies often take pride in the informal non-hierarchical
ways of working and therefore the modus operandi in innovative work is rather
flexible. Being able to maintain structure, transparency and functional organization while simultaneously nourishing an experimental mindset and cross-
functional operations may be a fruitful way of managing large innovative
organizations. In other words, managers need to orchestrate a work situation
wherein both mechanical and organic structures co-existing in simultaneity.
Tushman and O'Reilly (1996) describe such organizations as being "ambidextrous organizations", that is, organizations that are capable of being both exploring (managing innovation work) and exploiting (running full-scale production
activities). Being easier said than done, the movement between different coalitions and team organizations and the functionally oriented organization demands
leaders and co-workers capable of both accepting systematic and clear structure
and able to deal with ambiguities in settings where there are few opportunities for
predicting and estimating outcomes. The innovative bureaucracy is an organization that, similar to the biological organism, can adapt to new conditions
without losing its generic form, its innate structure. When they are able to shift
between positions while always returning to the bureaucratic model, large firms
can remain innovative without losing oversight and transparency.

Summary and conclusion

In the section "Outline of the book" in the first chapter (pages 24–25), this book
set itself three objectives: to critically review the literature on bureaucracy and

post-bureaucratic organizations; to report empirical studies on how innovation is organized and carried out in two large, functionally organized and hierarchical companies; and, finally, to theorize about bureaucracy in new – or at least not fully exploited – terms, recognizing the dual capacity of bureaucracies to maintain their form while ceaselessly adapting to external changes. The review of the literature shows that there is a long-standing theme of bureaucracy critique in the social sciences that more or less assumes that bureaucracy is an antiquated or ineffective form of organization. In order to undermine this *doxa*, empirical studies may prove this overtly negative image of bureaucracy too simplistic and one-sided. The two cases studies, set in the automotive and the pharmaceutical industry, respectively, of two multinational industries renowned for their use of advanced forms of specialized know-how and expertise, show that innovation work is by no means a linear and uncomplicated process. Innovation work is, instead, undertaken in domains wherein a number of competing objectives and goals intersect, where various expert groups claim their authority regarding various matters, and where work is always constrained by financial and temporal boundaries. Innovation work is a complex social practice wherein a variety of competing perspectives must be integrated. The studies show that such complex undertakings are dependent on an ability to develop and integrate a number of functionally organized expertise groups into one single unit. Therefore, advanced innovation work is organized in a bureaucratic form instituting clear boundaries between domains of expertise, hierarchical communication channels, and other rule-governed practices. Contrary to the predominant view in the literature addressing bureaucracy, the two case studies suggest that advanced innovation work is not only possible *despite* the bureaucratic organization but, in fact, innovation is possible *because* of the bureaucratic organization. The interviewees in the two case studies expressed their concerns regarding the day-to-day innovation work on a number of different topics, for instance, the transparency of decision-making, the use of management control systems and the lack of time for reflection and analysis. Such concerns were not primarily addressing bureaucratic shortcomings but were referencing the complexity of innovation work as such; the bureaucratic organization form was very much regarded among the interviewees as a *sine qua non* for being innovative in increasingly globalized hyper-competitive markets regulated by authorities.

At Volvo Cars, the sharing of R&D resources with Ford Motor Company was seen as an opportunity to maintain a qualitative new product development process. Volvo Cars, producing about 450,000 cars annually, was regarded as too small a player to be able to stay at the forefront of R&D work on its own. In AstraZeneca, the merger between British Zeneca and Swedish Astra gave new opportunities for sharing know-how and resources that, in turn, enabled advanced scientific research. In the two companies, the functional organization and the hierarchical structure were critical to the long-term performance of the innovation work. The bureaucratic organization form, as such, was therefore little criticized. Instead, specific managerial practices and tools and techniques were at times criticized for being poorly adapted to the day-to-day work of practising engineers, designers and laboratory researchers. If the interviewees were critical of the opportunities for innovation work, it is because innovation is a complex, time-consuming and costly matter, not because bureaucratic organizations as such are incapable of hosting innovative work. Thus, the black box of innovation needs to be opened and examined in greater detailed. Rather than criticizing bureaucracy offhand, innovation work activities in large, functionally organized companies may be examined as not, of necessity, fighting the bureaucratic organization but as, in fact, supported by and reinforced by the bureaucratic form. In the field of management studies, the innovative features of bureaucracy may be shown greater interest by researchers.

If we, once and for all, as suggested by Du Gay (2005: 3), abandon the idea that bureaucracy is a "singularity", a monolithic and unified standardized model, and instead think of bureaucracy as a "many-sided, evolving, diversified organizational device" (Du Gay, 2005: 3), then new opportunities for thoughtful research and reflections evolve.

The tedious denunciations of bureaucracy over the years need to be replaced by a practice-based view of bureaucracy; it is what bureaucrats do, not what formal documents prescribe and top-management visions declare, that matters at the end of the day. In an age like ours, wherein all sorts of fluid and fluxing social arrangements are praised as evidence of a forthcoming new world order, essentially embedded in a variety of technological machinery and new means of communication, the concept of bureaucracy needs to be reformulated and reappraised. This book has attempted to free bureaucracy from the predominant mechanistic and instrumental root metaphors and, instead, a biological organism metaphor has been used to portray how bureaucracy is a functionally organized, yet continuously adapting, social system. The contemporary episteme of fluidity, wherein social identities, subjectivities, organization forms and institutions are reinterpreted as being not fixed and immutable but, instead, conceived of as what-is-in-the-making (Urry, 2000, 2003), the mechanistic metaphors of the Fordist or mass-production era of capitalism are worn out. New metaphors enable new lines of thinking which, in turn – Foucault's (1972) idea of discursive formations as producing material effects is adhered to here – implies new practices and new institutions and new organization forms. It is noteworthy that the biological metaphor developed in this final chapter is marked by Bergsonian thinking; that is, a biological organism is not what is once and for all predetermined and fettered by its own hylemorphism and finalism but is, instead, an open-ended becoming. Similarly, bureaucracies are not predetermined to be capable of certain things and incompetent in dealing with others. On the contrary, the underlying idea here is that bureaucracy can develop in numerous directions. Rather than playing the supplementary role of merely being a less favoured organization form in a binary structure of opposites, the biological metaphor in Bergson's thinking defies all such Platonist epistemologies. Becoming is not the succession between binary states (e.g. "either/or", "1/0") but is a continuous and seamless transformation. Therefore, using the metaphor of the biological organism represents an opening for a process-based view of bureaucracy that is more in harmony with recent social theory favouring fluid and fluxing ontologies and epistemologies. Such a new beginning would benefit bureaucracy studies because this tradition of research is now too burdened with its own inability to present a more affirmative view of bureaucracy. Rethinking bureaucracies as organizations capable of innovating and orchestrating a great number of creative things would imply something new. To paraphrase Spinoza (1994: 72): We do not know what a bureaucracy can do. To rethink bureaucracy in an age of fluidity would imply a new beginning for bureaucracy studies.

Notes

1 Milburn's account of the implications of nanotechnology (2004: 123) may be cited at length here to support Virilio's idea:

> The birth of nanotechnology as a scientific discipline provokes the hyperreal collapse of humanistic discourse, punctuating the fragile membrane between real and simulation, science and science fiction, organism and machine, and heralding metamorphic futures and cyborganic discontinuities. In both its speculative-theoretical and applied-engineering modes, nanotechnology unbuilds those constructions of human thought, as well as those forms of human embodiment, based on the secularity of presence and stability – terrorizing presentist humanism from the vantage point of an already inevitable future.

2 Dougherty and Heller (1994) represent an opposing view, claiming that innovations are, in fact, by definition conflicting with predominant beliefs and institutions: "They [innovations] either violate prevailing practice, inside or outside of the firm, or require ways of thinking and acting that are 'undoable', or 'unthinkable', albeit in intractable or opaque ways. The activities of product innovation, therefore, are illegitimate" (1994: 202).

3 Du Gay (2000a: 67) defines discourse accordingly:

> A discourse ... is a group of statements that provide a way of talking about and acting upon a particular object. When statements about an object or topic are made from within a certain discourse, that discourse makes it possible to construct that object in a particular way.

4 Kline (1954: 430), speaking of the progress of mathematics, writes:

> Before 1800 every age had believed in the existence of absolute truth; men differed only in their choice of sources. Aristotle, the fathers of the Church, the Bible, philosophy, and science all had their day as arbiters of objective, eternal truths.

5 Before 1993, the company was a pharmaceutical division within ICI, a large British international chemical corporation.

6 A candidate drug exists in the final pre-clinical stage of drug development, which denotes the selection of a compound with the greatest potential to be developed into safe, effective medicines.

7 AstraZeneca, *Annual Report,* 2004.

8 www.astrazeneca.com.

9 AstraZeneca, *Annual Report,* 2004.
10 AstraZeneca, *Annual Report,* 2004.
11 Biological (or therapeutic) targets are membrane or cellular receptors (made of proteins) or genes, to which a molecule can be attached.
12 The study of causes of disease.
13 The human body is made up of several biological systems. For example, there is the nervous system, the cardiovascular system or the respiratory system.
14 The physical manifestation of the organism, such as cells, structures, organs or reflexes and behaviours; anything that is part of the observable structure, function or behaviour of a living organism.
15 The clinical research programme continues after the product's launch (Phase 4) by collecting data from outcome research and epidemiology data from patients; this might lead to new indications for the product.
16 A DASL is an expert on one specific disease, for instance in the field of gastrointestinal medicine where therapies for diseases like gastro-oesophageal reflux disease (GERD) or inflammatory bowel disease (IBD) are examined. The DASL is an in-house world-class expert on such a specific disease.
17 According to Keller (2000), one of the first "modern" definitions of organism was formulated by Kant in his *Critique of Judgment* and shares with Bergson the emphasis on both the concept of *organization* and the innate capacity of self-formation of the organism: *"An organized natural product is one in which every part is reciprocally both end and means.* In such a product nothing is in vain, without end, or to be ascribed to a blind mechanism of nature" (Kant, *Critique of Judgment,* cited in Keller, 2000: 107, emphasis in the original). Keller (2000: 108), discussing the concept of the gene as a biological entity, provides a similar definition, also underlining the dynamic self-formation of the organism:

> What is an organism? It is a bounded, physiochemical body capable not only of self-regulation – self-steering – but also, and perhaps most important, of self-formation. An organism is a material entity that is transformed into an autonomous and self-generating "self" by virtue of its peculiar and particular organization.

18 Ideas about a purposefulness of nature seems to be largely abandoned by Bergson's contemporary researchers and philosophers. For instance, Erwin Schrödinger (1958: 67) writes:

> Nature does not act by purposes. If in German we speak of purposeful (*zweckmässig*) adaptation of an organism to its environment, we know this to be only a convenient way of speech. If we take it literally, we are mistaken. We are mistaken within the frame of our world picture. In it there is only causal linkage.

However, it is important that the recent interest in genomics and other new biochemical scientific programmes in the life sciences seem to rejuvenate the idea of purposefulness (see extended argument below, note 20).
19 It is common in contemporary biology to distinguish between the *phenotype* of the organism, defined as "[t]he form of the organization, its 'body' and physical characteristics" (Malik, 2005: 479) and the *genotype,* "[t]he hereditary material, which is localized in most contemporary biology and medicine to the gene, which in turn is localized in the cell's chromosomes" (2005: 479).
20 Haraway (1997) speaks of "gene fetishism" in the Human Genome Programme and claims that one cannot assume that one single biological entity can single-handedly determine an entire biological organism. Rabinow (1999: 3) points out that, in the contemporary discourse on genomics, expressions such as "the book of life" were

used when speaking of the human genome. Contrary to such "simple locations" (in Alfred North Whitehead's formulation) and "logocentric epistemologies" (to use a Derridean expression), Haraways (2000: 94) says: "A gene is a knot in a field of relatedness. It's a material-semiotic entity; a concretization that *locates* (in the mapping sense of locates) and *substantializes* inheritance." Elsewhere she writes: "A gene is not a thing, much less a 'master molecule' or a self-contained code. Instead, the term *gene* signifies a node of durable action where many actors, humans and non-humans, meet" (1997: 142; see also Fujimura, 1995, 1996, for an overview of the concept of the gene). Keller (2000: 69) is also critical of what may be called a "gene-centric" explanation of life. In her review of a hundred years of genetics, Keller points at the "plasticity" of the concept and it situated nature:

> As we listen to the ways in which the term is now used by working biologists, we find that the gene has become many things – no longer a single entity but a word with great plasticity, defined only by the specific experimental context in which it is used".

The discovery of the importance of proteins and their ability to continuously change supports Haraway's (1997) thesis that life cannot be explained solely on the basis of the genome. The mapping of the human genome is not, it seems, the end of biological history. Biological models must seek models of life that are affirmative of change and becoming.

21 Deleuze and Guattari (1988: 409) speak of machinic phylum as a "flow of matter" that is "itinerate" and "ambulate". De Landa (1992: 151) defines machinic phylum as "a destratified, nonlinear flow of matter-energy" (for an extended discussion of the concept, see de Landa, 1991: 6–7, 20).

Bibliography

Abraham, John and Reed, Tim (2002) Progress, innovation and regulatory science in drug development: the politics of international standard-setting, *Social Studies of Science*, 32(3): 337–369.

Adamson, Stephen J., Doherty, Noeleen and Viney, Claire (1998) The meaning of career revisited: implications for theory and practice, *British Journal of Management*, 9: 251–259.

Adler, Niclas (1999) *Managing Complex Product Development*, PhD Thesis, The Economic Research Institute, Stockholm School of Economics.

Adler, N.B., Shani, A.B. and Styhre, A. (eds) (2004) *Collaborative Research in Organizations: Foundations for Learning, Change, and Theoretical Development*, London, Thousand Oaks and New Delhi: Sage.

Adler, Paul, S. and Borys, Bryan (1996) Two types of bureaucracies: enabling and coercive, *Administrative Science Quarterly*, 41: 61–89.

Ahrne, Göran (1990) *The Organizational Landscape*, London, Thousand Oaks and New Delhi: Sage.

Akrich, Madeleine, Callon, Michel and Latour, Bruno (2002a) The key success in innovation part I: the art of interessement, *International Journal of Innovation Management*, 6(2): 187–206.

Akrich, Madeleine, Callon, Michel and Latour, Bruno (2002b) The key success in innovation part II: the art of choosing good spokespersons, *International Journal of Innovation Management*, 6(2): 206–225.

Albrow, Martin (1970) *Bureaucracy*, London: Pall Mall Press.

Aldrich, Howard (1999) *Organizations Evolving*, Thousand Oaks: Sage.

Alexander, Marcus (1997) Getting to grips with the virtual organization, *Long Range Planning*, 30(1): 122–124.

Allcorn, Seth (1997) Parallel virtual organizations, *Administration & Society*, 29(4): 412–440.

Althusser, Louis (1984) Ideology and ideological state apparatuses, in *Essays on Ideology*, London and New York: Verso.

Anderson, P. (1999) Complexity theory and organization science, *Organization Science*, 10(3): 216–232.

Ansell Pearson, Keith (1997) *Viroid life: Perspectives on Nietzsche and the Transhuman Condition*, London and New York: Routledge.

Ansell Pearson, Keith (1999) *Geminal life: the Difference and Repetition of Deleuze*, London and New York: Routledge.

Ansell Pearson, Keith (2002) *Philosophy and the Adventures of the Virtual: Bergson and the Time of Life*, London and New York: Routledge.

Apic, G., Ignjatovic, T., Boyer, S. and Russell, R.B. (2005) Illuminating drug discovery with biological pathways. *FEBS Letters*, 579: 1872–1877.

Appadurai, Arjun (1996) *Modernity at Large: Cultural Dimensions of Globalization*, Minneapolis and London: Minnesota University Press.

Argyres, Nicholas S. and Silverman, Brian S. (2004) R&D, organization structure, and the development of corporate technological knowledge, *Strategic Management Journal*, 25: 929–958.

Arian, Edward (1971) *Bach, Beethoven, and Bureaucracy: the Case of the Philadelphia Orchestra*, University: University of Alabama Press.

Aristotle (1996) *Physics*, Oxford: Oxford University Press.

Aristotle (1998a) *Politics*, Indianapolis and Cambridge: Hackett.

Aristotle (1998b) *The Metaphysics*, London: Penguin.

Armitage, John (1999) From modernism to hypermodernism and beyond: an interview with Paul Virilio, *Theory, Culture & Society*, 16(5–6): 25–55.

Armstrong, Peter (2001) Science, enterprise and profit: ideology in the knowledge-driven economy, *Economy & Society*, 30(4): 524–552.

Ashby, W. Ross (1956) *An Introduction to Cybernetics*, London: Chapman & Hall.

Ashcraft, Karen Lee (2001) Organized dissonance: feminist bureaucracy as hybrid form, *Academy of Management Journal*, 4(6): 1301–1322.

Ashkenas, Ron, Ulrich, Dave, Jick, Todd and Kerr, Steve (1995) *The Boundaryless Organization: Breaking the Chains of the Organizational Structure*, San Francisco: Jossey-Bass.

AstraZeneca (2005) *Annual Report*.

Atkinson, Paul and Coffrey, Amanda (2003) Revisiting the relationship between participant observations and interviewing, in Gubrium, Jaber F. and Holstein, James A., (eds) *Postmodern Interviewing*, London, Thousand Oaks and New Delhi: Sage.

Augier, Mie and Thanning Vendelø, Morten (1999) Networks, cognitions and management of tacit knowledge, *Journal of Knowledge Management*, 3(4): 252–261.

Babbage, Charles (1833) *On the Economy of Machinery and Manufactures*, London: Charles Knight.

Bakhtin, Mikhail M. (1986) *Speech Genres and Other Late Essays*, trans. by Vern W. McGee, Austin: University of Texas Press.

Bakhtin, Mikhail M. (1993) *Toward a Philosophy of the Act*, trans. by Vadim Liapunov, Austin: University of Texas Press.

Balzac, Honoré de (2000) *Bureaucracy*, Trans. by Katharine Prescott Wormley, Cirencester: The Echo Library, originally published 1837.

Barker, James R. (1993) Tightening the iron cage: concertive control in self-managing teams, *Administrative Science Quarterly*, 38: 408–437.

Barley, Stephen R. (1986) Technology as an occasion of structuring: evidence from observations of CT scanners and the social order of radiology departments, *Administrative Science Quarterly*, 31: 78–108.

Barley, Stephen R. (1990) The alignment of technology and structure through roles and networks, *Administrative Science Quarterly*, 35: 61–103.

Barley, Stephen R. and Kunda, Gideon (1992) Design and devotion: surges of rational and normative ideologies of control in managerial discourse, *Administrative Science Quarterly*, 37: 363–399.

Barley, Stephen R. and Kunda, Gideon (2006) Contracting: a new form of professional practice, *Academy of Management Perspectives*, 20(1): 45–66.

Barley, Stephen R. and Tolbert, Pamela (1997) Institutionalization and structuration: studying the links between action and institution, *Organization Studies*, 18(1): 93–117.

Barney, Jay B. (1991) Firm resources and sustained competitive advantage, *Journal of Management*, 17: 99–120.

Barney, Jay B. (2001) Is the resource-based "view" a useful perspective for strategic management research? Yes, *Academy of Management Review*, 26(1): 41–56.

Barry, Andrew (2005) Pharmaceutical matters: the invention of informed materials, *Theory, Culture & Society*, 22(1): 51–69.

Bauman, Zygmunt (2000) *Liquid Modernity*, Cambridge and Malden: Polity Press.

Bauman, Zygmunt (2005) Time and class, in Leistyna, Pepi (ed.) *Cultural Studies: From Theory to Action*, Oxford and Malden: Blackwell, pp. 56–67.

Baxter, A.D. and Lockey, P.M. (2001) Hit-to-lead and lead-to-candidate optimisation using multi-parametric principles. *Drug Discovery World*, 2: 9–15.

Beauvoir, Simone de (1993) *The Second Sex*, London: Everyman's Library.

Beck, Ulrich (2000) *Welcome to the New World of Work*, trans. by Patrick Camiller, Cambridge: Polity Press.

Beckman, Jörg (2004) Mobility and safety, *Theory, Culture & Society*, 21(4/5): 81–100.

Bell, Daniel (1973) *The Coming Post-industrial Society*, New York: Basic Books.

Bendix, Reinhard (1956) *Work and Authority in Industry*, New York: Wiley.

Bendix, Reinhard (1971) Bureaucracy, in Bendix, Reinhard and Guenther Roth (eds) *Scholarship and Partisanship: Essays on Max Weber*, Berkeley, Los Angeles and London: University of California Press, pp. 129–155.

Benhabib, Selya (2002) *The Claims of Culture: Equality and Diversity in the Global Era*, Princeton and Oxford: Princeton University Press.

Bennis, Warren G. (1966) Changing organizations: essays on the development and evolution of human organization, New York: McGraw-Hill.

Bennis, Warren G. (1970) Post bureaucratic leadership, *American Bureaucracy*, 165–188.

Berggren, Christian (1990) *Det nya bilarbetet* (*The New Automotive Work*), Lund: Arkiv Förlag.

Berggren, Christian (1994) NUMMI vs. Uddevalla, *Sloan Management Review*, 36: 37–49.

Bergmann Lichtenstein, Benyamin M. (2000) Self-organized transitions: a pattern amid the chaos of transformative change, *Academy of Management Executives*, 14(4): 128–141.

Bergson, Henri (1975) *Mind-energy. Lectures and Essays*, trans. by H. Wildon Carr, Westport and London: Greenwood Press, originally published 1920.

Bergson, Henri (1977) *The Two Sources of Morality and Religion*, Notre Dame: University of Notre Dame Press, originally published 1935.

Bergson, Henri (1998) *Creative Evolution*, Mineola: Dover Publishers.

Bergson, Henri (1999) *An Introduction to Metaphysics*, Indianapolis: Hackett.

Berle, Adolf A. and Means, Gardiner C. (1991) *The Modern Corporation & Private Property*, New Brunswick: Transaction Publishers.

Best, Steven and Kellner, Douglas (1991) *Postmodern Theory: Critical Interrogations*, London: Macmillan.

Best, Steven and Kellner, Douglas (1997) *The Postmodern Turn*, New York: Guilford Press.

Bijker, Wiebe E. (1995) *Of Bicycles, Bakelites, and Bulbs: Toward a Theory of Sociotechnical Change*, Cambridge and London: the MIT Press.

Bijker, Wiebe E., Hughes, Thomas P. and Pinch, Trevor J. (eds), (1987) *The Social Construction of Technological Systems: New Directions in the Sociology and History of Technology*, Cambridge and London: the MIT Press.

Billing, Yvonne Due (2005) Gender equity – a bureaucratic enterprise?, in Du Gay, Paul (ed.) *The Values of Bureaucracy*, Oxford and New York: Oxford University Press, pp. 258–279.

Black, Janice A. and Edwards, Sandra (2000) Emergence of virtual or network organizations: fad or feature?, *Journal of Organization Change Management*, 13(6): 567–576.

Blackler, F., Crump, N. and McDonald, S. (1999) Managing experts and competing through innovation: an activity theoretical analysis, *Organization*, 6(1): 5–31.

Blau, Gary E., Pekny, Joseph F., Varma, Vishal A. and Bunch, Paul R. (2004) Managing a portfolio of interdependent new product candidates in the pharmaceutical industry, *Journal of Product Innovation Management*, 21: 227–245.

Blau, Judith R. and McKinley, William (1979) Ideas, complexity and innovation, *Administrative Science Quarterly*, 24: 200–219.

Blau, Peter M. (1956) *Bureaucracy in Modern Society*, New York: Random House.

Blau, Peter M. (1963) *The Dynamics of Bureaucracy: a Study of Interpersonal Relations in Two Government Agencies*, second edn, Chicago: University of Chicago Press.

Blau, Peter M. and Scott, W. Richard (1963) *Formal Organizations: a Comparative Approach*, London: Routledge & Kegan Paul.

Blauner, Robert (1964) *Alienation and Freedom – the Factory Worker and His Industry*, Chicago: Chicago University Press.

Bloch, Marc (1962) *Feudal Society, Vol. II: Social Classes and Political Organization*, trans. by L.A. Manyon, London: Routledge & Kegan Paul.

Boltzmann, Ludwig (1974) *Theoretical Physics and Philosophical Problems: Selected Writings*, ed. by Brian McGuinness, trans. by Paul Foulkes, Dordrecht and Boston: D. Riedel Publishing.

Bordo, Susan (1996) The Cartesian masculinization of thought, in Cahoone, L. (ed.) *From Modernism to Postmodernism*, Oxford: Blackwell.

Borgerson, Janet and Rehn, Alf (2004) General economy and productive dualisms, *Gender, Work and Organization*, 11(4): 455–474.

Borradori, Giovanna (2003) *Philosophy in a Time of Terror: Dialogues with Jürgen Habermas and Jacques Derrida*, Chicago and London: University of Chicago Press.

Bourdieu, Pierre (1977) *Outline of a Theory of Practice*, Cambridge: Cambridge University Press.

Bourdieu, Pierre (1990) *The Logic of Practice*, Cambridge: Polity Press.

Bourdieu, Pierre (2005) *The Economic Structures of Society*, Cambridge: Polity Press.

Bourdieu, Pierre and Passeron, J.-C. (1977) *Reproduction in Education, Society, and Culture*, London: Sage.

Bourdieu, Pierre and Wacquant, Loic J.D. (1992) *An Invitation to Reflexive Sociology*, Chicago and London: University of Chicago Press.

Boudreau, Marie-Claude, Loch, Karen D., Robey, Daniel and Straud, Dietmar (1998) Going global: using information technology to advance the competitiveness of the virtual transnational organization, *Academy of Management Executives*, 12(4): 120–128.

Bowker, Geoffrey C. and Leight Star, Susan (1999) *Sorting Things Out: Classification and its Consequences*, Cambridge and London: MIT Press.

Bragd, Annica (2002) *Knowing Management: an Ethnographic Study of Tinkering With a New Car*, Gothenburg: Bas Publisher (PhD Diss.).

Braidotti, Rosi (1994) *Nomadic Subjects: Embodiment and Sexual Difference in Contemporary Feminist Theory*, New York: Columbia University Press.

Braidotti, Rosi (2002) *Metamorphosis: Toward a Materialist Theory of Becoming*, Cambridge: Polity Press.

Braidotti, Rosi (2006) *Transpositions: On Nomadic Ethics*, Cambridge and Malden: Polity Press.

Braudel, Fernand (1992) *The Wheels of Commerce: Civilization & Capitalism 15th–18th century*, Vol. 2, Berkeley and Los Angeles. University of California Press.

Bresnen, Mike, Goussevskaia, Anna and Swan, Jacky (2004) Embedding new management knowledge in project-based organizations, *Organization Studies*, 25(9): 1535–1555.

Brewis, Joanna and Linstead, Stephen (2000) *Sex, Work and Sex Work*, London and New York: Routledge.

Briggs, Charles L. (2003) Interviewing, power/knowledge and social inequality, in Gubrium, Jaber F. and Holstein, James A. (eds) *Postmodern Interviewing*, London, Thousand Oaks and New Delhi: Sage, 243–254.

Britan, Gerald M. (1981) *Bureaucracy and Innovation: an Ethnography of Policy Change*, Sage: Beverly Hills.

Brown, Steven D. (1999) Caught up in the rapture: Serres translates Mandelbrot, paper presented at the CSTT/ESRC Workshop *Poststructuralism and Complexity*, Keele University, UK, 15 January.

Brown, Steven D. and Lightfoot, Geoffrey (2002) Presence, absence, and accountability: e-mail and the mediation of organizational memory, in Woolgar, Steve (ed.) *Virtual Society? Technology, Cyberbole, Reality*, Oxford and New York: Oxford University Press.

Brown, S.L. and Eisenhardt, K.M. (1998) *Competing on the Edge*, Boston: Harvard University Press.

Bunce, D. and West, M.A. (1996) Stress management and innovations at work, *Human Relations*, 49(2): 209–232.

Burawoy, Michael (1979) *Manufacturing Consent: Changes in the Labour Process Under Monopoly Capitalism*, Chicago: University of Chicago Press.

Burawoy, Michael (1985) *Politics of Production*, London: Verso.

Burns, T. and Stalker, G.M. (1961) *The Management of Innovation*, London: Tavistock Publications.

Burton-Jones, Alan (1999) *Knowledge Capitalism: Business, Work, and Learning in the New Economy*, Oxford: Oxford University Press.

Burwick, Frederick and Douglass, Paul (eds) (1992) *The Crisis in Modernism: Bergson and the Vitalist Controversy*, Cambridge: Cambridge University Press.

Busfield, Joan (2006) Pills, power, people: sociological understandings of the pharmaceutical industry, *Sociology*, 40(2): 297–314.

Bushe, Gervase R. and Shani, A.B. (Rami) (1991) *Parallel Learning Structures: Increasing Innovation in Bureaucracies*, Reading, MA: Addison-Wesley.

Butler, Judith (1993) *Bodies That Matter*, London and New York: Routledge.

Cálas, Marta and Smircich, Linda (1999) Past postmodernism? Reflections and tentative directions, *Academy of Management Review*, 24(4): 649–671.

Callon, Michel (ed.) (1998) *Laws of the Market*, Oxford: Blackwell.

Callon, Michel (2002) Writing and (re)writing devices as tools for managing complexity, in Law, John and Mol, Annemarie (eds) *Complexities: Social Studies of Knowledge Practices*, Durham and London: Duke University Press.

Callon, Michel and Latour, Bruno (1981) Unscrewing the big Leviathan, in Knorr-Cetina, K. and Cicourel, A.V. (eds) *Advances in Social Theory and Methodology: Toward an Integration of Micro and Macro Sociologies*, London: Routledge and Kegan Paul.

Canguilhem, Georges (1992) Machine and organism, in Crary, Jonathan and Kwinter, Sanford (eds) *Incorporations*, New York: Zone Books, pp. 45–69.

Cardinal, Laura B. (2001) Technological innovation in the pharmaceutical industry: the use of organizational control in managing research and development, *Organization Science*, 12(1): 19–36.

Cascio, Wayne F. (2000) Managing a virtual workplace, *Academy of Management Executives*, 14(3): 81–90.

Case, Peter (1999) Remember re-engineering? The rhetorical appeal of a management salvation device, *Journal of Management Studies*, 36(4): 419–441.

Casey, Catherine (2002) *Critical Analysis of Organizations: Theory, Practice and Revitalization*, London, Thousand Oaks and New Delhi: Sage.

Casper, Steven and Matraves, Catherine (2003) Institutional frameworks and innovation in the German and UK Pharmaceutical industry, *Research Policy*, 32: 1865–1879.

Castells, Manuel (1996) *The Information Age: Economy, Society and Culture, Vol. 1: the Rise of the Network Society*, Oxford: Blackwell.

Cavendish, Ruth (1982) *Women on the Line*, London: Routledge and Kegan Paul.

Chandler, Alfred D. (1977) *The Visible Hand: the Managerial Revolution in American Business*, Cambridge: Harvard University Press.

Cheng, Y.-T. and Van de Ven, A.H. (1996) Learning the innovation journey: order out of chaos?, *Organization Science*, 7(6): 593–605.

Chia, Robert (1996) The problem of reflexivity in organizational research: towards a postmodern science of organization, *Organizations*, 3(1): 31–59.

Chia, Robert (2004) The shaping of dominant modes of thought: rediscovering the foundations of management knowledge, in Jeffcut, Paul (ed.) *The Foundations of Management Knowledge*, London and New York: Routledge.

Chia, Robert and King, Ian W. (1998) The organizational structuring of novelty, *Organization*, 5(4): 461–478.

Chiari, Joseph (1992) Vitalism and contemporary thought, in Burwick, Frederick and Douglass, Paul (eds) *The Crisis in Modernism: Bergson and the Vitalist Controversy*, Cambridge: Cambridge University Press, pp. 245–273.

Chiesa, Vittorio (1996) Separating research from development: evidence from the pharmaceutical industry, *European Journal of Management*, 14(6): 638–647.

Cilliers, Paul (1998) *Complexity and Postmodernism*, London and New York: Routledge.

Cilliers, Paul (2005) Complexity, deconstruction and relativism, *Theory, Culture and Society*, 22(5): 255-267.

Clark, D.E. and Newton, C.G. (2004) Outsourcing lead optimisation – the quiet revolution. *Drug Discovery Today*, 9(11): 492–500.

Clark, Timothy and Salaman, Graeme (1996) The management gurus as organizational witchdoctors, *Organization*, 3(1): 85–107.

Clarke, Adele E., Mamo, Laura, Fishman, Jennifer R., Shim, Janet K. and Fosket, Jennifer Ruth (2003) Biomedicalization: technoscientific transformations of health, illness, and U.S. biomedicine, *American Sociological Review*, 68: 161–194.

Clawson, Dan (1980) *Bureaucracy and the Labor Process: The transformation of the U.S. industry, 1860–1920*, New York and London: Monthly Review Press.

Clegg, Stewart and Courpasson, David (2004) Political hybrids: Tocquevillean views of project organizations, *Journal of Management Studies*, 41(4): 525–547.

Clegg, Stewart R., Kornberger, Martin and Rhodes, Carl (2005) Learning/becoming/ organizing, *Organization*, 12(2): 147–167.

Coase, Ronald H. (1991) The nature of the firm, in Williamson, Oliver E. and Winter, Sidney G. (eds) *The Nature of the Firm: Origin, Evolution, and Development*, New York and Oxford: Oxford University Press, originally published 1937.

Collins, David (2000) *Management Fads and Buzzwords: Critical-Practical Perspectives*, London and New York: Routledge.

Collinson, David L. (1992) *Managing the Shopfloor: Subjectivity, Masculinity, and Workplace Culture*, Berlin: de Gruyter.

Cooke, Bill (2003) The denial of slavery in management studies, *Journal of Management Studies*, 40(8): 1895–1918.

Cooper, Robert (2005) Relationality, *Organization Studies*, 26(11): 1689–1710.

Courpasson, David (2000) Managerial strategies of domination: power in soft bureaucracies, *Organization Studies*, 21(1): 141–161.

Courpasson, David and Reed, Michael (2004) Introduction: bureaucracy in the age of enterprise, *Organization*, 11(1): 5–12.

Craig, Tim (1995) Achieving innovation through bureaucracy: lessons from the Japanese brewing industry, *California Management Review*, 38(1): 8–36.

Crozier, Michel (1964) *The Bureaucratic Phenomena*, Chicago: University of Chicago Press.

Cummings, Stephen and Thanem, Thorkild (2002) *Essai*: the ghost in the organism, *Organization Studies*, 23(5): 817–839.

Cusumano, Michael A. (1985) *The Japanese Automobile Industry: Technology and Management at Toyota and Nissan*, Cambridge: Harvard University Press.

Cuther-Gershenfeld, J., *et al.* (1994) Japanese team-based work systems in North-America, *California Management Review*, 37(1): 42–64.

Czarniawska, Barbara (1997) *Narrating the Organization: Dramas of Institutional Identity*, Chicago and London: University of Chicago Press.

Czarniawska, Barbara (1998) *A Narrative Approach to Organization Studies*, Thousand Oaks, London and New Delhi: Sage.

Czarniawska, Barbara and Genell, Kristina (2002) Gone shopping? Universities on their way to the market, *Scandinavian Journal of Management*, 18: 455–475.

Czarniawska, Barbara and Hernes, Tor (2005) *Actor-Network Theory and Organizing*, Malmö: Liber; Copenhagen: Copenhagen Business School Press.

Czarniawska-Joerges, Barbara (1992) *Exploring Complex Organizations*, London: Sage.

Dahlsten, Fredrik (2003) Avoiding the customer satisfaction rut, *Sloan Management Review*, Summer: 73–77.

Dahrendorf, Ralf (1959) *Class and Class Conflict in Industrial Society*. London: Routledge & Kegan Paul.

Damanpour, Fariborz (1992) Organization size and innovation, *Organization Studies*, 13(3): 375–402.

Davenport, Thomas and Pearlson, Keri (1998) Two cheers for the virtual office, *Sloan Management Review*, 39(3): 51–65.

Deetz, Stanley A. (1992) *Democracy in an Age of Corporate Colonialization*, Albany: State of New York University Press.

De Issekutz Wolsky, Maria and Wolsky, Alexander A. (1992) Bergson's vitalism in the light of modern biology, in Burwick, Frederick and Douglass, Paul (eds) *The Crisis in*

Modernism: Bergson and the Vitalist Controversy, Cambridge: Cambridge University Press, pp. 153–170.

De Landa, Manuel (1991) *War in the Age of Intelligent Machines*, New York: Zone Books.

De Landa, Manuel (1992) Nonorganic life, in Crary, Jonathan and Kwinter, Sanford (eds) *Incorporations*, New York: Zone Books, pp. 129–167.

De Landa, Manuel (1997) *A Thousand Years of Nonlinear History*, New York: Zone Books.

De Landa, Manuel (2002) *Intensive Science and Virtual Philosophy*, London and New York: Continuum.

Delbridge, Rick (1998) *Life on the Line in Contemporary Manufacturing: the Workplace Experience of Lean Production and the "Japanese Model"*, Oxford and New York: Oxford University Press.

Deleuze, Gilles (1988) *Bergsonism,* New York: Zone Books, originally published 1966.

Deleuze, Gilles (2004a) Gilbert Simondon, in *Desert Islands and Other Texts, 1953–1994*, ed. by David Lapoujade, trans. by Michael Taormina, New York and Los Angeles: Semiotext[e], pp. 86–89.

Deleuze, Gilles (2004b) Henri Bergson, 1859–1941, in *Desert Islands and Other Texts, 1953–1994*, ed. by David Lapoujade, trans. by Michael Taormina, New York and Los Angeles: Semiotext[e], pp. 22–31.

Deleuze, Gilles and Guattari, Félix (1988) *A Thousand Plateaus: Capitalism and Schizophrenia*, Minneapolis: University of Minnesota Press.

Deleuze, Gilles and Parnet, Claire (2002) *Dialogues II*, London and New York: Continuum.

Della Rocca, Guiseppe (1993) "Voice" and "exit" in the middle-management labor market, *International Studies of Management and Organization*, 22(1): 54–66.

Delmestri, Guiseppe and Walgenbach, Peter (2005) Mastering techniques or brokering knowledge? Middle managers in Germany, Great Britain and Italy, *Organization Studies*, 26(2): 197–220.

Denzin, Norman K. (2003) The cinematic society and the reflexive interview, in Gubrium, Jaber F. and Holstein, James A. (eds) *Postmodern Interviewing*, London, Thousand Oaks and New Delhi: Sage, pp. 141–155.

Der Derian, James (ed.) (1998) *The Virilio Reader*, Oxford: Blackwell.

Derrida, Jacques (1976) *Of Grammatology*, Baltimore: John Hopkins University Press, originally published 1967.

Dilthey, Wilhelm (1988) *Introduction to the Human Sciences: an Attempt to Lay a Foundation for the Study of Society and History*, Detroit: Wayne State University Press, originally published 1983.

DiMaggio, Paul J. and Powell, Walter W. (1991) *The New Institutionalism in Organizational Analysis*, Chicago: University of Chicago Press.

DiMasi, J.A. (2001) Risks in new drug development: approval success rates for investigational drugs, *Clinical Pharmacology Therapy,* 69: 297–307.

DiMasi, J.A, Hansen, R.W. and Grabowski, H.G. (2003) The price of innovation: new estimates of drug development costs, *Journal of Health Economics*, 22: 151–185.

Doan, T.N, Eilertson, C.D. and Rubinstein, A.L. (2004) High-throughput target validation in model organisms, *Drug Discovery Today*, 3(5): 192–197.

Dodgson, Mark (2000) *The Management of Technological Innovation*, Oxford and New York: Oxford University Press.

Dopson, Sue and Stewart, Rosemary (1990) What is happening to middle management?, *British Journal of Management*, 1: 3–16.

Dougherty, Deborah (1999) Organizing for innovation, in Clegg, S.R., Hardy, C. and Nord, W.R. (eds) *Managing Organizations*, London: Sage.

Dougherty, Deborah and Hardy, Cynthia (1996) Sustained product innovation in large mature organizations: overcoming innovation-to-organization problems, *Academy of Management Journal*, 39(5): 1120–1153.

Dougherty, Deborah and Heller, Trudy (1994) The illegitimacy of successful product innovation in established firms, *Organization Science*, 5(2): 200–218.

Drazin, Robert and Sandelands, Lloyd (1992) Autogenesis: a perspective on the process of organizing, *Organization Science*, 3(2): 230–249.

Drucker, Peter F. (1955) *The Practice of Management*, Melbourne, London and Toronto: Heineman.

Du Gay, Paul (1996) *Consumption and Identity at Work*, Sage, London.

Du Gay, Paul (2000a) Markets and meaning: re-imagining organizational life, in Schultz, Majken, Hatch, Mary Jo and Larsen, Mogens Holten (eds) *The Expressive Organization: Linking Identity, Reputation, and the Corporate Brand*, Oxford: Oxford University Press.

Du Gay, Paul (2000b) *In Praise of Bureaucracy*, London, Thousand Oaks and New Delhi: Sage.

Du Gay, Paul (2005) The values of bureaucracy: an introduction, in Du Gay, Paul (ed.) *The Values of Bureaucracy*, Oxford and New York: Oxford University Press, pp. 1–13.

Dupré, John (1993) *The Disorder of Things: Metaphysical Foundations of the Disunity of Science*, Cambridge and London: Harvard University Press.

Durkheim, É. (1933) *The Division of Labour in Society*, New York: Free Press, originally published 1893.

Durkheim, E. (1938) *The Rules of Sociological Method*, Glencoe: Free Press, originally published 1895.

Dyer, Frederick C. and Dyer, John M. (1965) *Bureaucracy vs. Creativity*, Coral Gables: University of Miami Press.

Dyer, Jeffrey H. and Nobeoka, Kentabo (2000) Creating and managing high-performance knowledge sharing networks: the Toyota case, *Strategic Management Journal*, 21: 345–367.

Ebrahimpour, M. and Cullen, J.B. (1994) Quality management in Japanese and American firms operating in the United States: a comparative study of styles and motivational factors, *Management International Review*, 33(1): 23–38.

Etzioni, Amitai (ed.) (1964) *Complex Organizations: a Sociological reader*, New York: Holt, Rinehart and Winston.

Farrell, Catherine and Morris, Jonathan (2003) The neo-bureaucratic state: professionals, managers and professional managers in schools, general practice and social work, *Organization*, 10(1): 129–156.

Fayol, Henri (1949) *General and Industrial Management*, London: Pitman, originally published 1916.

Feldman, Martha S. (2000) Organization routines as a source of continuous change, *Organization Science*, 11(6): 611–629.

Feldman, Martha S. and Pentland, Brian T. (2003) Reconceptualizing organization routines as a source of flexibility and change, *Administrative Science Quarterly*, 48: 94–118.

Feldman, Martha and Pentland, Brian (2005) Organizational routines and the macro-actors, in Czarniawska, Barbara and Hernes, Tor (eds) *Actor-Network Theory and Organizing*, Malmö: Liber; Copenhagen: Copenhagen Business School Press, pp. 91–111.

Feldman, Martha S. and Rafaeli, Anat (2002) Organizational routines as sources of connections and understandings, *Journal of Management Studies*, 39(3): 309–331.

Feldman, Steven P. (1989) The broken wheel: the inseparability of autonomy and control in innovation within organizations, *Journal of Management Studies*, 26(2): 83–102.

Feldman, Stephen P. (2004) The culture of objectivity: quantification, uncertainty, and the evaluation of risk at NASA, *Human Relations*, 57(6): 691–718.

Ferguson, Kathy E. (1984) *The Feminist Case Against Bureaucracy*, Philadelphia: Temple University Press.

Ferlie, Ewan, Ashburner, Lynn, Fitzgerald, Louise and Pettigrew, Andrew (1996) *The New Public Management in Action*, Oxford and New York: Oxford University Press.

Fine, Gary Alan (1996) *Kitchens: the Culture of Restaurant Work*, Berkeley, Los Angeles and London: University of California Press.

Fitzpatrick, William M. and Burke, Donald R. (2000) Form, functions, and financial performance realities for the virtual organization, *S.A.M. Advanced Management Journal*, 65(3): 13–21.

Fleck, Ludwik (1979) *Genesis and Development of a Scientific Fact*, Chicago and London: Chicago University Press.

Florida, Richard (2002) *The Rise of the Creative Class*, New York. Basic Books.

Florida, Richard and Kenney, Martin (1992) Transplanted organizations: the transfer of Japanese industrial organization to the U.S., *American Sociology Review*, 56: 381–398.

Floyd, Steven W. and Woolridge, Bill (1994) Dinosaurs or dynamos? Recognizing middle management's strategic role, *Academy of Management Executives*, 8(4): 47–57.

Floyd, Steven W. and Woolridge, Bill (1997) Middle management's strategic influence and organizational performance, *Journal of Management Studies*, 34(3): 465–485.

Follett, Mary Parker (1941) *Dynamic Administration: the Collected Papers of Mary Parker Follett*, Bath: Management Publications Trust.

Foucault, Michel (1972) *An Archaeology of Knowledge*, Routledge, London.

Foucault, Michel (2000) *Power: Essential Works of Michel Foucault, Vol. 3*, ed. by James D. Faubion, New York: New Press.

Fournier, Valerie (1998) Stories of development and exploitation: militant voices in the enterprise culture, *Organization*, 5(1): 55–80.

Frank, K.A. and Fahrbach, K. (1999) Organization culture as a complex system: balance and information in models of influence and selection, *Organization Science*, 10(3): 253–277.

Frank, Thomas (2000) *One Market Under God: Extreme Capitalism, Market Populism, and the End of Economic Democracy*, New York: Doubleday.

Fucini, J.J. and Fucini, S. (1990) *Working for the Japanese*, New York: Free Press.

Fujimura, Joan H. (1995) Ecologies of action: recombining genes, molecularizing cancer, and transforming biology, in Star, Susan Leigh (ed.) *Ecologies of Knowledge: Work and Politics in Science and Technology*, Albany: State University of New York Press.

Fujimura, Joan H. (1996) *Crafting Science: a sociohistory of the Quest for the Genetics of Cancer*, Cambridge: Harvard University Press.

Gadamer, Hans-Georg (1975) *Truth and Method,* London: Sheed and Ward, originally published 1960.

Galunic, D. Charles and Rodan, Simon (1998) Resource recombinations in the firm: knowledge structures and the potential for Schumpeterian innovation, *Strategic Management Journal*, 19: 1193–1201.

Gantt, H.L. (1919) *Work, Wages, and Profits*, second edn, New York: The Engineering Magazine Co., originally published 1913.

Garsten, Christina (1999) Betwixt and between: temporary employees as liminal subjects in flexible organizations, *Organization Studies*, 20(4): 601–617.

Garsten, Christina (2002) Flex fads: new economy, new employees, in Holmberg, Ingagill, Salzer-Mörling, Miriam and Strannegård, Lars (eds), *Stuck in the Future: Tracing the "New Economy"*, Stockholm: Bookhouse Publishing.

Gartman, David (2004) Three ages of the automobiles: the cultural logics of the car, *Theory, Culture & Society*, 21(4/5): 169–195.

Gatens, Moira (1996) *Imaginary Bodies: Ethics, Power, and Corporeality*, London and New York: Routledge.

Gergen, Kenneth J. (1992) Organization theory in the postmodern era, in Reed, Michael and Hughes, Michael (eds) *Rethinking Organization: New Directions in Organization Theory and Analysis*, London: Sage.

Gherardi, Silvia (1995) *Gender, Symbolism, and Organizational Cultures*, London, Thousand Oaks and New Delhi: Sage.

Giddens, Anthony (1990) *The Consequences of Modernity*, Cambridge: Polity Press.

Giddens, Anthony and Pierson, Christopher (1998) *Conversations with Anthony Giddens: Making Sense of Modernity*, Cambridge: Polity Press.

Gilbreth, Frank B. (1911) *Motion Study: a Method for Increasing the Efficiency of the Workman*, New York: Van Nostrand.

Gilbreth, Frank B. and Gilbreth, Lillian M. (1919) *Fatigue Study: the Elimination of Humanity's Greatest Unnecessary Waste: a First Step in Motion Study*, second edn, New York: Macmillan, originally published 1916.

Gleick, James (1999) *Faster: the Acceleration of Just About Everything*, New York: Vintage Books.

Gluckman, Max (1965) *Politics, Law, and Ritual in Tribal Society*, Oxford: Blackwell.

Goodsell, Charles T. (2004) *The Case for Bureaucracy: a Public Administration Polemic*, fourth edn, Washington, DC: CQ Books.

Goody, Jack (1986) *The Logic of Writing and the Organization of Society*, Cambridge: Cambridge University Press.

Gouldner, Alvin W. (1954a) *Patterns of Industrial Democracy*, Glencoe: The Free Press.

Gouldner, Alvin W. (1954b) *Wildcat Strike*, New York: Evanston and London: Harper Torchbooks.

Graham, L. (1995) *On the Line at Subaru-Isuzu: the Japanese Model and the American Worker*, Ithaca: ILR Press.

Greco, Monica (2005) On the vitality of vitalism, *Theory, Culture & Society*, 22: 15–27.

Greve, Heirich R. (2003) A behavioral theory of R&D expenditures and innovations: evidence from shipbuilding, *Academy of Management Journal*, 46(6): 685–702.

Greve, Henrich R. and Taylor, Alva (2000) Innovations as catalysts for organizational change: shifts in organizational cognition and search, *Administrative Science Quarterly*, 45: 54–80.

Grint, Keith (1997) *Fuzzy Management: Contemporary Ideas and Practices at Work*, Oxford: Oxford University Press.

Grosz, Elizabeth (1999) *Becomings: Explorations in Time, Memory, and the Future*, Ithaca and London: Cornell University Press.

Grosz, Elizabeth (2001) *Architecture from the Outside: Essays on Virtual and Real Spaces*, Cambridge: MIT Press.

Grosz, Elizabeth (2004) *The Nick of Time: Politics, Evolution and the Untimely*, Durham: Duke University Press.

Guattari, Félix (2000) *The Three Ecologies*, London and New Brunswick: Athlone Press.

Gubrium, Jaber F. and Holstein, James A. (eds) Postmodern sensibilities, in Gubrium, Jaber F. and Holstein, James A. (eds) *Postmodern Interviewing*, London, Thousand Oaks and New Delhi: Sage, pp. 3–16.

Guillén, Mauro F. (1994) *Models of Management: Work, Authority, and Organization in a Comparative Perspective*, Chicago and London: University of Chicago Press.

Gulati, Ranjay (1999) Network location and learning: the influence of network resources and firm capabilities on alliance formation, *Strategic Management Journal*, 20: 397–420.

Gulati, Ranjay, Nohria, Nitin and Zaheer, Akbar (2000) Strategic networks, *Strategic Management Journal*, 21: 203–215.

Habermas, Jürgen (1988) *On the Logic of the Social Sciences*, trans. by Shierry Weber Nicholsen and Jerry A. Stark, Cambridge: MIT Press.

Hacking, Ian (1998) Canguilhem amid the cyborgs, *Economy & Society*, 27(2 and 3): 202–216.

Hage, Jerald and Hollingsworth, J. Rogers (2000) A strategy for the analysis of idea innovation networks and institutions, *Organization Studies*, 21(5): 971–1004.

Hales, Collin (2002) "Bureaucracy-lite" and continuities in managerial work, *British Journal of Management*, 13: 51–66.

Handy, Charles (1997) The virtual organization, in Pugh, Derek S. (ed.) *Organization Theory: Selected Readings*, Harmondsworth: Penguin.

Hannan, Michael T. and Freeman, John (1989) *Organizational Ecology*, Cambridge and London: Harvard University Press.

Hara, Takuji (2003) *Innovation in the Pharmaceutical Industry: the Process of Drug Discovery and Development*. Cheltenham and Northampton: Edward Elgar.

Haraway, Donna (1997) *Modest = Witness@Second = Millenium. FemaleMan© = Meets = OncoMouse™*, London: Routledge.

Haraway, Donna J. (2000) *How Like a Leaf: an Interview with Thyrza Nichols Goodeve*, New York and London: Routledge.

Harding, Sandra (1998) *Is Science Multicultural? Postcolonialisms, Feminisms, and Epistemologies*, Bloomington and Indianapolis: Indiana University Press.

Hardt, Michael and Negri, Antonio (2000) *Empire*, Cambridge and London: Harvard University Press.

Hargadon, Andrew B. (1998) Firms as knowledge brokers: lessons in pursuing continuous innovation, *California Management Review*, 40(3): 209–227.

Hargadon, Andrew B. and Douglas, Yellowlees (2001) When innovations meet institutions: Edison and the design of the electric light, *Administrative Science Quarterly*, 46: 476–501.

Hargadon, A. and Sutton, R. (1997) Technology brokering and innovation in a product development firm, *Administrative Science Quarterly*, 42: 716–749.

Harrison, Denis and Laberge, Murielle (2002) Innovation, identities and resistance: the social construction of an innovation network, *Journal of Management Studies*, 39(4): 497–521.

Hayles, N. Katherine (1999) *How We Became Posthuman: Virtual Bodies in Cybernetics, Literature, and Informatics*, Chicago and London: University of Chicago Press.

Heckscher, Charles and Donnellon, Anne (eds) (1994) *The Postbureaucratic Organization: New Perspectives on Organizational Change*, Thousand Oaks, London and New Delhi: Sage.

Hedberg, Bo, Dahlgren, Göran, Hanson, Jörgen and Olve, Nils-Göran (2000) *Virtual Organizations and Beyond: Discovering Imaginary Systems*, New York: Wiley.

Hedgecoe, Adam and Martin, Paul (2003) The drug don't work: expectations and the shaping of pharmacogenetics, *Social Studies of Science*, 33(3): 327–364.

Heidegger, Martin (1959) *An Introduction to Metaphysics*, New Haven: Yale University Press.

Heidegger, Martin (1987) *Nietzsche, Vol. III: the Will to Power as Knowledge and as Metaphysics*, trans. by Joan Stambaugh, David Farrell Krell and Frank A. Capuzzi, San Francisco: Harper & Row, originally published 1961.

Heisenberg, Werner von (1958) *Physics and Philosophy*, London: George Allen & Unwin.

Hellström, Thomas, (2004), Innovation as social action, *Organization*, 11(5): 631–649.

Hernes, Tor and Bakken, Tore (2003) Implications of self-reference: Niklas Luhmann's autopoesis and organization theory, *Organization Studies*, 24(9): 1511–1535.

Hite, Julie M. and Hesterly, William S. (2001) The evolution of firm networks: from emergence to early growth of the firm, *Strategic Management Journal*, 22: 275–286.

Hitt, Michael E., Hoskisson, Robert E., Johnsson, Richard A and Moesel, Douglas D. (1996) The market for corporate control and firm innovation, *Academy of Management Journal*, 39(5): 1084–1119.

Hlavacek, James D. and Thompson, Victor A. (1973) Bureaucracy and new product innovation, *Academy of Management Journal*, 16(3): 361–372.

Hobday, Mike (2000) The project-based organisation: an ideal for managing complex products and systems?, *Research Policy*, 29: 871–893.

Hochschild, Arlie Russell (1983) *The Managed Heart*, Berkeley: University of California Press.

Hodgson, Damian E. (2004) Project work: the legacy of bureaucratic control in the post-bureaucratic organization, *Organization*, 11(1): 81–100.

Hofstede, Geert (1980) *Cultural Consequences: International Differences in Work-Related Values*, London: Sage.

Hoggett, Paul (2005) A service to the public: the containment of ethical and moral conflict by public bureaucracies, in Du Gay, Paul (ed.) *The Values of Bureaucracy*, Oxford and New York: Oxford University Press, pp. 167–190.

Holland, John H. (1998) *Emergence: From Chaos to Order*, Oxford: Oxford University Press.

Holmberg, Ingagill and Strannegård, Lars (2002) The ideology of the "new economy", in Holmberg, Ingagill, Salzer-Mörling, Miriam and Strannegård, Lars (eds), *Stuck in the Future: Tracing the "New economy"*, Stockholm: Bookhouse Publishing.

Homans, George C. (1950) *The Human Group*, London: Routledge & Kegan Paul.

Höpfl, Harro M. (2006) Post-bureaucracy and Weber's "modern" bureaucrat, *Journal of Organization Change Management*, 19(1): 8–21.

Howe, David (1992) Child abuse and the bureaucratization of social work, *The Sociological Review*, 40(3): 491–509.

Huczynski, A.A. (1996) *Management Gurus: What Makes Them and How to Become One*, London: Routledge.

Hughes, John A., O'Brien, Jon, Randall, Dave, Rouncefield, Mark and Tolmie, Peter (2001) Some "real" problems on "virtual" organisation, *New Technology, Work and Employment*, 16(1): 49–64.

Hullman, A. (2000) Generation, transfer and exploitation of new knowledge, in Jungmittag, A. Reger, A. and Reiss, G. (eds) *Changing Innovation in the Pharmaceutical Industry – Globalization and New Ways of Drug Development*, Berlin: Springer.

Hung, Shih-Chang (2004) Explaining the process of innovation: the dynamic reconciliation of action and structure, *Human Relations*, 57(11): 1479–1497.

Huy, Quy Nguyen (2002) Emotional balancing of organizational continuity and radical change: the contribution of middle managers, *Administrative Science Quarterly*, 47: 31–69.

Hynes, Timothy and Prasad, Pushkala (1997) Patterns of mock bureaucracy in mining disasters: an analysis of the Westray coal mine explosion, *Journal of Management Studies*, 34(4): 601–623.

Iedema, Rick (2003) *Discourses of Post-Bureaucratic Organization*, Amsterdam and Philadelphia: John Benjamins.

Ingold, Tim (1986) *Evolution and Social Life*, Cambridge: Cambridge University Press.

Irigaray, Luce (1985) *This Sex Which is Not One*, trans. by Catherine Porter and Carolyn Burke, Ithaca: Cornell University Press.

Irigaray, Luce (2002) *To Speak is Never Neutral*, London and New York: Continuum.

Jackson, Brad (2001) *Management Gurus and Management Fashions: a Dramatistic Inquiry*, London and New York: Routledge.

Jackson, Paul (ed.) (1999) *Virtual Working: Social and Organizational Dynamics*, London: Routledge.

Jacob, Merle and Ebrahimpur, Golaleh (2001) Experience vs expertise: the role of implicit understandings of knowledge in determining the nature of knowledge transfer in two companies, *Journal of Intellectual Capital*, 2(1): 74–88.

Jacoby, Sanford M. (1985) *Employing Bureaucracy: Managers, Unions, and the Transformation of Work in American Industry, 1900–1945*, New York: Columbia University Press.

Jacques, R. (1996) *Manufacturing the Employee*, London: Sage.

James, William (1912) *Essays in Radical Empiricism*, New York: Longmans, Green & Co.

James, William (1996) *A Pluralistic Universe*, Lincoln and London: University of Nebraska Press.

Janning, Finn (2005) *A Different Story: Seduction, Conquest and Discovery*, Copenhagen Business School (PhD Thesis).

Jasanoff, Sheila, Markle, Gerald E., Peterman, James C. and Pinch, Trevor (eds) (1995) *Handbook of Science and Technology Studies*, Thousand Oaks, London and New Delhi: Sage.

Jassawalla, Avan R. and Sashittal, Hemant C. (2002) Cultures that support product innovation processes, *Academy of Management Executives*, 16(3): 42–54.

Jermier, John M., Slocum, John W. Jr., Fry, Louis W. and Gaines, Jeannie (1992) Organizational subcultures in a soft bureaucracy: resistance behind the myth and façade of an official culture, *Organization Science*, 2(2): 170–194.

Jones, Campbell, Parker, Martin and Ten Bos, René (2005) *For Business Ethics*, London and New York: Routledge.

Jones, E. (2001) *The Business of Medicine*, London: Profile Books Ltd.

Jones, Oswald (2000) Innovation management as a post-modern phenomenon: the outsourcing of pharmaceutical R&D, *British Journal of Management*, 11: 341–356.

Jones, Richard A.L. (2004) *Soft Machines: Nanotechnology and Life*, Oxford and New York: Oxford University Press.

Jönsson, Sten (2004) *Product Development: Work for Premium Values*, Malmö: Liber; Copenhagen: Copenhagen Business School Press.

Josserand, Emmanuel, Teo, Stephen, and Clegg, Stewart (2006) From bureaucratic to post-bureaucratic: the difficulties of transitions, *Journal of Organization Change Management*, 19(1): 54–64.

Kallinikos, Jannis (2003) Work, human agency and organizational forms: an anatomy of fragmentation, *Organization Studies*, 24(4): 595–618.

Kallinikos, Jannis (2004) The social foundations of the bureaucratic order, *Organization*, 11(1): 13–36.

Kamoche, Ken and Pina e Cunha, Miguel (2001) Minimal structures: from jazz improvization to product innovation, *Organization Studies*, 22(5): 733–764.

Kärreman, Dan and Alvesson, Mats (2004) Cages in tandem: management control, social identity, and identification in a knowledge-intensive firm, *Organization*, 11(1): 149–175.

Kärreman, Dan, Svenningson, Stefan and Alvesson, Mats (2002) The return of the machine bureaucracy? Management control in the work setting of professionals, *International Studies of Management & Organization*, 32(2): 70–92.

Keller, Evelyn Fox (2000) *The Century of the Gene*, Cambridge and London: Harvard University Press.

Keller, Evelyn Fox (2002) *Making Sense of Life: Explaning Bbiological Development with Models, Metaphors, and Machines*, Cambridge and London: Harvard Univeristy Press.

Kenney, Martin and Florida, Richard (1993) *Beyond Mass Production: the Japanese System and its Transfer to the U.S.*, Oxford and New York: Oxford University Press.

King, Adelaide Wilcox, Fowler, Sally W. and Zeithaml, Carl P. (2001) Managing organizational competencies for competitive advantage: the middle-management edge, *Academy of Management Executives*, 15(2): 95–106.

Kittler, Friedrich (1990) *Discourse Networks 1800/1900*, trans. by Michael Metteer and Chris Cullens, Stanford: Stanford University Press.

Kline, Morris (1954) *Mathematics in Western Culture*, London: George Allen and Unwin.

Knights, David, Noble, Faith, Vurdubakis, Theo and Willmott, Hugh (2001) Chasing shadows: control, virtuality and the production of trust, *Organization Studies*, 22(2): 311–336.

Knorr Cetina, Karin D. (1981) *The Manufacture of Knowledge: an Essay on the Constructivist and Contextual Nature of Science*, Oxford: Pergamon Press.

Knorr Cetina, Karin D. (1983) The ethnographic study of scientific work: towards a constructivist interpretation of science, in Knorr Cetina, Karin D. and Mulkay, Michael (eds) *Science Observed: Perspectives on the Social Study of Science*, London, Beverly Hills and New Delhi: Sage, pp. 115–140.

Knorr Cetina, Karin (1995) How superorganisms change: consensus formation and the social ontology of high-energy physics experiments, *Social Studies of Science*, 25: 119–147.

Knorr Cetina, Karin (1999) *Epistemic Cultures: How Sciences Make Knowledge*, Cambridge: Harvard University Press.

Knorr Cetina, Karin (2005) How are global markets global? The architecture of the flow world, in Knorr Cetina, Karin and Preda, Alex (eds) *The Sociology of Financial Markets*, Oxford and New York: Oxford University Press. pp. 38–61.

Knorr Cetina, Karin and Bruegger, Urs (2002) Traders' engagement with markets: a post-social relationship, *Theory, Culture & Society*, 19(5/6): 161–185.

Kolakowski, Leszek (1985) *Bergson*, Oxford and New York: Oxford University Press.

Kotorov, Rodoslav P. (2001) Virtual organization: conceptual analysis of the limits of its decentralization, *Knowledge and Process Management*, 8(1): 55–62.

Kuhn, Robert Lawrence (ed.) (1993) *Generating Creativity and Innovation in Large Bureaucracies*, Westport and London: Quorum Books.

Kunda, Gideon (1992) *Engineering Culture*, Philadelphia: Temple University Press.

Kundera, Milan (1988) *The Art of the Novel*, trans. by Linda Asher, New York: Grove Press.

Kuzmetsky, George (1993) The growth and internationalization of creative and innovative management, in Kuhn, Robert Lawrence (ed.) *Generating Creativity and Innovation in Large Bureaucracies*, Westport and London: Quorum Books. pp. 3–18.

Laclau, Ernesto and Mouffe, Chantal (1985) *Hegemony and Socialist Struggle: Toward a Radical Democratic Politics*, London and New York: Verso.

Lakoff, George and Johnson, Mark (1980) *Metaphors We Live By*: Chicago and London: University of Chicago Press.

Lane, Jan-Erik (2000) *New Public Management*, London and New York: Routledge.

Lansing, Alexander Gordon (2001) Cybercentrism: the new virtual management, *Management Decision*, 39(8): 676–685.

Lash, Scott (2003) Reflexivity as non-linearity, *Theory, Culture & Society*, 20(2): 49–57.

Lash, Scott (2006) Life (vitalism), *Theory, Culture & Society*, 23(2–3): 323–329.

Latour, Bruno (1987) *Science in Action,* Cambridge: Harvard University Press.

Latour, Bruno (1995) Joliot: history and physics mixed together, in Serres, Michel (ed.) *A History of Scientific Thought*, Oxford: Blackwell.

Latour, Bruno (1996) *Aramis or the Love of Technology*, Cambridge: Harvard University Press.

Latour, Bruno and Woolgar, S. (1979) *Laboratory Life: the Construction of Scientific Facts*, New Jersey: Princeton University Press.

Law, John (ed.) (1991) *A Sociology of Monsters: Essays on Power, Technology and Domination*, London and New York: Routledge.

Law, John (1994) *Organizing Modernity*, Oxford and Cambridge: Blackwell.

Law, John (2002) *Aircraft Stories: Decentering the Object in Technoscience*, Durham: Duke University Press.

Lawlor, Leonard (2003) *The Challenge of Bergsonism: Phenomenology, Ontology, Ethics*, London and New York: Continuum.

Lawrence, Paul R. and Lorsch, Jay W. (1967) *Organization and Environment: Managing Differentiation and Integration*, Boston: Harvard Business School Press.

Le Goff, Jacques (1980) *Time, Work and Culture in the Middle Ages*, trans. by Arthur Goldhammer, Chicago: University of Chicago Press.

Lecourt, Dominique (1998) Georges Canguilhem on the question of the individual, *Economy & Society*, 27(2/3): 217–224.

Leidner, Robin (1993) *Fast Food, Fast Talk: Service Work and the Routinization of Everyday Life*, Berkeley: University of California Press.

Leonard-Barton, Dorothy (1995) *Wellspring of Knowledge: Building and Sustaining the Sources of Innovation*, Boston: Harvard Business School Press.

Levinthal, D.A. and Warglien, M. (1999) Landscape design: designing for local action in complex worlds, *Organization Science*, 20(3): 342–357.

Lévy, Pierre (1998) *Becoming Virtual: Reality in the Digital Age*, trans. by Robert Bononno, New York and London: Plenum Trade.

Liker, Jeffrey K. (2004) *The Toyota Way: 14 Management Principles from the World's Greatest Manufacturer*, Cambridge: Harvard Business School Press.

Lindkvist, Lars, Söderlund, Jonas and Tell, Fredrik (1998) Managing product development projects: on the significance of fountains and deadlines, *Organization Studies*, 19(6): 931–951.

Linstead, Alison and Brewis, Joanna (2004) Beyond boundaries: towards fluidity in theorizing and practice, *Gender, Work and Organization*, 11(4): 430–454.

Linstead, Alison and Thomas, Robyn (2002) 'What do you want from me?' A poststructuralist feminist reading of middle managers' identities, *Culture & Organization*, 8(1): 1–20.

Linstead, Stephen (ed.) (2004) *Organization Theory and Postmodern Thought*, London, Thousand Oaks and New Delhi: Sage.

Linstead, Stephen and Mullarkey, John (2003) Time, creativity and culture: introducing Bergson, *Culture and Organization*, 9(19): 3–13.

Littler, Craig R. and Innes, Peter (2004) The paradox of managerial downsizing, *Organization Studies*, 25(7): 1159–1184.

Lounsbury, Michael and Carberry, Edward J. (2005) From king to court jester? Weber's fall from grace in organization theory, *Organization Studies*, 26(4): 501–525.

Lyotard, Jean-François (1984) *The Postmodern Condition: a Report on Knowledge*, Manchester: Manchester University Press.

Luhmann, Niklas (1990) *Essays on Self-Reference*, New York: Columbia University Press.

Luhmann, Niklas (1995) *Social Systems*, Stanford: Stanford University Press.

Luhmann, Niklas (2003) Organization, in Bakken, Tore and Hernes, Tor (eds) *Autopoetic Organization Theory: Drawing on Niklas Luhmann's Social Systems Perspective*, Oslo: Abstrakt; Malmö: Liber; Copenhagen: Copenhagen Business School Press.

Lupton, Thomas (1963) *On the Shopfloor*, Oxford and New York: Pergamon Press.

Lynch, Michael (1985) *Art and Artifact in Laboratory Science: a Study of Shop work and Shop Talk in a Research laboratory*, London: Routledge & Kegan Paul.

Lynch, Michael and Woolgar, Steve (1988) Introduction: sociological orientation to representational practice in science, in Lynch, Michael and Woolgar, Steve (eds) *Representation in Scientific Practice*, Cambridge and London: MIT Press, pp. 1–18.

McGail, Brian A. (2002) Confronting electronic surveillance: desiring and resisting new technologies, in Woolgar, Steve (ed.) *Virtual Society? Technology, Cyberbole, Reality*, Oxford and New York: Oxford University Press.

MacIntosh, Robert and Maclean, Donald (1999) Conditioned emergence: a dissipative structures approach to transformation, *Strategic Management Journal*, 20: 297–316.

MacIntyre, Alasdair (1981) *After Virtue*, London: Duckworth.

Mackenzie, Adrian (2002) *Transductions: Bodies and Machines at Speed*, London and New York: Continuum.

McSweeney, Brendan (2006) Are we living in a post-bureaucratic epoch?, *Journal of Organization Change Management*, 19(1): 22–37.

Maguire, Steve and McKelvey, Bill (1999) Complexity and management: moving from fad to firm foundations, *Emergence*, 1(2), 5–49.

Mair, Andrew (1999) Learning from Honda, *Journal of Management Studies*, 36(1): 25–44.

Malik, Suhail (2005) Information and knowledge, *Theory, Culture & Society*, 22(1): 29–49.

Maniha, John K. (1975) Universalism and particularism in bureaucratizing organizations, *Administrative Science Quarterly*, 20: 177–190.

Manning, Peter K. (1979) Metaphors of the field: varieties of organizational discourse, *Administrative Science Quarterly*, 24(4): 660–671.

Maravelias, Christian (2003) Post-bureaucracy: control through professional freedom, *Journal of Organization Change Management*, 16(5): 547–566.

Marion, Russ (1999) *The Edge of Organization: Chaos and Complexity Theories of Formal Social Systems*, London, Thousand Oaks and New Dehli: Sage.

Martin, J., Knopoff, K. and Beckman, C. (1998) An alternative to bureaucratic impersonality and emotional labor: bounded emotionality at the Body Shop, *Administrative Science Quarterly*, 43: 429–469.

Marx, Karl and Engels, Friedrich (1970) *The German Ideology*, London: Lawrence & Wishart.

Mason, David, Button, Graham, Lankshear, Gloria and Coates, Sally (2002) Getting real about surveillance and privacy at work, in Woolgar, Steve (ed.) *Virtual Society? Technology, Cyberbole, Reality*, Oxford and New York: Oxford University Press.

Massumi, Brian (2002) *Parables of the Virtual: Movement, Affect, Sensation*, Durham and London: Duke University Press.

Maturana, Humberto R. and Varela, Francisco J. (1980) *Autopoesis and Cognition: the Realization of the Living*, Dordrecht, Boston and London: D. Riedle Publishing.

May, Christopher (2002) *The Information Society. a Sceptical View*, Cambridge: Polity Press.

Mayo, Elton (1946) *The Human Problems of an Industrial Civilization*, Cambridge: Harvard University Press.

Maznevsky, Martha L. and Chudoba, Katherine M. (2000) Bridging space over time: global virtual team dynamics and effectiveness, *Organization Science*, 11(5): 473–492.

Merton, Robert K. (1957) Bureaucratic structure and personality, in *Social Theory and Social Structure*, Glencoe: Free Press.

Michaels, Mike (2000) *Reconnecting Culture, Technology and Nature: from Society to Heterogeneity*, London and New York: Routledge.

Michels, Robert (1962) *Political Parties: a Sociological Study of the Oligarchical Tendencies of Modern Democracy*, New York: Free Press.

Midler, Christophe (1995) "Projectification" of the firm: the Renault case, *Scandinavian Journal of Management*, 11(4): 363–375.

Miettinen, Reijo and Virkkunen, Jaakko (2005) Epistemioc objects, artefacts and organizational change, *Organization*, 12(3): 437–456.

Milburn, Colin (2004) Nanotechnology in the age of posthuman engineering: science fiction as science, in Hayles, N. Katherine (ed.) *Nanoculture: Implications of the New Technoscience*, Bristol: Intellect Books, pp. 109–129.

Mills, Charles W. (1951) *White Collars: the American Middle Class*, Oxford: Oxford University Press.

Mises, Ludwig von (1969) *Bureaucracy*, second edn, New Rochelle: Arlington House, originally published 1944.

Morel, B. and Ramanujam, R. (1999) Through the looking glass of complexity: the dynamics of organizations as adaptive and evolving systems, *Organization Science*, 10(3): 278–293.

Morgan, Gareth (1980) Paradigms, metaphors, and puzzle solving in organization theory, *Administrative Science Quarterly*, 25: 605–622.

Morgan, Gareth (1986) *Images of Organization*, Thousand Oaks: Sage.

Mouritsen, Jan and Flagstad, Kirsten (2005) The making of knowledge society: intellectual capital and paradoxes of managing knowledge, in Czarniawska, Barbara and

Hernes, Tor (eds) *Actor-Network Theory and Organizing*, Malmö: Liber; Copenhagen: Copenhagen Business School Press, pp. 208–229.

Mullarkey, John (1999) *The New Bergson*, Manchester and New York: Manchester University Press.

Mumby, Dennis K. and Putnam, Linda L. (1992) The politics of emotion: a feminist reading of bounded emotionality, *Academy of Management Review,* 17(3): 465–486.

Nassehi, Armin (2005) Organizations as design machines: Niklas Luhmann's theory of organized social systems, in Jones, Campbell and Munro, Rolland (eds) *Contemporary Organization Theory*, Oxford and Malden: Blackwell, pp. 178–191.

Nelson, Richard R. and Winter, Sidney G. (1982) *An Evolutionary Theory of the Economic Change*, Cambridge: Belknap.

Newell, Helen and Dopson, Sue (1996) Muddle in the middle: organization restructuring and middle management careers, *Personnel Review*, 25(4): 4–20.

Newton, Janet (2005) Bending bureaucracy: leadership and multi-level governance, in Du Gay, Paul (ed.) *The Values of Bureaucracy*, Oxford and New York: Oxford University Press, pp. 191–209.

Nietzsche, Friedrich (1967) *The Will to Power*, New York: Vintage Books.

Nobel, R. and Birkinshaw, J. (1998) Innovation in multinational corporations: control and communication patterns in international R&D operations, *Strategic Management Journal*, 19: 479–496.

Nohria, Nitin and Gulati, Ranjay (1996) Is slack good for innovation?, *Academy of Management Journal*, 39(5): 1245–1264.

Nonaka, I. and Takeushi, H. (1995) *The Knowledge-Creating Company*, Oxford: Oxford University Press.

Nowotny, Helga (2005) The increased complexity and its reduction: emergent interfaces between the natural sciences, humanities and social sciences, *Theory, Culture & Society*, 22(5): 15–31.

O'Conner, E. (1999) Minding the workers: the meaning of "human" and "human relations" in Elton Mayo, *Organization*, 6(2): 223–246.

Ogbonna, Emmanuel and Wilkinson, Barry (2003) The false promise of organization culture change: A case study of middle managers in grocery retailing, *Journal of Management Studies*, 40(5): 1151–1178.

Oliver, Amalya L. (2004) On the duality of competition and collaboration: network-based knowledge relations in the biotechnology industry, *Scandinavian Journal of Management*, 20: 151–171.

Orlikowski, Wanda J. (2000) Using technology and constituting structures: a practice lens for studying technology in organizations, *Organization Science*, 11(4): 404–428.

Oseen, Collette (1997) Luce Irigaray, sexual difference and theorizing leaders and leadership, *Gender, Work and Organization*, 4(3): 170–184.

O'Shea, Anthony (2002) The (r)evolution of new product innovation, *Organization*, 9(1): 113–125.

Östholm, Ivan (1995) *Drug Discovery: a Pharmacist Story*, Stockholm: Swedish Pharmaceutical Press.

Oswick, Cliff, Keenoy, Tom and Grant, David (2002) Metaphor and analogical reasoning in organization theory: beyond orthodoxy, *Academy of Management Review*, 27(2): 294–303.

Parsons, Talcott (1991) *The Social System*, London and New York: Routledge.

Patriotta, Gerard (2003) *Organization Knowledge in the Making: How Firms Create, Use, and Institutionalise Knowledge*, Oxford and New York: Oxford University Press.

Paules, Greta Foff (1991) *Dishing It Out: Power and Resistance Among Waitresses in a New Jersey Restaurant*, Philadelphia: Temple University Press.

Pedraja, Luis G. (2002) Whitehead, deconstruction, and postmodernism, in Keller, Catherine and Daniell, Anne (eds) Process and difference: between cosmological and poststructuralist postmodernisms, Albany: State University of New York, pp. 73–90.

Peltonen, Tuomo (1999) Finnish engineers becoming expatriates: biographical narratives and subjectivity, *Studies in Cultures, Organizations and Societies*, 5: 265–295.

Penrose, Edith T. (1959) *The Theory of the Growth of the Firm*, Oxford: Blackwell.

Pentland, Brian T. and Rueter, Henry H. (1994) Organization routines as grammars of action, *Administrative Science Quarterly*, 39(3): 484–510.

Perrow, Charles (1986) *Complex Organizations: a Critical Perspective*, New York: McGraw-Hill.

Perrow, Charles (2002) *Organizing America: Wealth, Power, and the Origins of Corporate Capitalism*, Princeton and London: Princeton University Press.

Pettigrew, Andrew M. (1985) *The Awakening Giant: Continuity and Change in Imperial Chemical Industries*, Oxford: Blackwell.

Pfeffer, Jeffrey (1993) Barriers to the advance of organizational science: paradigm development as a dependent variable, *Academy of Management Review*, 18(4): 599–620.

Pfeffer, Jeffrey and Fong, Christina T. (2002) The end of business schools: less success than meets the eye, *Academy of Management Learning and Education*, 1(1): 78–95.

Pialoux, Michel and Beaud, Stéphane (1999) Permanent and temporal workers, in Bourdieu, Pierre, *et al.* (eds) *The Weight of the World: Social Suffering in the Contemporary Society*, Cambridge: Polity Press.

Pinsonneault, Alain and Kraemer, Kenneth L. (1997) Middle management downsizing: an empirical investigation of the impact of information technology, *Management Science*, 43(5): 659–679.

Piore, Michael J. and Sabel, Charles F. (1984) *The Second Industrial Divide – Possibilities for Prosperity*, New York: Basic Books.

Plato (1977) *Timaeus and Critias*, London: Penguin.

Polanyi, Karl (1944) *The Great Transformation,* New York: Rinehart.

Pollard, Sidney (1965) *The Genesis of Modern Management: a Study of the Industrial Revolution in Great Britain*, London: Edward Arnold.

Porter, Michael E. (1985) *Competitive Advantage, Creating and Sustaining Superior Performance,* New York: Free Press.

Poster, Mark (2001) *What's the Matter with the Internet?*, Minneapolis: University of Minnesota Press.

Power, Michael (1994) The Audit Society, in Hopwood, Anthony G. and Miller, Peter (eds) *Accounting as Social and Institutional Practice*, Cambridge: Cambridge University Press.

Potoski, J. (2005) Timely synthetic support for medicinal chemists, *Drug Discovery Today,* 10(5): 115–120.

Powell, Walter W. (1998) Learning from collaboration: knowledge and networks in the biotechnology and pharmaceutical industries, *California Management Review*, 40(3): 228–240.

Powell, Walter W. Koput, Kenneth W. and Smith-Doerr, Laurel (1996) Interorganizational collaboration and the locus of innovation: networks of learning in biotechnology, *Administrative Science Quarterly*, 41: 116–145.

Power, Michael (2004) Counting, control and calculation: reflection on measuring and management, *Human Relations*, 57(6): 765–783.

Prasad, Anshuman (ed.) (2003) *Postcolonial Theory and Organizational Analysis: a Critical Engagement*, Houndsmills and New York: Palgrave.

Prasad, Pushkala (2005) *Crafting Qualitative Research: Working in the Postpositivist Traditions*, Armonk and London: ME Sharpe.

Prigogine, Ilya (1997) *The End of Certainty: Time, Chaos, and the New Laws of Nature*, New York: Free Press.

Prigogine, Ilya and Stengers, Isabelle (1984) *Order Out of Chaos: Man's New Dialogue with Nature*, New York: Bantam Books.

Rabinow, Paul (1996) *Making PCR: a Story of Biotechnology*, Chicago and London: University of Chicago Press.

Rabinow, Paul (1999) *French DNA: Trouble in Purgatory*, Chicago and London: University of Chicago Press.

Rådberg Kohn, Kamilla (2005) *Continuous Change in Mature Firms*, Dept of Technology Management and Economics, Chalmers University of Technology (PhD Diss.).

Räisänen, Christine and Linde, Anneli (2004) Technologizing discourse to standardize projects in multi-project organizations: hegemony by consensus, *Organization*, 11(1): 101–121.

Reed, Michael I. (1992) *The Sociology of Organization: Themes, Perspectives, and Prospects*, New York: Harvester Wheatsheaf.

Reed, Michael (2001) From eating to meeting: the rise of the meeting society, *Theory, Culture & Society*, 18(5): 131–143.

Reed, Michael (2005) Beyond the iron cage? Bureaucracy and the democracy in the knowledge economy and society, in Du Gay, Paul (ed.) *The Values of Bureaucracy*, Oxford and New York: Oxford University Press, pp. 115–140.

Reis, Dayr A. and Betton, John H. (1990) Bureaucracy and innovation: an old theme revisited, *Industrial management*, 32(6): 21–25.

Rescher, Nicholas (1996) *Process Philosophy: an Introduction to Process Philosophy*, Albany: State University of New York Press.

Rheinberger, Hans-Jörg (1997) *Toward a History of Epistemic Things: Synthesizing Proteins in the Test Tube*, Stanford: Stanford University Press.

Riley, Alexander Tristan (2002) Durkheim contra Bergson? The hidden roots of postmodern theory and the postmodern "return" of the sacred, *Sociological Perspectives*, 45(3): 243–265.

Roberts, John (2005) The power of the "imaginary" in disciplinary processes, *Organization*, 12(5): 619–642.

Robertson, Maxine and Swan, Jacky (2003) "Control – what control?" Culture and ambiguity within a knowledge intensive firm, *Journal of Management Studies*, 40(4): 831–858.

Robertson, Maxine and Swan, Jacky (2004) Going public: the emergence and effects of soft bureaucracy within a knowledge-intensive firm, *Organization*, 11(1): 123–148.

Robey, D., Schwaig, K.S. and Jin, L. (2003) Intertwining material and virtual work, *Information and Organization*, 13: 111–129.

Roethlisberger, F.J. and Dickson, William J. (1943) *Management and the Worker*, Cambridge: Harvard University Press.

Romano, Claudio (1990) Identifying factors which influence product innovation: a case study approach, *Journal of Management Studies*, 27(1): 75–95.

Roth, Jonas (2003) Enable knowledge creation: learning from an R&D organization, *Journal of Knowledge Management*, 7(1): 32–48.

Rousseau, Jean-Jacques (1993) *The Social Contract and Discourses*, London: Everyman, originally published 1762.

Roy, William G. (1981) The process of bureaucratization in the U.S. State Department and the vesting of economic interests, 1886–1905, *Administrative Science Quarterly*, 26: 419–433.

Salaman, Graeme (2005) Bureaucracy and beyond: managers and leaders in the "post-bureaucratic" organization, in Du Gay, Paul (ed.) *The Values of Bureaucracy*, Oxford and New York: Oxford University Press, pp. 141–164.

Salaman, Graeme and Storey, John (2002) Managers' theories about the process of innovation, *Journal of Management Studies*, 39(2): 147–165.

Sampson, E.E. (1989) The deconstruction of the self, in Shotter, John and Gergen, Kenneth J. (eds) *Texts of Identity*, London, Thousand Oaks and New Delhi: Sage.

Sams-Dodd, F. (2005) Optimizing the discovery organization for innovation, *Drug Discovery Today*, 10(15): 1049–1056.

Savage, Mike and Witz, Anne (1992) *Gender and Bureaucracy,* Oxford: Blackwell.

Scarbrough, Harry, Bresnen, Michael, Edelman, Linda F., Laurent, Stephan, Newell, Sue and Swan, Jacky (2004) The process of project-based learning: an explorative study, *Management Learning*, 35(4): 491–506.

Schatzki, Theodore R. (2002) *The Site of the Social: a Philosophical Account of the Constitution of Social Life and Change*, University Park: Pennsylvania State University Press.

Schrödinger, Erwin (1946) *What is life? Physical Aspects of the Living Cell*, Cambridge: Cambridge University Press.

Schrödinger, Erwin (1958) *Mind and Matter*, Cambridge: Cambridge University Press.

Schroeder, Ralph (1992) *Max Weber and the Sociology of Culture*, London, Newbury Park and New Delhi: Sage.

Schroeder, R.G., Sakakibara, S., Flynn, E.J. and Flynn, B.B. (1992) Japanese plants in the U.S.: how good are they?, *Business Horizon*, 35(4): 66–72.

Schroeder, Roger G., Ven de Ven, Andrew H., Scudder, Gary D. and Polley, Douglas (2000) The development of innovation ideas, in Van de Ven, Andrew, Angle, Harold L. and Poole, Marshall Scott (eds) *Research on the Management of Innovation*, Oxford and New York: Oxford University Press, pp. 107–134.

Schultze, Ulrika and Orlikowski, Wanda J. (2001) Metaphors of virtuality: shaping an emergent reality, *Information and Organization*, 11: 45–77.

Schumann, Paul A. Jr. (1993) Creativity and innovation in large organization, in Kuhn, Robert Lawrence (ed.) *Generating Creativity and Innovation in Large Bureaucracies*, Westport and London: Quorum Books, pp. 111–130.

Schumpeter, Joseph A. (1934) *The Theory of Economic Development*, Boston: Harvard University Press.

Schumpeter, Joseph A. (1939) *Business Cycles*, Vol. 1, New York: McGraw-Hill.

Schumpeter, Joseph A. (1943) *Capitalism, Socialism, and Democracy*, New York: Harper & Row.

Schwartz, Sanford (1992) Bergson and the politics of vitalism, in Burwick, Frederick and Douglass, Paul (eds) *The Crisis in Modernism: Bergson and the Vitalist Controversy*, Cambridge: Cambridge University Press, pp. 277–305.

Scott, Susanne G. and Bruce, Reginald A. (1994) Determinants of innovative behavior: a path model of individual innovation in the workplace, *Academy of Management Journal*, 37(3): 580–607.

Seidl, David (2003) Organizational identity: Luhmann's theory of social systems, in

Bakken, Tore and Hernes, Tor (eds) *Autopoetic Organization Theory: Drawing on Niklas Luhmann's Social Systems Perspective*, Oslo: Abstrakt; Malmö: Liber; Copenhagen: Copenhagen Business School Press, pp. 123–150.

Selznick, Philip (1957) *Leadership in Administration*, Berkeley: University of California Press.

Sennett, Richard (1998) *The Corrosion of Character: the Personal Consequences of Work in the New Capitalism*, New York and London: W.W. Norton & Company.

Serres, Michel (1982) *The Parasite*, Baltimore: John Hopkins University Press.

Seufert, Andreas, von Krogh, Georg and Bach, Andrea (1999) Towards knowledge networking, *Journal of Knowledge Management*, 3(3): 180–190.

Sharma, Anurag (1999) Central dilemmas of managing innovation in large firms, *California Management Review*, 31(3): 146–164.

Shenhav, Yahouda (1995) From chaos to systems: the engineering foundations of organization theory, 1879–1932, *Administrative Science Quarterly*, 40: 447–585.

Shenhav, Yehouda (1999) *Manufacturing Rationality: the Engineering Foundation of the Managerial Revolution*, Oxford and New York: Oxford University Press.

Sheremata, Willow A. (2000) Centrifugal and centripetal forces in radical new product development under time pressure, *Academy of Management Review*, 25(2): 389–408.

Shields, Rob (2003) *The Virtual*, London and New York: Routledge.

Simondon, Gilbert (1992) The genesis of the individual, in Crary, Jonathan and Kwinter, Sanford (eds) *Incorporations*, New York: Zone Books, pp. 297–319, originally published 1964.

Sims, David (2003) Between the milestones: a narrative account of the vulnerability of middle managers' story, *Human Relations*, 56(10): 1195–1211.

Sköldberg, Kaj (2002) *The Poetic Logic of Administration: Styles and Changes of Style in the Art of Organizing*, London and New York: Routledge.

Slappendel, Carol (1996) Perspectives on innovation in organizations, *Organization Studies*, 17(1): 107–129.

Sloan, Alfred P. Jr. (1964) *My Years with General Motors*, New York: Doubleday.

Söderlund, Jonas (2004) Building theories of project management: past research, questions for the future, *International Journal of Project Management*, 22: 183–191.

Spencer, Jennifer W. (2003) Firms' knowledge-sharing strategies in the global innovation system: empirical evidence from the flat panel display industry, *Strategic Management Journal*, 24: 217–233.

Spinoza, Baruch (1994) *Ethics*, London: Penguin.

Stacey, Ralph D. (1995) The Science of Complexity: An Alternative Perspective for Strategic Change Processes, *Strategic Management Journal*, 16(6): 477–495.

Starbuck, William H. (1992) Learning by knowledge-intensive firms, *Journal of Management Studies*, 29(6): 713–740.

Starbuck, William H. (2003a) The origins of organization theory, in Tsoukas, Haridimos and Knudsen, Christian (eds) *The Oxford Handbook of Organization Theory: Meta-Theoretical Perspectives*, Oxford and New York: Oxford University Press.

Starbuck, William H. (2003b) Shouldn't organization theory emerge from adolescence?, *Organization*, 10(3): 439–452.

Stiegler, Bernard (1998) *Technics and Time, 1: the Fault of Epimetheus*, trans. by Richard Beardsworth and George Collins, Stanford: Stanford University Press.

Stinchcombe, Arthur (1959) Bureaucratic and craft administration of production: a comparative study, *Administrative Science Quarterly*, 4(2): 168–188.

Sturdy, Andrew (1998) Customer care in customer society: smiling and sometimes mean it, *Organizations*, 5(1): 27–53.

Styhre, Alexander (2006) Embracing the fluid: project management and feminist thinking, *Journal of Organization Change Management* (forthcoming).

Styhre, Alexander and Sundgren, Mats (2005) *Managing Organization Creativity: Critique and Practices*, Basingstoke and New York: Palgrave (forthcoming).

Styhre, Alexander, Ingelgård, Anders, Beausang, Peder, Castenfors, Mattias, Mulec, Kina and Roth, Jonas (2002) Emotional management and stress: managing ambiguities, *Organization Studies*, 23(1): 83–103.

Subramaniam, Mohan and Venkatraman, N. (2001) Determinants of transnational new product development capability: testing the influence of transferring and deploying new knowledge, *Strategic Management Journal*, 22: 359–378.

Subramaniam, Mohan and Youndt, Mark A. (2005) The influence of intellectual capital on the types of innovative capabilities, *Academy of Management Journal*, 48(3): 450–463.

Sundgren, Mats (2004) *New Thinking, Management Control, & Instrumental Rationality: Managing Organizational Creativity in Pharmaceutical R&D*, Gothenburg: Chalmers University of Technology (PhD Diss.).

Sundgren, Mats and Styhre, Alexander (2003) Creativity – a volatile key of success? Creativity in new drug development, *Creativity and Innovation Management*, 9(3): 145–161.

Sundling, S. (2003) *Per Aspera AD Astra: Astra 1913–1999*. Stockholm: Ekerlids.

Swedberg, Richard (1998) *Max Weber and the Idea of Economic Sociology*, Princeton: Princeton University Press.

Teilhard de Chardin, Pierre (1959) *The Phenomenon of Man*, trans. by Barnard Wall, London: Collins.

Thomas, Robyn and Linstead, Alison (2002) Losing the plot? Middle management and identity, *Organization*, 9(1): 71–93.

Thomas, Tom C. and Acuña-Narvaez, Rachelle (2006) The convergence of biotechnology and nanotechnology: why here, why now?, *Journal of Commercial Biotechnology*, 12(2): 105–110.

Thomke, Stefan (2001) Enlightened experimentation: the new imperative for innovation, *Harvard Business Review*, 79(2): 66–75.

Thompson, J.D. (1967) *Organizations in Action*, New York: McGraw-Hill.

Thompson, Paul and Alvesson, Mats (2005) Bureaucracy at work: misunderstandings and mixed blessings, in Du Gay, Paul (ed.) *The Values of Bureaucracy*, Oxford and New York: Oxford University Press, pp. 89–113.

Thompson, Victor A. (1969) *Bureaucracy and Innovation*, University: University Press of Alabama.

Todorov, Tzvetan (1983) *Symbolism and Interpretation*, trans. by Catherine Porter, London, Melbourne and Henley: Routledge & Kegan Paul.

Touraine, Alain (1971) *The Post-Industrial Society – Tomorrow's Social History: Classes, Conflicts and Culture in the Programmed Society*, trans. by Leonard F.X. Mayhew, New York: Random House.

Thrift, Nigel (1998) Virtual capitalism: the globalization of reflexive business knowledge, in Carrier, James G. and Miller, Daniel (eds) *Virtualism: a New Political Economy*, Oxford and New York: Berg.

Thrift, Nigel (2001) "It's the romance, not the finance, that makes the business worth pursuing": disclosing the new market culture, *Economy & Society*, 30(4): 412–432.

Thrift, Nigel (2005) *Knowing Capitalism*, London, Thousand Oaks and New Delhi: Sage.

Townley, B. (1993) Foucault, Power/Knowledge, and its Relevance for Human Resource Management, *Academy of Management Review*, 18(3): 518–545.

Traweek, Sharon (1988) *Beamtimes and Lifetimes: the World of High Energy Physicists*, Cambridge and London: Harvard University Press.

Tsoukas, Haridimous (1998) Introduction: chaos, complexity and organization theory, *Organizations*, 5(3): 291–312.

Tsoukas, Haridimous (2005) *Complex Knowledge: Studies in Organizational Epistemology*, Oxford and New York: Oxford University Press.

Tushman, Michael L. and Nelson, Richard R. (1990) Introduction: technology, organizations, and innovation, *Administrative Science Quarterly*, 35: 1–8.

Tushman, Michael L. and O'Reilly, Charles A. III. (1996) The ambidextrous organization: managing evolutionary and revolutionary change, *California Management Review*, 38(4): 8–30.

Turkle, Sherry (1996) *Life on the Screen: Identity in the Age of the Internet*, London: Weiderfeld & Nicolson.

Ure, Andrew (1967) *The Philosophy of Manufacturers*, London: Frank Cass & Co, originally published 1835.

Urry, John (2000) *Sociology Beyond Societies: Mobilities for the Twenty-first Century*, London and New York: Routledge.

Urry, John (2003) *Global Complexity*, Oxford and Malden: Polity.

Urry, John (2005) The complexities of the global, *Theory, Culture & Society*, 22(5): 235–254.

Van de Ven, Andrew (1986) Central problems in the management of innovation, *Management Science*, 32(5): 590–607.

Van de Ven, Andrew, Angle, Harold L. and Poole, Marshall Scott (eds) (2000) *Research on the Management of Innovation*, Oxford and New York: Oxford University Press.

Vattimo, G. (1992) *The End of Modernity*, Cambridge: Polity Press.

Veblen, Thorstein (1904) *The Theory of the Business Enterprise*, New York: Schreiber.

Ven de Ven, Andrew H. and Poole, Marshall Scott (2000) Methods for studying innovation processes, in Van de Ven, Andrew, Angle, Harold L. and Poole, Marshall Scott (eds) *Research on the Management of Innovation*, Oxford and New York: Oxford University Press, pp. 31–54.

Venkatraman, N. and Henderson, John C. (1998) Real strategies for virtual organizing, *Sloan Management Review*, Fall: 33–48.

Virilio, Paul (1991) *The Lost Dimension*, New York: Semiotext(e).

Virilio, Paul (2000) *A Landscape of Events*, trans. by Julia Rose, Cambridge: MIT Press.

Virilio, Paul (2002) *Desert Screen: War at the Speed of Light*, London and New York: Continuum.

Virilio, Paul (2004) *Unknown Quantity*, London: Thames and Hudson.

Virilio, Paul and Lotringer, S. (1997) *Pure War*, New York: Semiotext[e].

Von Hippel, Eric (1998) Economics of product development by users: the impact of "sticky" local information, *Management Science*, 44(5): 629–644.

Wajcman, Judy and Martin, Bill (2002) Narratives of identity in modern management: the corrosion of gender difference?, *Sociology*, 36(4): 985–1002.

Walker, M., Barrett, T. and Guppy, L.J. (2004) Functional pharmacology: the drug discovery bottleneck? *Drug Discovery Today*, 3(5): 208–215.

Wallace, Terry (1999) "It's a man's world!" Restructuring gender imbalance in the Volvo Truck Company, *Gender, Work and Organization*, 6(1): 20–31.

Walton, Eric J. (2005) The persistence of bureaucracy: a meta-analysis of Weber's model of bureaucratic control, *Organization Studies*, 26(4): 569–600.

Weber, Max (1947) *The Theory of Social and Economic Organization*, New York: Free Press.

Weber, Max (1949) *The Methodology of the Social Sciences*, New York: Free Press.

Weber, Max (1978) *Economy and Society: an Outline of Interpretative Sociology*, Berkeley, Los Angeles and London: University of California Press.

Weber, Max (1992) *The Protestant Ethic and the Spirit of Capitalism*, London: Routledge.

Weber, Max (1999) *Essays in Economic Sociology*, ed. by Richard Swedberg, Princeton: Princeton University Press.

Weick, Karl E. (1979) *The Social Psychology of Organizing*, New York: McGraw-Hill.

Weick, Karl E. and Roberts, K.H. (1996) Collective mind in organizations: heedful interrelating on flight decks, in Cohen, M.D. and Sproull, L.S. (eds) *Organizational Learning*, London: Sage.

White, Hayden (1987) *The Content of Form: Narrative Discourse and Historical Representation*, Baltimore and London: John Hopkins University Press.

Whitehead, Alfred N. (1925) *Science and the Modern World*, Cambridge: Cambridge University Press.

Whitehead, Alfred N. (1978) *Process and Reality*, New York: Free Press.

Whitley, Richard (2000) The institutional structuring of innovation strategies: business systems, firm types, and patterns of technical change in different market economies, *Organization Studies*, 21(5): 855–886.

Whyte, William H. (1956) *The Organization Man*, New York: Simon and Schuster.

Wickelgren, Mikael (2005) *Engineering Emotion: Values as a Means in Product Development*, Department of Business Administration, Gothenburg School of Economics and Commercial Law, Gothenburg University (PhD Thesis).

Wiener, Norbert (1948) *Cybernetics, or Control and Communication in the Animal Machine*, New York: John Wiley.

Williamson, Oliver E. (1975) *Market and Hierarchies*, New York: Free Press.

Wilms, W.W., Hardcastle, A.J. and Zell, D.M. (1994) Cultural transformation at NUMMI, *Sloan Management Review*, Fall: 99–113.

Wittgenstein, Ludwig (1953) *Philosophical Investigations*, Oxford: Blackwell.

Wolfe, Richard A. (1994) Organization innovation: Review, critique and suggested research directions, *Journal of Management Studies*, 31(3): 405–431.

Wood, Martin (2005) The fallacy of misplaced leadership, *Journal of Management Studies*, 42(6): 1101–1121.

Wood, Martin and Ferlie, Ewan (2003) Journeying from Hippocrates with Bergson and Deleuze, *Organization Studies*, 24(1): 47–68.

Woolgar, Steve (ed.) (2002) *Virtual Society? Technology, Cyberbole, Reality*, Oxford and New York: Oxford University Press.

Wren, Daniel A. (1972) *The Evolution of Management Thought*, New York: The Ronald Pres Company.

Young, Ann P. (1999) Rule breaking and a new opportunistic managerialism, *Management Decision*, 37(7): 582–588.

Yu, H. and Adedoyin, A. (2003) ADME–Tox in drug discovery: integration of experimental and computational technologies, *Drug Discovery Today*, 8(18): 852–861.

Zivin, J.A. (2000) Understanding clinical trials, *Scientific American*, April: 49–55.

Žižek, Slavoj (1989) *The Sublime Object of Ideology*, New York and London: Verso.

Zuccato, C., Tartari, M., Goffredo D., Cattaneo, E. and Rigamonti, E. (2005) From target identification to drug screening assays for neurodegenerative diseases, *Pharmacological Research*, 52(3): 245–251.

Zucker, Lynne G. and Darby, Michael R. (1997) Present at the biological revolution: transformation of technological identity for a large incumbent pharmaceutical firm, *Research Policy*, 26: 429–446.

Index